SCHIZOANA
CARTOGRA

SCHIZOANALYTIC CARTOGRAPHIES

Félix Guattari

Translated by Andrew Goffey

B L O O M S B U R Y

LONDON • NEW DELHI • NEW YORK • SYDNEY

Bloomsbury Academic

An imprint of Bloomsbury Publishing Plc

50 Bedford Square
London
WC1B 3DP
UK

175 Fifth Avenue
New York
NY 10010
USA

www.bloomsbury.com

Originally published in French as *Cartographies Schizoanalytiques* © Éditions Galilée, 1989

British Library Cataloguing-in-Publication Data

A catalogue record for this book is available from the British Library.

ISBN: HB: 978-1-4411-5727-0
PB: 978-1-4411-6727-9

Library of Congress Cataloging-in-Publication Data
Guattari, Félix, 1930-1992.
[Cartographies schizoanalytiques. English]
Schizoanalytic cartographies / Félix Guattari ; translated by Andrew Goffey.
p. cm.-- (Impacts)
Includes bibliographical references (p.) and index.
ISBN 978-1-4411-5727-0 (hardcover)-- ISBN 978-1-4411-6727-9
(pbk.)-- ISBN 978-1-4411-4679-3 (ebook epub)-- ISBN
978-1-4411-8947-9 (ebook pdf) 1. Psychoanalysis and philosophy. 2.
Semiotics--Psychological aspects. 3. Social psychiatry. I. Title.

BF175.4.P45G8313 2012
194--dc23

2012017053

Typeset by Fakenham Prepress Solutions, Fakenham, Norfolk NR21 8NN

CONTENTS

ACKNOWLEDGEMENTS

N umerous people have contributed to the final shape of this translation, both directly and indirectly. I would like to thank in particular Éric Alliez and the Centre for Research in Modern European Philosophy at Kingston University, whose efforts made it possible to purchase the English language rights for *Schizoanalytic Cartographies* in the first place, Paul Bains, Sarah Campbell, Rachel Eisenhauer, Camilla Erskine, Matthew Fuller, Jeremy Gilbert, Emmanuelle Guattari, Brian Massumi and Isabelle Stengers. Sue Cope risked her sanity copy-editing the translated text, Joe Gerlach his when compiling the index, and Kim Storry hers getting the whole thing ready to print. A special thanks goes to Lynne, without whose support this translation would never have seen the light of day.

ACKNOWLEDGEMENTS

Numerous people have contributed to the final shape of this translation, both directly and indirectly. I would like to thank in particular Éric Alliez and the Centre for Research in Modern European Philosophy at Kingston University, whose efforts made it possible to purchase the English language rights for *Schizoanalytic Cartographies* in the first place, Paul Bains, Sarah Campbell, Rachel Eisenhauer, Camilla Erskine, Matthew Fuller, Jeremy Gilbert, Emmanuelle Guattari, Brian Massumi and Isabelle Stengers. Sue Cope risked her sanity copy-editing the translated text, Joe Gerlach his when compiling the index, and Kim Storry hers getting the whole thing ready to print. A special thanks goes to Lynne, without whose support this translation would never have seen the light of day.

LIST OF FIGURES AND TABLES

The original French publication of *Schizoanalytic Cartographies* included black and white reproductions of three paintings by Balthus, which are the subject of the discussion in the final essay in the collection 'Cracks in the Street'. It also included reproductions of eight photographs (of Ricardo Bofill, Joseph Beuys x 2, Laura Betti, Bram van Velde, Christian Boltanski, François Truffault and Arman) by the Japanese photographer Keiichi Tahara. These form part of the discussion of the penultimate essay in the collection 'Keiichi Tahara's Faciality Machine'. Neither set of images have been included in this translation for reasons of cost. Digital reproductions of most of the images can be readily located on the Internet.

6 The Domain of Phyla

7 The Domain of Universes

8 Enunciative Recursion

The Refrains of Being and Sense

TRANSLATOR'S INTRODUCTION

The artifice of jargon. On Guattari's style

Schizoanalytic Cartographies is perhaps one of the last big books of French 'theory' – that extraordinary efflorescence of thinking that occurred in the wake of the events of 1968 – to be translated into English. Chapters and sections of it have appeared in translation already, in readers, edited collections and journals, but in its integrity, as published in France by Editions Galilée, it has not. The book was not a great success when first published and despite the tribute later paid to its 'marvellous four-headed system' by Gilles Deleuze,[1] David Hume's comments about his *Treatise of Human Nature* (1789) (which he described as falling 'deadborn from the press') are apt. Maybe this is why, unlike other single-authored Guattari texts, such as *Chaosmosis*, the *Cartographies* has experienced little of the (often ambiguous) benefits of critical commentary. From some points of view this is regrettable, but the failure of the text to resonate through the amplifiers of academic reception – even in the momentary form of a yowling feedback loop – can be considered a positive thing: readers will be able to come fresh to a kind of writing that still possesses much of its singular experimental charge without too much fear of having their readings inflected by what they know of it from secondary criticism.

Custom dictates that a translator should comment on difficulties encountered in the process of translating a text from one language to another – and the *Schizoanalytic Cartographies* presented enough challenges in this regard for that to be a substantial task in its own right (only Whitehead's *Process and Reality* presents more apparent textual inconsistencies, and hence editorial challenges). Considered as a kind of multi-dimensional semiotic mapping, translation creates all sorts of problems – re-establishing stabilized quanta of signification, a conventional propositional structure (with associated schema of judgement) or even phonemic texture where an original text is perhaps more decoded, abrupt or jarring, for example. In this respect, the translator's undertaking is one that typically presents far less interest to the reader than it should, because it is precisely the untranslateable idiosyncrasies of language use that provide the indices of a writer's (or indeed, a culture's)[2] movements of thought. In the case of a figure such as Guattari, this is an idiosyncrasy vindicated as such in the construction of a kind of *mathesis singularis* manifest through a peculiar – and peculiarly inventive – jargon. In this respect, the mode of theorizing that *Schizoanalytic Cartographies* develops – on the planes of expression *and* content – is inseparable from a very characteristic pragmatics of style.

In some respects, the *Cartographies* pushes to a paroxystic extreme ideas expressive of tendencies and movements of thinking that one can find elsewhere in Guttari's work, those nominally authored alone as well as the more celebrated works co-written with Gilles Deleuze – an almost subterranean discussion of the Spinozist semiotics of Hjelmslev, for example, that have actually continued unabated in both writers' works since the early 1970s; a re-working of ideas about machinic Phyla or about transversality. But the highly idiosyncratic vocabulary developed by *Schizoanalytic Cartographies* – like its myriad diagrams (commented on by Janell Watson)[3] – marks out a way of thinking and developing ideas that are perhaps singular to Guattari, even (perhaps especially) where they are heavily inflected by his work with Deleuze. Encountering this strange machinery of expression, which is evident on almost every page, the reader of *Schizoanalytic Cartographies* will doubtless experience an assortment of feelings – bewilderment, surprise, amusement, frustration and perhaps irritation at its exorbitantly baroque qualities. The expressive resources of a conceptual terminology, running from the unusual – existential 'cutouts' (découpes) and 'Constellations of Universes of reference' – to the nigh on untranslateable – 'déclinaisons logicielles' and 'ritornellization' – is assembled here with a marvellously abstracted syntax for exploring the metadynamics of the four-headed matrix of entities ΦFTU at work in forms of content ranging from the pathological (an autistic child's experience of a housing estate), through the mundane (opening the automatic barrier in a car park), to the avant garde (the proto-Surrealist aesthetics of Witkiewicz) and abstract (quantum physics, complexity theory).

Appropriately, it is Gilles Deleuze who puts his finger on this very particular trait of Guattari's style. In an interview from 1974 (published in translation in the collection *Negotiations*), he contrasts his own practice, in which a page of writing flies off 'in all directions' and at the same time closes in on itself 'like an egg', with Guattari's 'schizoid flow carrying along all sorts of things'.[4] Where Deleuze's writing has a fullness and formal perfection – organized with the construction of what could now be called his *oeufre* permanently in mind (sometimes to Guattari's frustration)[5] – the latter's writing often bears the marks both of its circumstantial occurrence and its partially unfinished quality in a way that renders consideration of it in canonic terms problematic. Guattari was not a professional philosopher (he described himself, appropriately enough, as the Douanier Rousseau of philosophy)[6], and whilst this might cause some difficulties in the reception of his ideas, there is no doubt that it equally allowed him to avoid the 'thinking in grooves' that can be the cost of the entitlement to make professional judgements. In fact, in view of his decidedly pragmatic understanding of concepts, the asperities and snagging awkwardness of some of Guattari's writing is actually rather felicitous. Jargons don't have authors and the conventional judgements about status and ability (could he write, couldn't he write…?) that usually form part of the author function become more difficult to apply as a result. More so than Deleuze perhaps – whose work can easily be situated in relationship to canonical issues and central problems in the history of philosophy – Guattari's work calls for, first and foremost, an experimental *use*.

Discussion of Guattari's writing has tended to develop in the context of his readily professed admiration for modernist writers such as Proust, Joyce and Kafka. Indeed it has been argued that his obsession with Joyce, for example, was something of an inhibition for him in so far as it allegedly cemented an inability to write – 'he was too obsessed by Joyce throughout his life'.[7] But from the pragmatic point of view of use, such claims would be better situated in relationship to the question of what *kind* of writing is best fitted to the operations of machinic thinking. In this respect – and perhaps in spite of Guattari's admiration for some of the most canonical of modernist writers – the notion of jargon may well be better suited as a way to characterize his writing. The varied senses and etymology of the term are invaluable indicators – the twittering of birds, barbarous or debased language, the use of difficult to understand terms or expressions, and so on. Whilst his writing might not quite be considered jargon in any of these historically stabilized senses, their relevance is undeniable when considering the qualities of his writing.[8] However, if the notion of jargon is invoked here, this is not as an excuse to permit consideration of Guattari's writing in purely linguistic terms, illuminating though this may be, because to do so would be to miss the very particular role that jargon plays in the *functioning* that Guattari ascribes to theory. His recurrent strictures about pragmatics are in this respect crucial, not least because they require us to *start* from the transformational role of language, rather than add it on once we've got clarity about syntax and semantics. In a footnote discussing Chomsky in his *Machinic Unconscious*, for example, Guattari makes the point that 'pragmatic transformational components [...] are first in relation to components "generative" of effects of signification and subjectification.'[9] From this point of view, actions generative of machinic sense 'flush with the real' always take precedence over any kind of contract, ideal speech situation or tacit (and tacitly exclusionary) consensus about meaning, a theoretical claim of critical, even decisive, importance.[10]

Guattari's insouciance with regard to explicit or tacit norms of language use in his thinking should not, then, simply be considered evidence of wilful obfuscation or a peculiarly Gallic taste for rebarbative abstruseness (from the poverty of theory to fashionable nonsense)[11], or at least should not be so considered for anyone looking for a way out of the tired rituals and institutionalized fictions of intellectual endeavour. Criticism of jargon – rather like the criticism of sophistry – resurges throughout the history of Western thinking, and when journalists today fustigate it, one should bear in mind that it is not just the anti-intellectual protagonists of media debate who call for considered and controlled language use. One might, for example, recall Hobbes's strictures against the 'Iargon' of Scholasticism in his *Leviathan*, Heidegger's attack on Spinoza in his essay on Schelling or Adorno's polemic against Husserl and Heidegger in his *Jargon of Authenticity*, as evidence of this recurrent bringing to order of language. Indeed, Wittgenstein's well-known comment about language – his seventh and final proposition in the *Tractatus* – 'Whereof one cannot speak, thereof one must be silent' – encapsulates much of this regulatory zeal, particularly when translated into French, where it acquires a repressive nuance which is symptomatic of a problem that jargon creates: 'Ce dont on ne peut parler, *il faut* le taire'.[12] Whilst it is often tempting to consider the awkward or abstruse vocabulary of jargon as exemplifying the conceptual weaknesses or semantic difficulties of fashionable nonsense, or the protective defensiveness of sects and secret societies, a point of view that doesn't presuppose some tacit linguistic normativity is obliged to read such asperities differently.

The very particular style developed by *Schizoanalytic Cartographies* is in some respects the living embodiment of a point made by Deleuze and Guattari in *What is Philosophy?* concerning the specific necessity of the vocabulary that a philosopher uses 'some concepts must be indicated by an extraordinary and sometimes even barbarous or shocking word, whereas others make do with an ordinary, everyday word that is filled with harmonics so distant that it risks being imperceptible to a non-philosophical ear [...] In each case there must be a strange necessity for these words and for their choice, like an element of style'.[13] The question becomes even more pressing here because the odd, dissonant resonances of Guattari's vocabulary are so evident. This is a question about the specificity of his theoretical practice, in the sense that the idiom, the idiosyncracy – the idiocy, even – of a jargon testifies to what it is that matters to it, what cannot be captured by the self-evidences of the day.[14] Guattari's intellectual and practical formation marks him out as somewhat different to many of the French intellectuals associated with the developments of 'theory' in the 1960s and 1970s. As he once put it 'I'm a sort of inveterate auto-didact, a do-it-yourself guy, a sort of Jules Verne – *Voyage to the Centre of the Earth*'.[15] This auto-didacticism, which was allied to a collective research practice extending over many years in Guattari's work with Centre d'Études, de Recherches et de Formation Institutionelles certainly helps us understand the peculiar mobility of his thinking, the ease with which he could, for example, bring together discussions of Marcel Proust with the findings of ethological studies of the behaviour of monkeys.[16] Likewise his involvement in politics from an early age – from youth movements to the communist left, and then his work with patients – impatients – at the La Borde clinic gave his writing a different set of connections, and, crucially, a different set of constraints in its production, to those that one finds in many of his contemporaries. Where structuralist Marxism and its descendants found common cause with Lacanian structuralism (to the point of seeing in revolutionary movements a kind of 'hysteria' of the social)[17] – for Guattari (as well as for Deleuze), it is more appropriate to understand everything as revolving around psychosis, and the failure of the symbolic, structural order to 'take hold'.

Tackling a blindspot in the structuralist theorizing of analysis, Guattari's on-going work with psychotic patients and the need to find effective ways into and out of their peculiarly coiled up worlds – and words, when spoken – meant that theoretical work, for him, had always to pay careful attention to lived experience, a phenomenological watchword that could only be suspicious to structuralists. Attention to 'lived experience' was, in any case, the signal virtue of the most clinically acute of work on psychosis – beginning, perhaps, with Karl Jaspers' phenomenologically inspired existential psychiatry – a lesson that was clearly not lost on Guattari, given the continued reference even in the present text to that rich tradition. What this passage through the peculiarities of psychotic experience gave Guattari was a sensitivity to the ways in which group practices enveloped a dynamic that could not be imputed or reduced to an algebraic logic of position or the regulated interplay of the synchronic and diachronic aspects of structure. In some respects, such experience could only lead to a critique of the particular position assumed by structuralist theory, as made evident in some of his early writings in *Psychanalyse et transversalité*. Discussing his conception of the 'group-subject', for example, he remarks,

> the group-subject is not incarnated in a delegated individual who could pretend to speak in its name. First of all, it is a project resting on a provisional totalisation, producing a truth in the unfolding of its action. Unlike Althusser, the group-subject is not the theorist who produces concepts. It produces signifiers, not signification. It produces the institution, institutionalisation, not the party and the line…[18]

Yet as the previous quote suggests, Guattari was not immune to the charms of the structuralist thinking of a Lacan and one might want to understand his own approach to 'doing' theory in part as a response to the peculiarly performative equivocations of 'the master'. But even here curious theoretical conjunctions and subtle shifts of emphasis open up different pathways – the identification of the structural operations of the signifier with the 'nihilating' movement of the existential consciousness, for example, maintains the possibility of a connection between linguistic structures and forms of praxis. And even in his most evidently Lacanian of moments, there is a room for manoeuvre that the later encounter with Deleuze will exploit considerably. In a piece on 'The Transference' from 1964, commenting on a trend in the wake of Heidegger to develop a 'perverse practice of etymology', he comments,

> everything Freud was able to utilise, whether rightly or wrongly, in the order of mythology to translate his conceptual distributions, should not, in my opinion, be taken in the 'spirit of the image'. It is 'the letter', in all its artificiality, indeed, the number, which is the key to interpretation (…) Ancient reference myths, on the theme of Oedipus, for example, have nothing to do with the imaginary wellsprings and symbolic articulations of today's conjugal family, nor with our system of social coordinates.[19]

Whilst the Lacanian influence is rather obvious here, what is more striking perhaps is the element of artificiality with which it is connected. And it will take but the tiniest shift of emphasis to displace one's focus of concern from the 'letter' to its 'artifice' and thence to the multiplicitous code of the unconscious 'not so much a language as a jargon, an open-ended, polyvocal formation'.[20]

In the encounter with Deleuze, that displacement and shift of emphasis will occur to dramatic effect. It is in *Anti-Oedipus* that the strange operations of the schizoanalytic unconscious, and its polyvocal jargon 'flush with the real' are thought and explored for themselves, without the overcoding benefits of linguistic structure. But it is by himself, in the writings collected in *The Anti-Oedipus Papers* and in *La révolution moléculaire*, that Guattari developed a more focused and nuanced attention to the ways in which signs operate beyond the regulated interplay of signification, of paradigm and syntagm evident in the structuralist framework.[21] In these texts, we see the emergence of a vocabulary – of power-signs, the Plane of Consistency, machinic Propositions, micro-redundancies, anti-black hole and so on – that flags the taking off of the Guattarian jargon machine.

This terminology, later evident in an extended and modified form in *Schizoanalytic Cartographies,* with its existential tensors, mutational filters, transistence, contingencing, etc., is the result of the exploration of semiotic operations the existence of which Guattari had evidently started to hypothesize in the early 1970s (and which Anglophone readers will be partly familiar with from the later work with Deleuze in *A Thousand Plateaus*). If the outcome can sometimes be rather ugly (and there is nothing pretty about words like 'deterritorialization' or the later 'Point of Contingencing'), they are decidedly not to be confused with the precautionary operations of other forms of expressive operation in theory – the textual, deconstructive play of *différance*, for example. Rather, they acquire a necessity that relates to a sense of signs as prospective, prospecting devices operating as part of a specific, experimental understanding of theory, in which theory acquires greatest contact with the real through its very artifice ('the real is the artificial and not (as Lacan says) the impossible').[22] Discussing the practice of contemporary science in *La révolution moléculaire*, Guattari discerns a semiotic functioning, in which, as he puts it, the distinction between the sign and the referent

> seems to lose a certain degree of pertinence. Today, one no longer requires the furnishing of a positive proof for the existence of a particle. It is enough to make it function without contradiction in the overall semiotics of the theory.

Theoretical physics exemplifies the operation of an a-signifying semiotic, in which the theory fabricates entities for which no positive proof is needed, entities that are effectively prospectively posited as necessarily entailed for the consistency of the theory. These are a-signifying *sign-particles*, entities that have passed beyond the coordinates of space and time.[23] Guattari's comments here point towards a practice of theory that operates as a kind of quasi-experimental *modelling* of semiotico-material entities that cannot be adequately grasped in semiological terms. But the point about such theory is not that it should provide a privileged starting point for the explication and understanding of what is – with the theorist profiting from an underhand authority analogous to that which accrues to the analyst in the process of 'transference' – but rather that it should find ways of generating and working with new forms of existence, to make non-discursive 'nuclei' of machinic sense perceptible and tractable. If science provides Guattari with a model here it is because of the way that its semiotic artifices offer a means of leaping into the unknown[24] through a materially effective abstraction from spatio-temporal coordinates. As he puts it, 'between the sign and the referent, a new type of relation is established, no longer a direct relation but a relation putting into play the ensemble of a theoretico-experimental assemblage.'[25] Far from taking us away from materiality and the real, the endogenous development of theory, which abstracts language from the phenomenological coordinates of personological enunciation (embodied in the reciprocities of communication), operates as a specific kind of praxis which follows 'as closely as possible the points of singularity, of non-sense, the semiotic asperities which, phenomenologically, appear the most irreducible'.[26] But the theory itself offers no guarantee – indeed, in this speculative, experimental pragmatics, the transitive, pre-personal nature of affect and the generalized 'existential transference' that *Schizoanalytic Cartographies* explores as its consequence gives rise only to a heterogenetic labour, 'a potential praxis':

> Affect is the process of existential appropriation by the continuous creation of heterogeneous durations of being. For this reason, we would certainly be well advised to give up treating it under the aegis of scientific paradigms so as to turn deliberately towards ethico-aesthetic paradigms.[27]

With this dimension of heterogenesis, we come back to the question of style. Although his *Essays Critical and Clinical* doesn't offer an analysis of Guattari's work, the conception of style that Deleuze proposes there explores the operations of language 'far from equilibrium' and the generation of non-linguistic visions and auditions necessarily draws on Guattari's arguments about semiotic regimes[28] and his endeavours to explore the possibility of 'escaping' language. What Deleuze says of canonical figures such as Michaux, Melville or Mandelstam captures something of this endeavour.

> Everyone can talk about his memories, invent stories, state opinions in his language; sometimes he even acquires a beautiful style, which gives

him adequate means and makes him an appreciated writer. But when it is a matter of digging under the stories, cracking open the opinions and reaching regions without memories, when the self must be destroyed, it is certainly not enough to be a 'great' writer, and the means must forever remain inadequate. Style becomes nonstyle, and one's language lets an unknown foreign language escape from it, so that one can reach the limits of language and become something other than a writer.'[29]

PRELIMINARY

Classical thought kept the soul at a distance from matter and the essence of the subject at a distance from the cogs of the body. Marxists, for their part, opposed subjective superstructures to the infrastructural relations of production. How should we talk today about the production of subjectivity? A first observation leads us to recognize that the contents of subjectivity depend more and more on a multitude of machinic systems. From now on, no domain of opinion, thought, image, affect or narrativity can pretend to escape from the invasive grip of 'computer-assisted' data banks, the telematic, etc. Consequently, one is even starting to ask if the essence of the subject – this famous essence, after which Western philosophy has been chasing for centuries – doesn't find itself threatened by this new 'machine addiction' of subjectivity. The curious mixture of enrichment and impoverishment that has resulted from it so far is well known: an apparent democratization of the access to data, to knowledge, associated with a segregative closing down of the means for their elaboration; a multiplication of the anthropological angles from which it is approached, a planetary stirring up of cultures that paradoxically is contemporaneous with a growth of particularisms and racisms; an immense extension of techno-scientific and aesthetic fields of investigation unfolding in a moral context of greyness and disenchantment. But rather than associating with the fashionable crusades against the misdeeds of modernism, rather than preaching the rehabilitation of ruined transcendental values, or giving in to the disillusioned delights of postmodernism, we can try to challenge the dilemma of contorted refusal or cynical acceptance of the situation.

Because machines are in a position to articulate statements and record states of fact at the rhythm of the nanosecond and, perhaps tomorrow, the picosecond[1] does not mean that they are diabolical powers that threaten to dominate man. In fact, people are all the less justified in turning away from machines given that, after all, they are nothing other than hyperdeveloped and hyperconcentrated forms of certain aspects of human subjectivity and, let us emphasize, precisely not those aspects that polarize humans into relations of domination and power. A double bridge will have been set up from human to machine and machine to human, across which new and confident alliances between them will be easier to foresee, once it has been established that:

1 current informatic and communication machines do not just convey representative contents but equally contribute to the preparation of new (individual and/or collective) Assemblages of enunciation;

2 all machinic systems, whatever domain they belong to – technical, biological, semiotic, logical, abstract – are, by themselves, the support for proto-subjective processes, which I will characterize in terms of modular subjectivity.

I will refer here to the first aspect of these questions only, reserving myself the right to tackle the second, which turns around problems of self-reference, self-transcendence, etc. elsewhere.

Before going any further, we have to ask ourselves if this 'entry' of subjectivity into 'the machine' (like one used to say 'entering into religion') really is all that new. Weren't 'precapitalistic' or 'archaic' subjectivities also engendered by diverse initiatory, social, rhetorical machines embedded in clan, religious, military, corporational, etc. institutions, institutions that I will group together here under the general rubric *collective apparatuses* [équipements] *of subjectification*? This, for example, was the case with the monastic machines, which carried down the memories of Antiquity to us, stimulating, in passing, our passage to modernity. What else were they than the software, the 'macro-processors', of the Middle Ages – the Neo-Platonics having in their own way been the first to conceptualize a processuality capable of crossing time and stases. And what else was the Court at Versailles, with its meticulous management of the flows of power, money, prestige, competence and its very precise etiquette, if not a machine deliberately conceived to secrete a replacement aristocratic subjectivity that was much more submissive to the royalty of the state than were the lords of the feudal tradition, and to activate other relations of subjection to the values and customs of the growing bourgeoisie?

I cannot retrace here the background history of these collective apparatuses of subjectification in a thumbnail sketch. Besides, to my mind, neither history nor sociology would really be in a position to give us the analytico-political keys to the processes in play. I would like simply to bring to light some fundamental voices/pathways – French here allows a homophonic link between path and enunciation – that these apparatuses have produced, and whose interlacing remains at the base of the processes of subjectification of contemporary Western societies. I will distinguish three series of voices/pathways:

1   voices/pathways of *power*, circumscribing and circumventing human groups from the outside, either by direct coercion and the panoptic hold on bodies, or by the seizure of the soul through the imaginary;

2   voices/pathways of *knowledge* articulated to techno-scientific and economic pragmatics from inside subjectivity;

3   voices/pathways of *self-reference* developing a processual subjectivity (which some time ago I related to the category of 'group-subject') that founds its own coordinates and is self-consistantial, which doesn't stop it from establishing itself transversally to social and mental stratifications.

Powers over external territorialities, deterritorialized knowledges of human activities and machines, and, finally, the creativity proper to subjective mutations: although inscribed at the heart of historical diachrony and enduringly incarnated in sociological divisions and segregations, these three voices/pathways don't stop mixing together in strange ballets, alternating fights to the death and the promotion of new figures.

Let us note in passing that in the schizoanalytic point of view on the elucidation of subjectification only a very restricted use will be made of dialectical, structuralist, systemic and even genealogical (in Michel Foucault's sense) approaches. This is because, in a certain fashion, all modelling systems are valid, all are acceptable, in my opinion. This is solely to the extent that their principles of intelligibility give up any universalist pretention and admit that they have no other mission than to contribute to the cartography of existential Territories, implying sensible, cognitive, affective, aesthetic, etc. Universes, for clearly delimited areas and periods of time. Besides, from an epistemological point of view, there is nothing shameful about this relativism. It derives from the fact that the regularities, the more or less stable configurations that subjective occurrences offer up for deciphering, arise precisely and above all, from the self-modelling systems mentioned earlier, with the third voice/pathway, of self-reference. Here the discursive chains – of expression and of content – only respond very distantly, or against the grain or in a disfiguring way, to the ordinary logic of discursive sets. In other words, at this level, everything is good! Any ideology or cult, even the most archaic, can do the job, as it is no longer a matter of anything other than of using them as existential materials. The primary purpose of their expressive chains is no longer one of denoting states of facts or of organizing states of sense in the axes of signification, but, I repeat, of enacting existential crystallizations that somehow install themselves on this side of the basic principles of classical reason: those of identity, of the excluded middle, of causality, of sufficient reason, of continuity…What is most difficult to bring out here is that these materials, on the basis of which subjective processes of self-reference may be set off, are themselves extracted from radically heterogeneous, if not heteroclite, elements: the rhythms of lived experience, obsessive refrains, identificatory emblems, transitional objects, fetishes of all sorts…What is affirmed, during this traversing of regions of being and modes of semiotization, are traits of singularization – kinds of existential stamps – that date, eventalize, 'contingentialize' states of fact, their referential correlates and the Assemblages of enunciation that correspond to them. This double capacity of intensive traits to singularize and transversalize existence, to confer on it a local persistence, on the one hand, and a transversalist consistency – a transistency – on the other, cannot be fully grasped by rational modes of discursive knowledge. It is only given through an apprehension of the order of the affect, a global transferential seizure. The most universal finds itself conjoined with the most contingent facticity here: the most detached ordinary moorings of sense find themselves anchored in the finitude of being-there. But diverse traditions of what can be called a 'limited rationalism' continue to maintain a systematic, quasi-militant ignorance with regard to everything which, at the heart of these meta-modellings, can thus refer to virtual, incorporeal Universes, to all the vague worlds of uncertainty, of the aleatory, the probable…For a long time, this 'limited rationalism' has, at the heart of anthropology, tracked modes of categorization that it characterized as 'pre-logical' whilst in reality they were only metalogical, paralogical, their objectives being essentially to give a consistency to individual and/or collective Assemblages of subjectivity. Now, here one would have to manage to think a continuum that would go from children's games, through haphazard rituals during psychopathological efforts to recompose 'schizzed' worlds, to the complex cartographies of myths and of the arts, so as finally to join up again with the sumptuous speculative edifices of theologies and philosophies that have sought to apprehend these same dimensions of existential creativity. (Let it suffice here for me to evoke the 'forgetful souls' of Plotinus, or the 'immobile motor' that, according to Leibniz, pre-exists all dissipation of potential.)

But let us come back to our three primordial voices/pathways. Our problem now is to position the third voice/pathway, that of self-reference, appropriately in relation to those of powers and of knowledges. I defined it as being the most singular, the most contingent – that which anchors human realities in finitude, and also the most universal – that which brings about the most dazzling traversals between heterogeneous domains. One should put it a bit differently: it is not universal in the strict sense, it is the richest in *Universes of virtuality*, the best furnished with lines of processuality. And at this point in my exposition, I beg you not to hold the plethora of characterizations, the semantic overload of certain expressions and, doubtless, a certain vagueness in their understanding, against me too much: there is no other recourse possible here!

The voices/pathways of power and knowledge were inscribed in coordinates of exo-reference that guaranteed an extensive use and a precise circumscription of sense for them. The Earth was the basic referent of powers of bodies and populations, whereas Capital was the referent for economic knowledges and the mastery of the means of production. For its part, the Body without organs of self-reference, with neither figure nor ground, opens up for us the completely different horizon of a processuality considered as the point of continuous emergence of every form of creativity.

I must stress that the triad of territorialized Power, Capital of deterritorialized knowledge and processual Self-reference has no other ambition than to clarify certain problems such as, for example, the current resurgence of neo-liberal ideologies or other, even more pernicious, archaisms. Of course it remains the case that it is not on the basis of so summary a model that one might pretend to tackle the cartographies of concrete processes of subjectification. Let's say that it is only a matter here of instruments for a speculative cartography, without any pretention with regard to a universal structural foundation nor an on-the-ground effectiveness. This is another way of recalling that these voices have not always existed and doubtless will not always exist, at least in the same form. Consequently it is perhaps not without relevance to seek to localize their historical emergence and the crossing of thresholds of consistency that was to allow them to put themselves enduringly in the orbit of our modernity.

It is to be expected that such taking consistency relies on collective systems for the 'putting into memory' of data and of knowledges but equally on material apparatuses of a technical, scientific and aesthetic order. One can thus attempt to date these fundamental subjective mutations as a function of the birth of the great collective religious and cultural Apparatuses, on the one hand, and of the invention of new materials, new energies, new machines to crystallize time and, finally, new biological technologies, on the other. I am not saying that it is a matter here of material infrastructures conditioning collective subjectivity directly, but only of components essential to its taking consistency in space and time as a function of technical, scientific and artistic transformations.

These considerations lead me, then, to distinguish three zones of historical fracture on the basis of which, over the last millennium, the three fundamental capitalistic components saw the light of day:

- *the age of European Christianity*, marked by a new conception of the relations between the Earth and Power;
- *the age of the capitalistic deterritorialization of knowledges and techniques,* founded on the principles of generalized equivalence;
- *the age of planetary computerization,* which opens up the possibility that a creative and singularizing processuality might become the new basic reference.

Let us make it clear straightaway, concerning this last point, that few objective elements yet allow us to count on such a shift from oppressive mass-mediatic modernity to a postmedia era that would give the Assemblages of subjective self-reference their full scope. Yet it appears to me that it is only in the context of the new 'deals' of the production of computational and telematic subjectivity that this voice/pathway of self-reference will succeed in acquiring its full capacity. Evidently, nothing can be relied on in advance! Nothing, in this domain, can compensate for innovative social practices. Here it is only a matter of noting that unlike other revolutions of subjective emancipation – Spartacus, the French Revolution, the Paris Commune…– the individual and social practices of self-valorization and self-organization of subjectivity, which today are in reach, are in a position (perhaps for the first time in history) of leading to something more enduring than crazy and ephemeral spontaneous effervescences: namely, a fundamental repositioning of man in relation to his machinic and natural environments (which, moreover, tend to coincide).

The age of European Christianity

On the ruins of the Late Roman and Carolingian Empires, a new figure of subjectivity was erected in Western Europe, which can be characterized by its double articulation to:

1   basic relatively autonomous territorial entities of an ethnic, national, religious character, which at the outset were to constitute

the texture of Feudal segmentarity but which were due to remain, in different forms, down to the present day;

2 the deterritorialized entity of subjective power borne by the Catholic Church and structured as a collective Apparatus on a Europe-wide scale.

Unlike the previous formulae for imperial power, the central figure of power here no longer has a direct, totalitarian-totalizing hold on the basic territories of the socius and subjectivity. Much more precociously than Islam, Christianity will have had to give up the constitution of an organic unity. But far from weakening the processes of the integration of subjectivity, the disappearance of a Caesar in flesh and bone and the promotion, which one might dare to call a substitution, of a deterritorialized Christ will on the contrary have reinforced them. And it seems to me that a sort of fault, a metastable equilibrium, favourable to the proliferation of other equally partial processes of autonomy may have resulted from the conjunction between the partial autonomy of the political and economic spheres proper to Feudal segmentarity and the hyper-fusional character of Christian subjectivity (manifest in the Crusades or the adoption of aristocratic codes such as the 'Paix de Dieu' described by Georges Duby). They will be found in:

- the schismatic vitality of sensibility and religious reflection characteristic of this period;
- the explosion of aesthetic creativity that has been uninterrupted since;
- the first big 'taking off again' of technologies and commercial exchange, characterized by historians as the 'industrial revolution of the eleventh century' and which was correlated to the appearance of new figures of urban organization.

What gave this ambiguous, unstable, tortured formula the additional consistency that was to allow it to survive the dreadful historical ordeals – barbarian invasions, epidemics, permanent wars – that were awaiting it? Schematically, a series of six factors:

1 The promotion of a monotheism that was to turn out, in use, to be rather supple, evolving, relatively capable of adapting to the particular subjective positions of the barbarians, the slaves, etc. The fact that the suppleness of a system of ideological reference might become a fundamental asset in allowing it to last will constitute a basic given that will be found at all the important crossroads of the history of capitalist subjectivity. (One thinks, for example, of the surprising capacity of contemporary capitalism to adapt, which allows it literally to phagocytose the so-called socialist economies.) Consolidation of the new ethico-religious patterns of the Christian West will result in a parallel double market of subjectification: one of the permanent refounding, whatever its setbacks, of the basic territorialities, and the redefinition of the filiations and networks of suzerainty; the other, of a predisposition to the free circulation of the flows of knowledge, of monetary signs, of aesthetic figures, of technology, of goods, of people, etc., clearing the path for the assumption of the second, deterritorialized capitalistic voice.

2   The putting into place of a division of Christian populations by a new type of religious machine, resting in particular on the parish schools created by Charlemagne and which survived the disappearance of his Empire.

3   The long-term installation of bodies of crafts, guilds, monasteries, of religious orders...as so many 'data banks' for the knowledges and techniques of the epoch.

4   The generalization of the use of iron and mills powered by natural energy sources; the development of artisanal and urban mentalities. But this first development of machinism, it must be emphasized, was only established in a sort of parasitical fashion, 'encycsted' at the heart of the big human Assemblages on which the bulk of the big systems of production continued to rest. In other words, one doesn't escape here from the fundamental man/machine relation.

5   The appearance of the first machines, bringing about a much more sustained drive to subjective integration:

- clocks, which beat the same canonical time throughout Christendom;
- the step-by-step invention of religious musics enslaved by their written support.

6   The selection of animal and vegetable species, which will be the basis of the quantitative growth of demographic and economic parameters, and, consequently, of the change in dimensions of the Assemblages in question.

In spite, or because, of colossal pressures – of territorial repression, but also cultural enrichment – exercised by the Byzantine Empire (relayed by Arab Imperialism), on the one hand, and by the barbarian and nomad powers (who were bearers of innovations in metallurgy in particular), on the other, the melting pot of proto-capitalist Christian culture will achieve a relative stabilization (of long duration) of its three fundamental poles of aristocratic, religious and peasant subjectification, ruling over relations of power and knowledge. Thus, the 'machinic surges' linked to urban development and to the growth of civil and military technologies will find themselves encouraged and held back at the same time. This sort of state of nature of relations between man and tool will continue in the paradigmatic reterritorializations of the type 'Work, Family and the Nation' to the present day.

The age of capitalist deterritorialization of knowledges and techniques

This second component of capitalistic subjectivity will be affirmed principally starting in the eighteenth century. It will be marked by a growing disequilibrium of the relations between man and machine. Man will lose the social territorialities that he had hitherto thought permanent. His reference points of physical and social corporeality will find themselves profoundly disrupted. The universe of reference for the new generalized exchangism will no longer be a segmentary territoriality but Capital, as a semiotic mode of reterritorialization of human activities and structures turned upside down by machinic processes. Previously, it was the real Despot or the imaginary God who served as the operational cornerstone for the local recomposition of existential Territories. Now, it will be a symbolic capitalization of the abstract values of power, bearing on economic and technological knowledges, articulated to two deterritorialized social classes and leading to a generalized equivalence amongst all the modes of valorization of goods and human activities. Such a system will only manage to conserve a historical consistency in so far as it will remain engaged in a sort of perpetual racing ahead and by a constant relaunching of its stakes. The new 'capitalistic passion' will sweep away everything in its passage, in particular the cultures and territorialities that had succeeded, for better or for worse, in escaping from the steamrollers of Christianity. The principal factors in the consistency of this component are:

1   the general penetration of the printed text throughout the gears of social and cultural life, corresponding to a certain collapse of direct oral performances, but which, in compensation, will authorize a much greater capacity for the accumulation and treatment of knowledges;

2   the primacy of steel and of steam engines which will multiply the penetrative power of machinic vectors, on earth, at sea, in the air, as much as in the ensemble of technological, economic and urban spaces;

3   a manipulation of time, which finds itself literally emptied of its natural rhythms by:

   • chronometric machines, which will lead to the Taylorist dividing up of work;

   • techniques of economic semiotization, by means of credit money, for example, which imply a general virtualization of capacities for human initiative and a predictive calculus bearing on the domains of innovation – sort of writing cheques on the future – that allow the imperium of market economies to expand indefinitely;

4   biological revolutions, on the basis of the discoveries of Pasteur, which will increasingly link the future of living species with the development of the biochemical industries.

Consequently, man finds himself in a quasi-parasitic position of adjacency with regard to machinic Phyla. Each one of his organs, his social relations, will, in sum, find itself re-patterned, so as to be re-affected, overcoded, as a function of the global requirements of the system (it is in the oeuvres of Leonardo da Vinci, of Brueghel and, above all, of Achimboldo, that the most striking and premonitory representations of these corporeal modifications will be found).

Paradoxically, whilst obstinately referring to universalizing perspectives, this functionalism of organs and of human faculties, and its regime of the generalized equivalence of systems of valorization has never been able, historically, to do anything other than fold back on itself, in reterritorializations of a nationalist, classist, corporatist, racist, paternalist order…reducing it inexorably and sometimes caricaturally, to the most conservatives paths of power. The 'Age of Enlightenment' that marked the advent of this second figure of capitalistic subjectivity, was, in fact, to remain doubled by a hopeless fetishisation of profit – a libidinal formula for a specifically bourgeois power which for all its demarcation from the ancient emblematic systems of control over territories, people and goods by recourse to more deterritorialized mediations, nevertheless secreted the most obtuse, asocial and infantilizing subjective background. Whatever the appearances of free thinking the new capitalist monotheism liked to cloak itself in, it has always presupposed an irrational and archaicizing hold over unconscious subjectivity, in particular by means of apparatuses of hyper-individuated responsibilization and culpabilization which, pushed to their paroxysm, lead to self-harming compulsions and morbid cults of blame, catalogued perfectly in the Kafkaesque universe.

The age of planetary computerization

Here the previous pseudo-equilibria will find themselves upset in a completely different way. Now, it is the machine that will be under the control of subjectivity, not a reterritorialized human subjectivity but a machinic subjectivity of a new type. Listed below are some characteristics of the taking on of consistency of this new age:

1   Media and telecommunications tend to 'overtake' the old oral and scriptural relations. It is to be noted that the resulting polyphony will associate not only human voices but also machinic voices, with databanks, artificial intelligence, etc. Opinion and collective taste, for their part, will be worked over by statistical apparatuses and apparatuses for modelling such as those produced by publicity and the film industry.

2   Little by little, natural raw materials are replaced by a multitude of new materials made to order by chemistry (plastic matters, new alloys, semi-conductors, etc.). The growth of nuclear fission, and tomorrow, of nuclear fusion, allows one to foresee a considerable expansion of energy resources, unless pollution leads it to irreversible disasters! Here, as elsewhere, everything will depend on the capacities of collective reappropriation of new social Assemblages.

3   With the temporality put to work by microprocessors, enormous quantities of data and problems can be processed in minuscule periods of time, in such a way that the new machinic subjectivities keep on jumping ahead of the challenges and stakes with which they are confronted.

4   For its part, biological engineering opens up the path to an indefinite remodelling of living forms, which may equally lead to a radical modification of the conditions of life on the planet and, as a consequence, all the ethological and imaginary references relating to it.

The question that returns here in a haunting fashion is to know why the immense processual potentialities carried by all these computational, telematic, robotic, bureaucratic, biotechnological revolutions so far still only result in a reinforcement of previous systems of alienation, an oppressive mass-mediatization, infantilizing consensual politics. What will enable them finally to lead to a postmedia era, setting them free from segregational capitalist values and giving a full lease of life to the beginnings of a revolution in intelligence, sensibility and creation? Various varieties of dogmatism claim to find a way out of these problems by violently affirming one of these three capitalistic paths, to the detriment of the others. In matters of power, there are those who dream of returning to the legitimacies of yesteryear, to the well-delimited circumscriptions of people, race, religion, caste, sex, etc....Paradoxically, neo-Stalinists and social-democrats, who can only think the socius in the framework of a rigid insertion into Statist functions and structures, are to be classed in this category. There are those whose faith in capitalism leads them to justify all the havoc wreaked by modernity – on man, culture, the environment...– because they gauge that as a last resort they will be the bringers of benefits and of progress. Finally, there are those whose phantasms of the radical liberation of human creativity ended up being relegated to chronic marginality, in a world of pretences, or who turned back to seek refuge behind a façade of socialism or communism.

It is for us, on the contrary, to try to rethink these three necessarily interwoven voices/pathways. No engagement in the creative Phyla of the third voice/pathway is tenable without at the same time creating new existential territories. Whilst they don't arise from the post-Carolingian ethos, they nonetheless call for a protective disposition with regard to the person, the imaginary and the constitution of an environment of gentleness and devotion. As for the mega-enterprises of the second voice/pathway, the great collective industrial and scientific adventures, the management of the large markets of knowledge, they evidently also retain all their legitimacy. This, however, is on condition that their purpose, which today remains desperately deaf and blind to human truths, be redefined. Is it still enough to pretend that this purpose is only profit? Whatever the case may be, the purpose of the division of labour, like that of emancipatory social practices, will have to end up being re-centred on a *fundamental right to singularity*, an ethics of finitude that is all the more demanding with regard to individuals and social entities the less it can found its imperatives on transcendent principles. One sees here that ethico-political Universes of reference are called on to establish themselves in the continuation of aesthetic universes, without anyone for all that being authorized here to speak of perversion or sublimation. It will be noted that, for the same reason as aesthetic operators, the existential operators bearing on these ethico-political matters imply inevitable passages via points where sense is ruptured, irreversible processual engagements, whose actants are most frequently incapable of accounting for anything, to anyone (even themselves), exposing them to the risk of madness. Only the taking consistency of the third voice/pathway, in the direction of self-reference – the passage from the consensual mediatic era to a dissensual postmediatic era – will allow each person to take on fully his or her processual potentialities and perhaps to transform this planet, which is lived as a hell by four-fifths of its population today, into a universe of creative enchantments.

I imagine that this language will ring false to many jaded ears, and that the least badly intentioned will accuse me of being utopian. Yes, utopia does not get good press today, even when it acquires a charge of realism and effectiveness, as conferred on it by the Greens in Germany. But one should not be deceived: these questions of the production of subjectivity no longer only concern a handful of visionaries. Look closely at Japan, the model of models for new capitalist subjectivities! It has never been emphasized enough that one of the essential ingredients of the miracle cocktail that it presents to visitors consists in the fact that collective subjectivity, which is massively produced there, associates the most 'hi-tech' components with archaisms inherited from the depths of the past. There again one finds the reterritorializing function of an ambiguous monotheism – Shinto-Buddhism, a mixture of animism and universal powers – which contributes to the establishing of a supple formula for subjectification, which, it is true, goes well beyond the triadic filter of Christian capitalist paths. There's a lot to learn!

But let us consider instead another extreme, the case of Brazil. Here is a country where the phenomena of the redeployment of archaic subjectivities have taken an entirely different turn. We know that whilst a considerable proportion of the population stagnates in such poverty that it falls outside the monetary economy, this doesn't stop Brazilian industry being ranked sixth amongst Western powers. In this society, a dual society if ever there was one, we are witness to a double sweeping away of subjectivity: on the one hand, by a somewhat racist Yankee wave – whatever some people might think – that finds itself conveyed by one of the most powerful television networks in the world and, on the other, by a wave with an animist character, involving syncretic religions like that of Candomblé. More or less directly inherited from an African cultural background, these religions tend to escape their original confinement in the ghettos so as to contaminate the whole society, including the most well-connected milieus in Rio and São Paulo. In this context, it is impressive to see how mass-mediatic impregnation precedes capitalistic enculturation. Do you know what happened when President Sarney wanted to strike a decisive blow to inflation, which had reached upwards of 400 per cent per year? He went on television; he brandished a piece of paper in front of the cameras and he declared that from the moment that he signed the decree-law that he held in his hand, every one of the people watching him would become his personal representative and would have the right to arrest traders who did not respect official prices. It seems that it was a formidably effective time. But at the price of what regression with regard to the matter of the law!

The subjective impasse of the capitalism of permanent crisis (Integrated World Capitalism) seems total. It knows that the voices/pathways of self-reference are indispensible to its expansion and thus to its survival, and yet everything leads it to block their proliferation. A sort of Superego – the loud, Carolingian voice – dreams only of crushing them by reterritorializing them on its archaic images. But, to try to escape from this vicious circle, let us try, now, to resituate our three capitalistic voices/pathways in relation to the geopolitical coordinates used to hierarchize the big subjective ensembles in the first, second and third worlds. For the subjectivity of the Christian West, everything was (and remains) simple: it tolerates no restriction in latitude or longitude. It is the transcendent centre around which everything is obliged to turn. For their part, the voices/pathways of Capital haven't stopped rushing forward, first towards the West, in search of ungraspable 'new frontiers' and, more recently, to the East, to the conquest of what remains of the old Asiatic empires – Russia included. Except that this crazy race reaches its limit with California on one side and Japan on the other. The second pathway for Capital has looped back on itself, the world has closed up and the system is saturated. (The last power to notice will doubtless be France, perched on its atoll in Muroroa!) Consequently, it is perhaps along the North-South axis that the fate of the third voice/pathway, of self-reference, will be played out. That is what I would like to call the barbarian compromise. The old walls of the limits of barbarianism have been irremediably disintegrated, deterritorialized. The last shepherds of monotheism have lost their sheep, because the new subjectivity is no longer of the sort that can be gathered in a flock. And now it is Capital that is starting to shatter into animist and machinic polyvocity. Would it not be a fabulous reversal if the old aboriginal African subjectivities pre-Columbus became the ultimate recourse for the subjective reappropriation of machinic self-reference? These same Negroes, these same Indians, the same Oceanians many of whose ancestors chose death rather than submission to the ideals of power, slavery and the exchangism of Christianity and then capitalism?

I hope no-one will object to the rather too exotic character of my last two examples. Even in the countries of the Old World, like Italy, it has been observed for some years now that at the heart of the North-East-Centre triangle, a multitude of little family enterprizes have started to operate in symbiosis with the cutting edge manufacturers of the electronics and telematic industries. It has got to the point that if an Italian Silicon Valley were to see the light of day, it would be thanks to the redeployment of subjective archaisms having their origin in the country's old patriarchal structures. And perhaps you are not unaware that certain futurologists, who aren't in the least fantasists, claim that in several decades certain Mediterranean countries, like Italy and Spain, are set to overtake the major economic poles of Northern Europe. So, you see that in the matter of dreams and utopias, the future remains largely open! My wish is that all those who remain attached to the idea of social progress – for whom the social has not become a trap, a 'semblance' – turn seriously towards these questions of the production of subjectivity. The subjectivity of power does not fall out of the sky; it is not inscribed in the chromosomes that the divisions of knowledge and of labour must necessarily lead to the atrocious segregations that humanity experiences today. The unconscious figures of power and knowledge are not universals. They are attached to reference myths that are deeply anchored in the psyche, but which can be inflected towards liberating pathways. Today, subjectivity remains massively controlled by apparatuses of power and knowledge which place technical, scientific and artistic innovations at the service of the most retrograde figures of sociality. And, yet, other modalities of subjective production – those that are processual and singularizing – are conceivable. Tomorrow, these alternative forms of existential reappropriation and of self-valorization may become the *reason for living* of human collectives and individuals who refuse to give themselves up to the deathly entropy characteristic of the period through which we are passing.

1 ANALYTIC CARTOGRAPHIES

Assemblages of enunciation

For more than ten years I have endeavoured to extract from the debris of psychoanalysis what still stands up, what deserves to be rethought on the basis of theoretical scaffoldings that are different to and, if possible, less reductionist than those of the Freudians and Lacanians.

I'm concerned to make clear immediately that I have never conceived of the undertaking that I have called schizoanalysis as a self-enclosed specialism obliged to position itself in the ranks of the psy domain.

In my opinion, its ambitions should be both more modest and more grand. More modest because if this schizoanalysis really is going to exist one day, it is because *it already exists a little bit everywhere today*, in an embryonic fashion, in diverse modalities, and has no need of an institutional foundation in due form. More grand, to the extent that its vocation is, in my opinion, to become a discipline for reading *other modelling systems*. Not as a general model, but as an instrument for deciphering modelling systems in diverse domains, a meta-model, in other words. One might object that the limit between a model and a meta-model does not appear to be a stable frontier. And it is true that in one sense, subjectivity is always more or less an activity of meta-modelling (in the perspective proposed here *the transfer of modelling*, transversal passages between problems of different kinds).

But what matters to me is precisely a displacement of the analytic problematic, making it drift from systems of *statements* and preformed subjective *structures* towards *Assemblages of enunciation* able to forge new coordinates for reading and to 'bring into existence' new representations and propositions.

Schizoanalysis will thus be essentially eccentric in relation to professional 'psy' practices, with their corporations, societies, schools, didactic initiations, the 'pass', etc. Its provisional definition could be *the analysis of the impact of Assemblages of enunciation on semiotic and subjective productions in a given problematic context.*

I won't really be able to expand on these notions of 'problematic context', of 'scene', of 'bringing into existence' in the framework of this exposition. I will limit myself to signalling in passing that they can refer to things as different as a clinical tableau, an unconscious phantasm, a diurnal fantasy, an aesthetic production, a micro-political fact…What counts here is the idea of an existential circumscription that implies the deployment of intrinsic references – one might also say, a process of self-organization or singularization.

Why this leitmotif of a return to *Assemblages of enunciation*? So as to avoid, as far as possible, getting bogged down in the concept of the 'unconscious'. So as not to reduce the facts of subjectivity to drives, affects, intra-subjective instances and inter-subjective relations. Obviously, this sort of thing will have a certain place in the preoccupations of schizo-analysis, but only as a component, and always only in certain kinds of scenario. One will note, for example, that there exist Assemblages of enunciation not including any components of the semiotics of signification, Assemblages that do not have subjective components and others that have no consciousness component. The Assemblage of enunciation will thus be led to 'exceed' the problematic of the individuated subject, the thinking monad delimited by consciousness, the faculties of the soul (the understanding, the will…) in their classically accepted sense. It seems necessary to me to emphasize that one will always be dealing with ensembles that at the outset are indifferently material and/or semiotic, individual and/or collective, actively machinic and/or passively fluctuating.

The question will then become that of the status of these Assemblage components, which find themselves 'straddling', and interacting with, radically heterogeneous domains. I once said, I no longer remember where, that we wanted to construct a science in which dishcloths and napkins would be mixed up, along with other things that are more different still,[1] in which dishcloths and napkins could no longer even be encompassed under the general rubric of linen. A science in which one would be prepared instead to accept with good grace that dishcloths are differentiated in singularized becomings and have a cortège of contextual repercussions, in which it could just as easily be a question of a landlord drying glasses with a dishcloth as of soldiers launching a cleanup operation [a 'coup de torchon'] on a pocket of resistance. In a classic analytic perspective one only takes this kind of contextuality into account in its signifying incidences and never as a referent generative of pragmatic effects in given institutional and material social fields. It seems to me that it is this micro-politics of sense that needs to be overturned. The presumed analytic effect no longer resides in a derivation of interpretable signifying chains, but in an 'a-signifying' mutation of a 'Universe-context', that is to say, the Constellation of registers called into question. Collective and/or individual Assemblages of enunciation then become objects of investigation that take priority in relation to those of the imagos and structures that are supposedly constitutive of subjectivity. In a contingent fashion, certain Assemblages are put into the position of the 'analyser'[2] of formations of the Unconscious. It matters little whether these analysers are conscious of their 'mission' or are invested by other instances so as to occupy such a position. An analytic Assemblage can be laid out in different ways, according to whether it is incarnated in:

- an individual – when Freud 'invents' psychoanalysis, for example;
- a sociologically defined group such as a gang of youths who 'reveal' the potentialities of a ghetto;
- more diffuse social phenomena, such as mutations of collective sensibility or uncontrolled movements of opinion;
- a pre-personal practice; a style, a creative mutation that binds an individual or a group without them even being aware of it.

All these cases and many others are combinable in multiple fashions. Thus the schizoanalytic undertaking will never limit itself to an interpretation of 'givens'; it will take a much more fundamental interest in the 'Giving', in the Assemblages that promote the concatenation of affects of sense and pragmatic effects. As they do not escape from this general plasticity of Assemblages themselves, these 'analysers' do not present themselves as pre-established apparatuses and never pretend to institute themselves as legitimate structures of enunciation – as is the case with the classic psychoanalytic cure. Not only will there not be any normalized schizoanalytic protocol, but a new fundamental rule, an anti-rule rule, will enforce a constant calling into question of analyser Assemblages, as a function of their feedback effects on the analytic givens.

This feedback, which is negative when it leads to a simple re-equilibrating of the Assemblage, and positive, when it sets off processes of splitting, or even of catastrophe, constitutes the analytic matter *par excellence*. How does one Assemblage relay another Assemblage so as to 'administer' a given situation? How does an analytic Assemblage, or one that is alleged such, mask another? How do several Assemblages enter into relation and what is the result? How are the potentialities for the constitution of new Assemblages to be explored in a context that appears totally blocked? How are the relations of production, of proliferation and the micropolitics of these new Assemblages to be 'aided' in such a case? This is the kind of question that schizoanalysis will be led to pose. This work of subjectivity – in the sense that one works iron – or on musical scales on or fecund moments in the weft of existence – is identified here with the production of [a] referent, or more precisely, a *meta-modelling of trans-Assemblage relations*. Far from coinciding with what is ordinarily understood by subjectivity, it no longer relates to I don't know what subtle and ineffable essence of a subject in search of a vertiginous adequation to himself (with God as the only witness). Schizoanalytic subjectivity is established at the intersection of Flows of signs and machinic Flows, at the junction of the facts of sense, of material and social facts, and, above all, in the wake of transformations resulting from their different modalities of Assemblage. It is these last that make it lose its character as human territoriality and project it towards the most original and the most 'futuristic' processes of singularization at the same time – becomings animal, vegetable, cosmos, becomings immature, multivalent sex, becomings incorporeal…Without entirely ceasing to be thinking reeds,[3] through this subjectivity, humans are at present adjacent to a reed that 'thinks for them', an abstract machinic Phylum that carries them well beyond their previous possibilities.

Archaic forms of enunciation rested in the main on speech and direct communication, whereas the new Assemblages have more and more recourse to mediatic informational Flows, carried by machinic channels (the machines in question not only being of a technical order but also scientific, social, aesthetic, etc.), which everywhere exceed the old individual and collective subjective territories. Whilst territorialized enunciation was logocentric and implied a personal mastery of the ensembles that it discursivized, deterritorialized enunciation, which can be characterized as machinocentric, relies on non-human procedures and memories to deal with semiotic complexes that for the most part escape from direct conscious control.

But we will not pay attention to this first dichotomy, which risks proving far too reductive. On account of the preceding considerations, we are quite naturally led to setting out the various different modalities of Assemblages of enunciation, as a function of what happens, or does not happen, to prevail of the components of semiotization, subjectification and conscientialization (this list can always be extended as a function of descriptive needs).

Non-semiotic Assemblages

The stigmergic constructions of bees or termites provide us with a first example: highly elaborated forms that result from 'modular codings' that are evidently neither semiotic, nor subjective, nor consciential. In the order of human enunciation, similar systems, such as those of endocrine regulation, may be led to hold a determining place at the heart of Assemblages, the semiotic components of which they in some way put in brackets. I'm thinking in particular of the probable role of self-intoxication (self-addiction) on the basis of ß-endorphines in the 'hardening' of certain sado-masochist tableaus or in acute forms of mental anorexia.

Non-subjective semiotic Assemblages

For example, the psychosomatic tableaus relative to the 'character armour' studied by Wilhelm Reich. The subjective representations here pass to 'one side' of the somatic semiotization.

Subjective, non-conscientialized semiotic Assemblages

Assemblages arising from human ethology, for example, that set off learning processes through unconscious imprinting, delimitations of Territory, reception, display, submission and hostile behaviours, etc.

I imagine that a psychoanalyst, especially if he is of a Lacanian persuasion, would be tempted to object that what I am talking about is all well and good but has nothing to do with the Unconscious, the true psychoanalytic Unconscious, which is only conceivable within the snare of language…We know the tune! To which I would reply that schizoanalytic Assemblages take the keenest interest in the reductionist structures centred on the Oedipal triangle and the symbolic castration that the production of subjectivity effectively leads to in a capitalistic context. However, that doesn't in the slightest mean they can dispense with taking into consideration productions of subjectivity in other domains of psychopathology, or anthropology…respecting their specific characteristics. In this sense, the claim of schizoanalysis is indeed, I repeat, to constitute itself as a meta-modelling Assemblage of all these heterogenenous domains, which it will consider as so many 'optional matters'.

We will start, then, from the broadest hypothesis, namely, that of the existence, for humans, of an unconscious domain associating, on an equal footing, facts of sense borne by structures of representation and language, and very different systems of coding, moulding, tracing, imprinting, relative to organic, social, economic, components, etc. The putting into play of phenomena of subjectification, that is to say, the establishment of lived territories, accepted as such in a relation to a world of objects and alter-egos, will only be occasional, optional. In other words, neither the question of the subject, nor that of the linguistic signifier, will necessarily be at the centre of the problematics posed in this unconscious domain. It will be the same with the question of consciousness. Different processes of conscien-tialization, succeeding and/or being superposed on one another could be put into play here. To illustrate these kinds of connections and disconnec-tions, a good example seems to me to be that of driving a car. On the road, it is not rare for a state of wakeful dreaming to establish itself on the basis of a pseudo-sleep. In fact, the subject is not sleeping; she allows several systems of consciousness to function in parallel, some of which remain on guard, whilst others shift to the foreground. This is what happens when a traffic signal, a traffic incident or the yelling of a passenger re-establish a sequence of hyper-vigilance. The Assemblage of enunciation, in the enlarged sense that I am giving it here, thus passes via several levels of *machinic enslavement* (to take up an old notion from cybernetics). Consequently, rather than returning constantly to the same, supposedly foundational, structures, the same archetypes, the same 'mathemes', schizoanalytic meta-modelling will choose to map compositions of the unconscious, contingent topographies, evolving with social formations, technologies, arts, sciences, etc. Even when it is led to typify some unconscious scenarios – on the basis of egoistic, personological, conjugal, familial, domestic organizing formulae – it will never do so – I repeat – as a structural prototype.

Consciousness and subjectivity

Let us pause on some of the implications of this 'unsticking' of consciousness and subjectivity. At first I had thought that it would be necessary to differ-entiate between:

- an absolute unconscious, at a molecular level, which would escape radically from any re-presentation and whose manifestations would only arise from a-signifying figures;[4]
- a relative unconscious, at a molar level, which would, on the contrary, be organized in more or less stable representations.

I was then concerned about falling into a topographical freezing of psychic instances, like that which led Freud to separate, on opposite sides, the

Unconscious and the Conscious (accompanied by the Preconscious); and later, the Id and the Ego (with its subsidiaries); or indeed which led Lacan to erect a symbolic order, as the armature of the Real and the Imaginary.

Since first inspection, such a circumscribing of the molecular Unconscious has proved to be shaky. In effect, this type of Assemblage can adapt perfectly well to the existence of consciential components. We know that the molecular processes that are at work in a hysterical or obsessional neurosis are inseparable from a particular type of consciousness and even – in the case of the second – a hyper-consciousness. Whilst operating on the basis of an a-signifying matter (which doesn't prevent it from also conveying images and signifying chains, but it only retains from them what it can treat as a-signifying figures)[5], an oneiric Assemblage or a delirious Assemblage also includes idiosyncratic modes of conscientialization. I believe that one gains nothing from wanting to endow all these Assemblages with the same consciential essence, always identical to itself. Little by little, one arrives at 'limit-consciousnesses', with the experiences of trance, mystic rupture with the world, catatonia or even, proximate to this, unlocalizable organic tensions or more or less deep comas. So, then, every instance of enunciation can be simultaneously conscious and unconscious. It is a question of intensity, of proportion, of scope. Conscious and unconscious states are relative to Assemblages that authorize their composite assembly, superpositions, slidings and disjunctions. And one senses here that at a tangent to them, an absolute consciousness, coinciding with the absolute Unconscious of a non-thetic self-presence, escaping any alterity or life of society, establishes itself.

It thus seems essential to me not to set up an opposition of the 'primary process-secondary elaboration' type again. Especially if it has to be based on the idea that the passage from one to the other would correspond to a rupture in the level of modes of differentiation, as in Freud's second topography (id, ego, superego): chaos on the side of the primary process, and structuration on the side of the secondary elaboration. Just because we are forbidden a digitalized, binarized access to the molecular unconscious doesn't mean that we are condemned to fall into an entropic abyss of disorder.

We believe that as far possible, it is necessary for the rectification of the analysis of formations of the Unconscious to minimize the use of notions like those of subjectivity, consciousness, significance…as transcendental entities that are impermeable to concrete situations. The most abstract, radically incorporeal, references mesh with the real; they cross the most contingent of Flows and Territories. On account of this, nothing protects them against historical alteration and cosmogenetic mutations. In other words, the signifying structure does not transcend the libido. In this respect, one could easily demonstrate that Lacan progressively substituted his concept of the signifier for that of the libido. In certain contexts, sense can be massively opposed to material and signaletic Flows, conceived in an essentially passive mode. But in other contexts it may originate on the basis of a 'machinic' of fluctuations, exceeding strata and homeostases. It is this processual option, this refusal of a generalized economy of equivalences, this choice of a 'clinamen' that singularizes repetition, which makes us refuse maps that are fixed and invariant, as of right, in the domain of subjectivity, even if in fact they are established in certain areas of an Assemblage (as is the case for the Oedipal triangle in the Capitalist field of production). Thus we have made up our mind only to consider situations from the angle of the junction of Assemblages that, to a certain point, secrete their own meta-modelling coordinates. A junction can certainly impose connections, but it does not impose a fixed constraint, it can be bypassed; its connective power can decrease when certain of its components lose their consistency.

Let us try to illustrate this point. A singer loses her mother. The following week, she also loses two octaves in her tessitura; she starts going out of tune; her abilities to interpret suddenly seem to become useless. This woman's singing was established on the basis of several Assemblages, certain of which exceeded the limit of the person. At present, the component of enunciation that was grafted onto her relations with her mother is put to the test by the death, but that is not in the slightest synonymous with its extinction. The element of it that is not actual (the past that one cannot recapture) gains the upper hand over the element of open possibility, and an erratic, vaguely threatening representation of her mother finds itself put into circulation. This image of death, sheltered from any test of reality, is the bearer of a sort of power of petrification. The subject, as Freud writes, 'clings' to the lost object.[6] But in this particular case the only manifest consequence of this semiotic 'contraction' seems to be localized on the vocal element of musical activity. It is conceivable that a more sustained exploration might have revealed other incidences of it. But would such an investigation have been absolutely necessary?

Nothing is less sure, because in such circumstances one should always fear inducing new symptoms on the basis of the transference and interpretation (either by forcing the hand of an etiological tableau that seems to 'fit well', or – what amounts to the same thing – that the subject brings to you the appropriate symptoms on a plate, of their own accord). As it happens, it is a matter of being wary of the temptations that lead to the 'work of mourning' that originates in the difficulties that the libido experiences in turning to substitute objects. Here, as elsewhere, a description in terms of an object, rather than in terms of an Assemblage of enunciation, would present the drawback of obscuring the fields of possibility that escape psychoanalytic programming. Where Freud only envisaged two options – the slow and melancholic liquidation of the libido invested in the lost object, or, in extreme cases, a 'hallucinatory wishful psychosis'[7] – we have to be ready to be receptive to reorganizations of an Assemblage that escape from the curses of primary identification or the relation of 'oral incorporation', without any complex. And that is precisely what happened with this singer, who – if you will allow me the expression –'took the blow' perfectly well, by even managing to conquer several new degrees of freedom on this occasion and by starting, from then on, to control her Superego in a clearly more accommodating way. This time, the loss of consistency of a component will thus not have been accompanied by a chain of inhibitions. Rather, it will have served as a sensory plate, a revealer, an alarm signal! To which it is appropriate not to hasten to respond, because perhaps it doesn't need any response properly so-called. An a-signifying index – the restriction of vocal performance – marks the stopping of something, without, as the context reveals, preventing something else from occurring. That is all one can say about it! Certain long marked out pathways – singing, the moralizing overcoding of the mother – undergo a pragmatic transformation. Should these facts be recorded in the column of debts and losses? Nothing is less sure! But nothing is played out either. Because many things will depend on the positive or negative judgement with which this event will be connoted. Every transferential induction, even the most subtle, the most allusive, which would allow guilt of an Oedipal origin to be supposed to exist behind this symptomatic manifestation, could have devastating effects, or, at least, bring us back to the depressive tableau that is 'normally' expected in similar circumstance by a psychoanalyst. Is it not preferable to ask oneself about the material qualities of this component of expression, which perhaps allowed the singer to avoid other damage? Wouldn't the fact of having a component as luxurious as singing have allowed an alarm to be sounded and to induce a bifurcation of the Assemblage? Consequently, what had been vegetating in the form of an inhibition was transformed into a process of singularization. Without the existence of the singing, other things would doubtless have happened. Maybe this patient would have lost other kinds of octaves in other registers! But nothing is assured in this domain. Everything in this is domain is, I repeat, a question of the threshold of consistency, of the quanta of transformation, of the probability of the accumulation of effect. Certain faciality traits were unlinked from the face of the mother, were detached from the coordinates of the Superego, to work on their own count, on other lines of possibility, other

Constellations of Universes, whilst certain scrutinizing frowns paralysed the extreme ends of the scale, transformed for the occasion into a sort of altar on which the sacrificial offerings will finally turn out not to be very costly. One will perhaps find this kind of description closer to myths and tales than to the scientific schemas of psychology and psychoanalysis – such as those of the celebrated 'globus pharynges' or the comings and goings of Kleinian objects, the ruptures of identification consequent to melancholic introjection, or even the disentangling of the death drive. But what is wrong with that?

The functors of deterritorialization

The category of deterritorialization should allow us to separate out the problematic of consciousness – and as a consequence, the unconscious – from that of the representation of the Ego and the unity of the person. The idea of a totalizing, even totalitarian, consciousness ('I am the master of myself and of the universe') participates in a founding myth of capitalist subjectivity. In fact, there are only diversified processes of conscientialization, resulting from the deterritorialization of existential Territories that are themselves multiple and tangled. But in their turn, these different instruments for the catalysis of a for-itself and of modes of singularization of the relation to the worlds of the in-itself and of other egos can only acquire the consistency of an existential monad to the extent that they succeed in affirming themselves in a second dimension of deterritorialization, which I will characterize as energetic discursivization (Figure 1.1).

By virtue of their relations of reciprocal presupposition (indicated on the abcissae), and their relations of composition (indicated on the ordinates), the four functors FTΦU deploy four domains:

- material and signaletic Flows;
- existential Territories;
- abstract machinic Phyla;
- incorporeal Universes (qualified as 'consciential' in this particular case).

It is on the basis of these two sets of coordinates that we expect to be able to map the configurations of subjectivity, desire, drive energy and the diverse modalities of discourse and consciousness relating to them, without having recourse to the traditional apparatuses of somatic infrastructure,

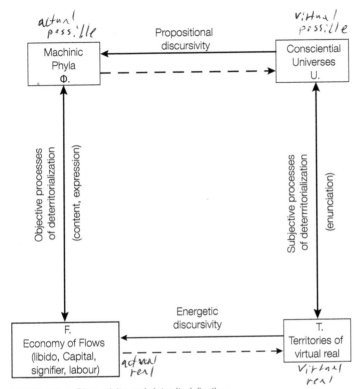

FIGURE 1.1 Discursivity and deterritorialization

instinctual propping, determinism (founded on need and lack), behavioural conditioning, etc. To this effect, the entities arising from these four domains will not have any fixed identity. They will only be able to sustain their own configurations through the relations that they entertain with each other; they will be required to change state and status as a function of their overall Assemblage. In other words, they will not arise from a structural topography, and it is to their systems of transformation that the task of 'administering' their modelling is allotted. To be in a position to support such a traversing of orders (which classical thought dedicated itself to keeping separate), these functors will depend on the laws of composition between two couples of categories: the actual and the virtual, the possible and the real, whose matrix of cross-relations is illustrated in Figure 1.2.

Inscribed according to objective and subjective coordinates of deterritorialization, the relations of inter-entitarian presupposition do not put

	Actual	Virtual
Possible	Φ.: Phylum of actual possibility	U.: Universe of virtual possibility
Real	F.: Flux of actual real	T.: Territories of virtual real

FIGURE 1.2 The matrix of cross-relations of the four categories

the Flows and the Territories of the real on an equal footing with the Phyla and Universes of the possible – the latter envelop and subsume the former in such a way that the reality of the possible always has primacy over the possibility of the real. In these conditions, the Phyla will constitute the 'integrals' of Flows, as it were, and the Universes, the 'integrals' of Territories (Figure 1.3).

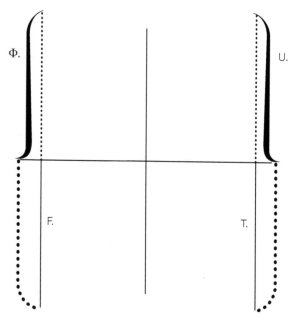

FIGURE 1.3 The integration of the four categories

Although it entails shifting onto the terrain of the Freudian heritage – the majority of psychoanalysts for more than 50 years having invoked Freud's texts as though bearers of a sacred truth – it seems to me to be useful to try to define how the present attempt at refounding the unconscious on deterritorialization is inscribed in its continuation, and how it differs from it.

Unconscious versus libido

Freud's first concern was to give a scientific foundation to psychology by introducing into it *abstract quantities*.[8] It is this preoccupation that led him to renounce the idea of the 'faculties of the soul' of classical theories and to promote a deterritorialization of the psyche operating on an unconscious 'scene', one unlocalizable in ordinary phenomenological coordinates. But although one might have expected that such a treatment of the psyche would have had an essentially reductionist function, it was, on the contrary, correlative to an enrichment manifesting itself in a veritable explosion of new interpretations of the discourse of hysteria, of dreams, of lapsus, of witticisms, etc. It is no mean paradox that mechanistic presuppositions[9] directly inspired by the psychotherapy of Fechner and the physicalism of Helmholtz and Brücke could thus coexist with an 'abyssal' exploration, for which scarcely anything other than Dadaism and Surrealism would have an equivalently adventurous character.[10] Everything seems to have happened as if the support that Freud had drawn from the scientific schemas of his epoch gave him sufficient confidence to allow him to give free rein to his creative imagination. Whatever the case may be, it has to be admitted that his discovery of the unconscious processes of semiotic singularization – the celebrated 'primary process' – would have much difficulty finding a place in the rigid associationist framework that he developed simultaneously in the wake of his 'Project for a Scientific Psychology' of 1895.[11] Yet he was never to break the links with his initial neuronal models completely.[12] (In the definitive 1929 edition of the *Traumdeutung*, for example, he will maintain his first professions of reflexological faith,[13] resulting in the Unconscious such as he conceived it finding itself sandwiched between perception and motricity.[14])

This incessant coming-and-going, between an impenitent scientism and a lyrical inventiveness reminiscent of Romanticism, results in a series of reterritorializations in response to the diverse advances of the deterritorialization of the psyche. I will invoke this phenomenon here with regard to only a couple of concepts, the libido and the Unconscious.

The *libido* finds that it has two statuses conferred on it. That of a processual energy making dynamic relations drift far from their equilibrium position, or that of a static energy contributing to the stratification of psychic formations. But Freud never succeeded in articulating them in a coherent way, even when he postulated the coexistence of an object libido and an Ego libido. It will be different from our point of view, as these two statuses will no longer arise from the hazards of a libidinal economic balance, but from fundamental micro-political choices. The libido will consequently find itself 'denaturalized', deterritorialized: it will become a sort of abstract matter of possibility. The generic choice will become: either the deterritorialized option of the schizoanalysis of a *libido-Phylum* as the integral of the (material and signaletic) transformational Flows of desire (on the left abscissa of Figures 1.1 and 1.3); or the reterritorialized option of the Freudianism of a *libido-Flow* first encysted in the somatic part of the drives (the drive and the source, by contrast with the aim and the object), then organized in psychogenetic stages, to finally be made prisoner of a timeless face-to-face confrontation with an entropic death (the opposition Eros-Thanatos).

For the *unconscious*, the generative choice will be to constitute it either as a *Universe* of reference of an ensemble of lines of alterity, virtual possibilities, unprecedented new becomings (on the right abscissa of Figures 1.1 and 1.3), or as a *refuge-Territory* for the repressed, kept on a leash by the censor of the Conscious-Preconscious system in the first topography, and by the Ego-Superego system in the second.

Freud abandoned the first terrain very early on to theorists like Jung, who, moreover, were barely able to exploit it.[15] On the other hand, he did not stop reterritorializing the unconscious from several points of view, on:

- a spiritual plane, as I have just recalled, by circumscribing it in a topographical instance that he will end up emptying of all substance and reducing to an indifferent chaos;[16]

- a temporal plane, with his hypothesis of psychogenetic stages, which was literally to ruin his discovery of the new continent of child sexuality that he had nevertheless managed to endow with a paradoxical historical dimension (with his theory of phantasmatic deferred action) destined to thwart the realist implications of his first formulations concerning the traumas of precocious seduction. If only he had stuck to his initial intuitions, namely that the unconscious fundamentally escapes the ordinary knowledge/experience of time![17]

There is the same reversal of situation concerning the object of desire. At the time of the *Traumdeutung* it is presented in a rich and ambiguous fashion. Like Proust's Albertine, 'a goddess with several heads' (and probably several sexes as well), it still, to a certain extent, escapes from binary and phallic capitalistic logics. For example, the Irma of the inaugural dream of the *Traumdeutung* is described as a 'collective figure' represented by a 'generic image' unifying: 1) The patient of whom it is a question in the dream; 2) a woman that Freud might have treated; 3) his own eldest daughter; 4) a child that he is examining in consultation at the hospital; 5) yet another woman and 6) Mrs Freud in person,[18] whilst elsewhere 'localities are often treated like persons'.[19] The object thus functions like a 'knot' of overdetermination,[20] the 'navel' of the dream, 'the point by which it is attached to the unknown'[21] and on the basis of which it makes indefinite lines of singularization proliferate. Deterritorialization will score a few more points with the Kleinian escape of the object from its personological framework so as to become 'partial'. From that point, could the door towards other, non-human, animal, vegetable, cosmic, abstract machinic becomings have been opened? And yet it was closed again in every way possible: because an exhaustive list of typical partial objects in question will be set out; because they will be used as the normative landmarks that the 'combatant's journey' to any subjectivity aspiring to reach the supreme stage of 'oblative genitality' is supposed to stick to; because from 'bad objects' to 'good objects', from the 'object relation' and 'transitional objects' to 'objects little a', successive generations of Freudians will end up making a function that is generic, robbing it of its traits of singularity.

It will be the same with alterity: although Freud introduced it as a requirement for truth in the most barricaded of psychopathological tableaus, it too will find itself reterritorialized in personological relations (to the point of becoming prohibited from remaining on the supposedly fusional pre-Oedipal scene) and structuralized in an initiatic complex of symbolic castration, under the murderous eye of the analytic Sphinx.

In summary, the 'optional matter' of the face-to-face of the Libido and the Unconscious, could be figured as in the diagram overleaf (1.4).

The maps of subjectivity

Before going any further with our examination of the cartographic possibilities opened up by our four functors FTΦU, we must ask ourselves about the status of the present theoretical undertaking. Our principal concern is

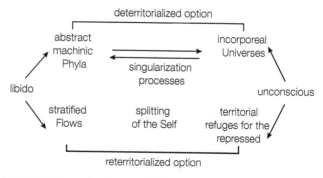

FIGURE 1.4 The optional matter Libido-Unconscious

to develop a conceptual framework that might protect schizoanalysis from every temptation to give in to the ideal of scientificity that ordinarily prevails in the 'psy' domains, like a collective Superego. We will seek instead to find a foundation for it that will make it similar to the aesthetic disciplines, by its mode of valorization, its type of truth and its logic. All the professional specializations that deal with the psyche are generally enveloped in an aura that, paradoxically, mixes the scientific spirit and magic inextricably. As far as I'm concerned, in principle I am not all hostile with regard to magic. I even think that, in many cases, it constitutes a mode of mapping of psychic Assemblages of great interest, sometimes capable – in the context of traditional medicines – of setting up an opposition to the sterile and reductionist approaches of the shrinks in white smocks! Still, it would be a good idea for this magic dimension to be recognized and accepted as such! This is evidently not the case with the specialists in question. Too frequently they offer us the spectacle of people who cloak themselves in a bookish knowledge, cut off from reality and whose uncertainties are badly dissimulated by a façade of professional assurance. Moreover, it needs to be recognized that all the protagonists in the 'psy' theatre are complicit in this deception: the users, the health administrators, the media, etc. Everything rests on the idea that a person can only legitimately consecrate his activities to the psychological difficulties of his fellow humans in the name of science. When 'shrinks' meet each other, they hold 'scientific' meetings, they give addresses characterized in the same fashion. Their way of expressing themselves, their social pretences, their attitude, their posture and even their dress codes are imprinted with this ideal of scientificity. One has to admit that overall the whole thing is generally in painfully bad taste and unbearably affected.

One could list at least three modes of articulation between the scientistic mythology of shrinks and their domains of application – the three, additionally overlapping in every way possible: an ascetic pathway, an identificatory pathway and a pathway of propping.

The ascetic pathway consists in the specialist setting himself up directly in the position of a scientist in the exact sciences – or at least, the position that he imagines they have. At the end of the nineteenth century and during the first half of the twentieth century, the 'psy' domains, which were in the process of being explored, appeared as the last nooks and crannies of reality that still escaped from the divisions of scientific reason. So nothing seemed more urgent than to submit them to the reigning experimental procedures of the day. This implied that, as a prerequisite, one distinguish within them perfectly defined objects on the basis of which one would endeavour to establish correlations and laws. The epitome of this approach had been promoted in the psychophysics of Fechner, who believed he had discovered a decisive law (called the 'Weber-Fechner Law'), which continues to lie around in the manuals, establishing a correlation between sensation and excitation, such that the first varies as the logarithm of the second. The study of conditioned reflexes, the growth of 'behaviourism', seemed at first equally to be inscribed in this direction. But given that they were to find it impossible to invent a corpus of algorithms that would be sufficiently coherent to allow continuous scientific development, the proponents of this way of thinking were very quickly to become disillusioned. It nonetheless continues to fester in the laboratories of psychology and, in recent years, has even experienced a spectacular revival, with the massive return of methods of conditioning and the growth of currents of family therapy based on the systems theory of Ludwig von Bertalanffy.[22] But however much the packaging has changed, it still remains a prisoner of the basic options of scientism.

I characterized the second pathway as one of hysterical identification because it consists in a mimetic appropriation of scientificity, one which cares little for 'sticking to' reproducible experimental procedures, or for relying on testable and falsifiable theories, in Karl Popper's sense.[23] The most significant example of this scientific 'bluffing' is provided by psychoanalysis. Conceived at the outset by Freud from a point of view that was close, precisely, to that of Fechner, Helmholtz and the 'Physicalist' school, as it became institutionalized and acquired gravity in society, it came to consider that its doctrinal assertions could only really be understood by a caste of initiates having had access to the benefits of a didactic cure. Consequently, it was no longer a question for them of a scientificity with a direct connection to commonsense! One would, however, be wrong to relate this kind of procedure to a simple mystification or to a first degree of obnubilation, like that of the scientist Cosinus, who was at the origin of the famous episode of the 'sniffer planes',[24] because psychoanalysis effectively enlists much more elaborate phenomena of belief, to which we will return.

The third pathway, that of propping, makes a lateral use of science, the statements of which retain a character of exteriority in relation to the discipline under consideration, or are only used metaphorically. It is in this mode that psychoanalysis in part functioned too. For example, when Freud referred to Carnot's Principle – seriously 'revised' – to justify his bipolarization of the drives between Eros and Thanatos. Or, subsequently, when the apostles of the Signifier plunder structural linguistics or get started on a mathematical topology, which, unfortunately, is of no help at all!

Evidently I don't wish to see schizoanalytic cartographies oriented in any of these directions! I think that they will only avoid the swamps of reductionism in which psychologists and psychoanalysts naturally get bogged down, on condition that they resolutely and without regret get rid of every scientific reference. And don't let me be misunderstood! It is not a question here of a shameful renunciation, of the admission of a congenital weakness in our means of investigation, but of an indispensible weaning with regard to a fundamentally illusory and pernicious viewpoint. In fact scientific methods are even less in a position to help in the analysis of the psyche because they only succeeded in 'taking off' as a specific semiotic Phylum from the moment that they committed to a systematic bracketing off of questions relating to their enunciation, to idiosyncratic modes of valorization and to irreducibly singular processes – in other words, the essential dimensions of subjectivity! Not only do the cartographies of subjectivity have nothing to gain from aping science, but the latter can perhaps expect a great deal from the problematics that they carry along in their wake. In this regard, let us recall the warning issued by Merleau-Ponty in the introduction to the *Phenomenology of Perception*:

> all my knowledge of the world, even my scientific knowledge, is gained from my own particular point of view or from some experience of the world without which the symbols of science would be meaningless. The whole universe of science is built upon the world as directly experienced, and if we want to subject science itself to rigourous scrutiny and arrive at a precise assessment of its meaning and scope, we must begin by reawakening the basic experience of the world of which science is the second order expression.[25]

One is indeed obliged to note that a certain positivistic progressivism continues to be an obstacle to a truly analytic and micropolitical approach to subjective formations. Whatever the waves of religiosity sweeping across the world today may be, capitalistic subjectivity persists in presenting itself as an historical accomplishment. Basically, we still remain more or less under the Comtian law of the 'three states'. However, is it not evident that the famous theological, metaphysical and positive ages have *never* stopped overlapping to different degrees? The subjectivity at work within the most elaborate scientific paradigms still functions in part in terms of animism and transcendental abstractionism. All scientific approaches, all forms of logico-mathematical rationality, establish themselves on the basis of the same fabric of perceptual schemes, affects, imaginary activities and representations as one also finds in everyday life, in dreams, madness or creation. It is just that the Assemblages and the intensity of the components put into play change. Reciprocally, these same concrete, oneiric, pathological or aesthetic Universes enrol in specific modalities, problematic traits, highly differentiated machinic Propositions that find themselves as if buried under the banality of their ordinary manifestations.

Thus, from our point of view, the cartographies of unconscious subjectivity ought to become the indispensible complements of the systems of rationality that circulate in the sciences, in politics and all other regions of knowledge and human activity. The complements to or instruments of contestation and transformation, as the case may be! And last but not least, irreplaceable instruments for throwing light on and reading zones of hyper-complexity, the elucidation of which no longer arises from habitual logical treatments. Why? Because above all the map here loses its primary vocation of having to represent the Territory.[26] The logic of discursive sets should thus agree to step aside with good grace in the face of cartographic procedures able to position singularities and processes of singularization, what I call ontological pragmatics. And it would be vain, on this occasion, to howl about the failure of rationality because, in a sense, it is ultimately really a question of its consolidation. It is a matter of exploring and of rendering produceable zones of semiotization that no longer only have as their task the articulation, the placing of collections of: 1) figures of expression; 2) mental entities; 3) objects referred to (real or virtual) into plurivocal correspondence; but also, as a supplement to these classical functions of *representation* and *denotation*, of setting in motion a function of *existentialization*, proper to these ontological pragmatics, which consists in deploying and putting into intensive concatenation specific existential qualities. Let it suffice for me to emphasize at this stage that the intensive indices, the diagrammatic operators implied by this existential function do not have any universal character: this is what will lead schizoanalysis to differentiate them from Kleinian 'part objects' or from the Lacanian 'object little a', despite certain similarities. Rather, they are like crystals of singularization, points of bifurcation outside the dominant coordinates, on the basis of which mutant universes of reference can spring up. But perhaps these cartographic entities will seem mysterious to some! It is true that we no longer have spontaneous access to them, like in the good old days of 'animist' thought, or, as is still the case, during certain experiences of rupture with 'normality'. The necessity of constructing apparatuses of analytic enunciation from scratch – which are not unrelated to those of artistic creation[27] – to rediscover their effectiveness, follows from this. Finally, let us emphasize that the stake of the promotion of these 'analysers' largely exceeds psychoanalysis and art, because it concerns the capacity of our societies to conquer new degrees of freedom in relation to existing economic and social constraints, and recentre the collective and individual purposes of human activity on new objectives.

From postmodernism to the postmedia era

A certain conception of progress and of modernity has gone bankrupt, compromising in its collapse collective confidence in the very idea of emancipatory social practice. In parallel, a sort of glaciation has taken over social relations: hierarchies and segregations have rigidified, poverty and unemployment tend to be accepted today as inevitable evils, the unions cling onto the last institutional branches conceded to them and are imprisoned in corporatist practices leading them to adopt conservative attitudes that are sometimes close to those of reactionary milieus. The communist left is irremediably stuck in sclerosis and dogmatism, whilst socialist parties concerned to present themselves as reliable technocratic partners have given up any progressive questioning of existing structures. It is not surprising, after all that, if the ideologies that once claimed to serve as a guide to rebuilding society on a less unjust, less unequal basis have lost their credibility.

Does it follow that we are henceforth condemned to stand around like idiots in the face of the growth of the new order of cruelty and cynicism that is on the point of submerging the planet, with the firm intention, it seems, of staying? It is this regrettable conclusion that numerous intellectual and artistic milieus effectively seem to have reached, in particular those who invoke the fashion of postmodernism.

I will leave to one side here the major promotional operations launched by the managers of contemporary art that were christened Neo-Expressionism in Germany, 'Bad Painting' in the United States, 'New Painting' in Italy, 'Trans-Avant-Garde' in France, 'Figuration libre', 'Nouveaux Fauves', etc. Otherwise I would make it too easy to demonstrate that postmodernism is a final twitch of modernism, in reaction to and in some way a mirror of the formalist and reductionist abuses of the latter, from which it is not really distinguishable. Without a doubt some genuine painters will emerge from these schools, and their personal talent will protect them against the pernicious effects of this type of infatuation maintained by means of publicity. But they will surely not relaunch the creative Phyla that they had the pretention of re-animating.

In being more securely attached to the profoundly reterritorializing tendencies of current capitalistic subjectivity, architectural postmodernism seems to me, on the other hand, to be much less skin-deep and much more suggestive of the place allotted to art by the dominant power formations. Let me explain: for all times, and whatever its historical avatars might be, the capitalistic drive has always knotted together two fundamental components: one, that I characterize as deterritorializing, of the destruction of social territories, collective identities and traditional systems of value. The other, of the recomposition, even by the most artificial of means, of individuated personological frameworks, schemes of power and models of submission that are, if not formally similar to those that it has destroyed, at least homothetic to them from a functional point of view. It is this latter that I characterize as a movement of reterritorialization. To the extent that deterritorializing revolutions, linked to the development of the sciences, of techniques and of the arts, sweep away everything in their passage, a compulsion to subjective reterritorialization is mobilized. And this antagonism is aggravated even more by the prodigious development of communicational and informational machinisms to the extent that their deterritorializing effects are focused on human faculties such as memory, perception, understanding, the imagination, etc. It is a certain formula for anthropological functioning, a certain ancestral model of humanity that thus finds itself expropriated from within. And I think that it is for want of the capacity to face up to this prodigious mutation appropriately that collective subjectivity has given in to the absurd wave of conservatism that we are currently experiencing. As for knowing under what conditions it would become possible to make the levels of these cursed waters drop, and what role might be played by the remaining islands of the will to liberation still able to emerge from this deluge, that is precisely the question that is subjacent to my proposition regarding the transition to a postmedia era. Without going any further with this theme, I would say that it seems to me that the seesaw that has carried us to a dangerously retrograde subjective reterritorialization could be inverted spectacularly the day that new emancipatory social practices, and, above all, alternative Assemblages of subjective production – capable of being articulated with the molecular revolutions that work over our epoch in a different mode to that of conservative reterritorialization – are sufficiently affirmed.

Let's come back now to our postmodern architects. For some amongst them, Léon Krier for example – when he proposes quite simply to rebuild traditional cities, with their streets, squares and districts – the question of reterritorialization really isn't figurative.[28] With Roberto Venturi, it is less a matter of reterritorializing space than of cutting the bridges of time, by refusing the crossing-out of the future by Modernists such as Le Corbusier, as well as the backward-looking dreams of the Neo-Classicists. From now on it is good form for the present state of things to be accepted as it is. Better, Robert Venturi accepts its most prosaic aspects: he goes into raptures over the 'commercial strips', bordered with 'decorated sheds' that rip apart the urban fabric of the United States; he even goes as far as eulogizing over the kitsch ornamentation on the lawns of prefabricated satellite towns, which he compares to the urns of Le Notre's parterres.[29] Whilst in the domain of the plastic arts, young painters were required to submit to the ambient conservatism through the mediation of the masters of the marketplace – failing which they would find themselves condemned to stagnate in the margins – here being equal to the most retrograde of neo-liberal values happens without hesitation. It is true that for the ruling classes painting has only ever been a business of prestige value, of providing a little extra soul, whereas architecture has always occupied a major place in the making of the territories of power, in the fixing of its emblems, in the proclamation of its eternity.

Are we not, therefore, at the centre of what Jean-François Lyotard calls the postmodern condition,[30] which (unlike this author) I understand to be the paradigm of all the submissions, all the compromises with the status quo? As a result of the collapse of what he calls the master narratives of legitimation (the discourse of the Enlightenment, for example, that of Hegel on the accomplishment of the Spirit, or that of the Marxists on the emancipation of the workers), it would be suitable – still according to Jean-François Lyotard – to be suspicious of the slightest impulse to concerted social action. All consensual values, he explains to us, have become outdated and suspect. Only the little narratives of legitimation, in other words, the multiple, heterogeneous 'pragmatics of language particles' (whose performativity must have spatio-temporal limits) can still save some of the values of justice and freedom. Here, Jean-François Lyotard joins other theorists, such as Jean Baudrillard, for whom the social and the political have only ever been traps, 'semblances' from which it would be a good idea to free oneself as quickly as possible. All social agitation being summed up as language games (one senses that the Lacanian signifier is not far away), the only kitsch slogan that Lyotard – an old organizer of the leftist journal *Socialisme ou barbarie* – manages to save from disaster is the right to free access to computer memories and data banks.

Whether they are painters, architects or philosophers, the heroes of postmodernity share an assessment that the crises the artistic and social practices are experiencing today can no longer lead into anything other than irrevocable refusal of any collective projectuality of any scale. Let's tend to our garden then and preferably in conformity with the habits and customs of our contemporaries. No waves. Just vogues, modulated on the markets of art and opinion by means of publicity campaigns and opinion polls. As for ordinary sociality, a new principle of 'sufficient communication' will have to provide for the maintenance of its equilibria and ephemeral consistency. If one thinks about it, how much distance has been travelled since the epoch in which one could read on the banners of French sociology: 'social facts are not things'! For the postmoderns, they are now nothing more than erratic clouds of floating discourse in a signifying ether!

But where, for that matter, do they get the idea from that the socius can thus be reduced to the facts of language, and these latter in turn to binarisable, 'digitisable' signifying chains? On this point the postmoderns have hardly innovated! They are directly inscribed in the very modernist tradition of structuralism, whose influence on the human sciences it seems must have been relayed, in the worst conditions, by Anglo-Saxon systemism. The secret link between all these doctrines, it seems to me, derives from their having been marked by the reductionist ideas conveyed in the immediate post-war period by information theory and the first cybernetic research. The references that they continued trying to extract from the new communication and information technologies were so hasty, so badly mastered, that they projected us way back behind the phenomenological research that had preceded them.

One must come back to the simple obvious fact – but how heavy in consequences – namely that concrete social Assemblages, which should not be confused with the 'primary groups' of American sociology (which still only arise from opinion) call into question many other things than linguistic performances: ethological and ecological dimensions, economic, aesthetic, corporeal, phantasmatic semiotic components that are irreducible to the semiology of language, a multitude of incorporeal Universes of reference, which do not willingly becoming integrated into the coordinates of the dominant empiricity…However much postmodern philosophers flutter around research in pragmatics, they remain faithful to a structuralist conception of speech and language that will never allow them to articulate subjective facts with the formations of the unconscious, aesthetic and micropolitical problematics. To say it without beating about the bush, I believe that this philosophy is not one: it is only an ambient state of mind, a 'condition' of opinion, which takes its truths from the trends of the day. Why would it go to the bother of elaborating serious speculative support for its thesis relative to the inconsistency of the socius? Don't the currently all-powerful media amply complement the demonstration that effectively no matter what social link can lend itself, with no apparent resistance, to the desingularizing and infantilizing reduction of capitalistic productions of the signifier? An old adage of Lacan's, according to which 'a signifier represents the subject for another signifier' could be the epigraph for this new ethic of disengagement. Because in effect that is what it has come to! Only there really is nothing to be proud of, in the way the postmodernists are. The whole question is rather one of knowing how it is possible to get out of such an impasse!

That the production of our signaletic primary matter is increasingly tributary to the intervention of machines[31] does not imply that human freedom and creativity are inevitably condemned to being alienated by mechanical procedures. Rather than the subject passing into the clutches of the machine, nothing prohibits machinic networks from engaging in a sort of process of subjectification, in other words, the possibility that machinism and humanity might one day start to entertain fruitful symbiotic relations. In this regard it would perhaps be appropriate to establish a distinction between the aforementioned signaletic matter and the optional matters of subjectivity, by which I mean all the domains of decisionality, enacted by (collective and/or individual) Assemblages of enunciation. Whilst signaletic matters arise from the logic of discursive sets whose relations can be referred to objects that are deployed according to extrinsic (energetico-spatio-temporal) coordinates, optional matters arise from logics of self-reference that engage/enrol traits of existential intensities that refuse all submission to the axioms of set theories. These logics, which I also call logics of bodies without organs, or logics of existential Territories, have this particularity: that their objects are ontologically ambiguous, they are bifaced objects-subjects that can neither be discernibilized nor discursivized as figures represented on a background of coordinates of representation. Thus they cannot be apprehended from the outside; one can only accept them, take them upon oneself, through an existential transfer.

The 'transversalist' function of these ambiguous objects, which confers on them the possibility of cutting across the circumscriptions of time and space, and of transgressing identitarian assignments, is found again at the heart of the Freudian cartography of the unconscious and also in the preoccupations of the linguists of enunciation, although from a different angle.

The primary process, identification, the transference, part objects, the deferred action function of the phantasm, all these notions familiar to psychoanalysts imply, in one way or another, the existence of a ubiquity and a recursivity-prospectivity of the entities that it calls into question. But by making the logic of the unconscious depend indirectly on the logic of dominant realities – interpretation being awarded the task of making the first translateable into the terms of the second – Freud lost the specificity of his discovery, namely that certain semiotic segments, being led to escape from the frame of their ordinary 'mission' of signification could acquire a particular power of existential production (universes of neurosis, perversion, psychosis, sublimation, etc.). Far from improving things, the tripartite Lacanian division of Real, Imaginary and Symbolic has, from this point of view, only aggravated the compartmentalization of topographic instances in relation to one another.

For their part, the linguists of enunciation and of speech acts[32] have brought out the fact that certain linguistic segments, in parallel with their classically recognized functions of signification and denotation, could acquire a particular pragmatic effectiveness by making the respective positions of enunciating subjects crystallize or by putting into place, de facto, certain situational framings. (The classic example: the president who declares 'the session is open' and who, so doing, effectively opens the session.) But they also believed they had to restrict the scope of their discovery to the register of their specialism only. Whereas in reality this third, 'existentializing' function, which they emphasized, ought logically to imply a definitive breaking up of the structuralist corset in which they continue to keep language.[33] It is not with the sole aim of indexing general subjective positions – those of deictics – or of positioning the contextualization of discourse within statements, that language thus escapes from itself. It is also, first and foremost, so as to make pragmatic singularities crystallize, to catalyse the most varied processes of singularization (the cutting-out of sensible Territories, deployments of incorporeal Universes of endo-reference…). It goes without saying that this pragmatics of 'setting into existence' is not the exclusive privilege of language; all the other semiotic components, all the other procedures of natural and machinic encoding, contribute to it. The linguistic signifier does not occupy the royal place that capitalistic subjectification has offered it (because it constitutes an essential support for its logic of generalized equivalence and its politics of the capitalization of the abstract values of power) as of right. Other regimes of semiotization are able to make the affairs of the world work and, in so doing, relieve this symbolic-signifying imperium, in which the current hegemony of mass-mediatized powers are rooted, of its position of transcendence in relation to the Rhizomes of realities and imaginaries. But they will not arise through spontaneous generation: they are there to be constructed, within our reach, at the crossroads of new analytic, aesthetic and social practices, which no postmodern spontaneity will serve up to us on a platter.

The emergence of these new practices of subjectification of a postmedia era will be greatly facilitated by a concerted reappropriation of information and communication technologies in so far as they will increasingly authorize:

1 the promotion of innovative forms of consultation and collective interaction, and, in the long run, a reinvention of democracy;

2 the miniaturization and personalization of apparatuses, a resingularization of mediatized means of expression. One may assume, in this respect, that it is the extension into a network of databanks that will have the biggest surprises in store for us;

3 the multiplication to infinity of 'existential shifters' permitting access to creative mutant Universes.

Finally, let us note that the multicentring and subjective autonomization of postmedia operators will not be correlative to their closing on themselves or a disengagement of a postmodernist type. The postmedia revolution to come would have to be called on to relay, with an efficacity without any common measure, the minoritarian groups who are still today alone in having become aware of the mortal risk to humanity of questions such as:

- the nuclear arms race;
- famine;
- irreversible ecological catastrophe;
- the mass-mediatic pollution of subjectivity.

If the future fails to orient itself in these directions, I have to say, I don't rate our chances for the end of the present millennium!

Schizoanalytic meta-modellings

Psychoanalysis is not a science; it is not an art, it is not for all that a religion – although it does mobilize powerful phenomena of belief, Freud is venerated like a Father of the Church, his first patients are celebrated like holy martyrs, his writings treated like the Gospel and the congregations that invoke him practise the excommunication of schismatics just like in the good old days of the Inquisition...I have already mentioned the difference in position of religious and psychoanalytic subjectivity with regard to scientific rationality, the first ostensibily separating itself from it, the second endeavouring to absorb it in various ways. Two other differences equally deserve to be noted: 1) psychoanalysis requires a more active participation of its users in its rituals; 2) its myths are more deterritorialized than those of religion.

Psychoanalysis and the monotheistic religions have in common that they seek to grip subjectivity in ethical axes in conformity with the requirements of what I will call capitalistic logics, that is to say, systems of judgement proceeding by generalized equivalence, the conjuring and repression of animist intensities, the conversion of singular trajectories, the system of reiteration and circulation of formal entities on deterritorialized 'markets' (those of the economy, of morality, of art...). Whilst, to achieve their ends, religions act by direct suggestion, by the imprint of standardized representations and statements, at least to begin with psychoanalysis gives free reign to a certain individual expression, the better subsequently to take it over and to submit of its own accord to other, perhaps even more tyrannical, kinds of stereotypes. The original and insidious character of the psychoanalytic method thus resides in its conducting a minimal lifting of the constraints that weigh on discourse ordinarily, and in engendering the illusion that through it certain singularities of desire might gain expression, especially in the field of sexuality. Whilst religion, dare I say it, straitjackets subjectivity in the open air, psychoanalysis gets rid of some of the ballast of statements in order to concentrate its efforts on remodelling enunciation. Consequently one may consider that it is only a religion in the second degree, a religion of pure form, its sacred texts – Freud's Old Testament, Lacan's New Testament – having no other role than to fix an extrinsic armature to ritual practices all but emptied of content: some all-purpose formulae, some encouragement on the basis of which, in principle, a free expression is authorized. But only in principle! Because, in fact, very little use will be made of this enunciative licence, any slight impulse to free up the 'analysand' running into the apparatus of the cure – the ceremony of the sessions, the straitjacket of the transference, the incisive interpretations that impose themselves in such a way that the analyst doesn't even have to utter them, and who, under the cover of the neutrality of the pure listening to the plays of signifiers, is increasingly led to withdraw behind an ostentatious silence and a cheap priestliness. However, I emphasize, even if it turns out, in practice, that the so-called 'free interpretation' is rapidly channelled by a pitiless semiotic remote control, appearances are nonetheless safe: something might have happened, nothing expressly prohibited subjectivity from renewing the light that it casts on itself. If that wasn't how it was – aside from the miniscule storms in a teacup of the Oedipal transference – it must be clear, in the eyes of the patient-subject, that it can only be his fault. He was not worthy of the line that was thrown to him and he will, as a consequence, find additional reinforcement for his guilt and alienation in the person of his analyst. A masochistic passion on an inglorious Way of the Cross! That is how psychoanalysis, like one of our modern tourist grottos, will only dispense its vestiges of freedom marked out, trapped and assisted by 'son et lumière' programmes that are so well interiorized that they spare their guides the need for any intervention, all commentary having become superfluous.

The importance aquired by psychoanalysis in developed societies, amongst their elites as much as in their mass-mediated subjectivity, poses another problem as well. What virtue, what magic, must it be the bearer of to have been capable of being reborn in this way from all the crises that haven't stopped shaking it since its first appearance? My hypothesis is that we can only understand such a phenomenon if the whole of the psychoanalytic movement is considered – with its variants, its permanent dissidences – as a sort of hydra with multiple probe-heads, all aimed at seizing mutant forms of subjectivity, corresponding to machines of enunciation for the interiority and transference of subjectivities that are noticeably more deterritorialized than those that were common prior to it. Everything would then be an affair of supplementary coefficients of deterritorialization. That is to say what? The history of capitalist subjectivity appears to me to be inseparable from a double tension, which pulls it in opposite directions: towards a deterritorialization expelling it from its 'native lands' – of the orders of childhood, filiation, life situation, professional guarantee, ethico-national identity…and towards an existential reterritorialization that is strictly imbricated with the functionality of the system as a whole. What confers a capitalistic character on this antagonism is that when all is said and done it always leans in the same direction, that of the neutralization and expulsion of processual singularities, that of the active ignorance of contingency and finitude and, consequently, an infantilization of its protagonists that is more and more marked.

Despite certain appearances, this subjectivity isn't in the least the object of an eternal return on itself; it is caught in an immense spiral of regression that it belongs to the myths conveyed by the narrativity of the media, and to the pseudo-scientific references of the 'psy' operators to express. Freud discovered that adult subjectivity was permanently doubled by an infantile subjectivity. However, what he was not in a position to grasp is that this 'standing in for' did not arise from a psychogenetic programming anchored in universal 'complexes' but from particular modes of production of subjectivity, namely, exactly those of the modes of production of capitalist subjectivity.

It is certainly not for nothing that one senses a sort of complementarity between the subjective figures produced serially by television (based on the elimination of every 'disturbing' singularity, on a cult of the upmarket family, on purifying, securitarian compulsions…), and the structural models of psychoanalysis. Their common trait, I repeat, is not to be sought in a correspondence of contents, but in a similarity of their procedures for deterritorializing-reterritorializing enunciation, and, as it happens, in a progress backwards, which leads us to ever more platitudes, ever more superficiality. McLuhan said of subjectivity that it is in the process of becoming flat like the telly, and Lewis Carroll drew up the map of flat affects in *Alice in Wonderland*. But the ultimate reductionist model belongs neither to literature nor to the mass media. Until further notice, it seems to belong to psychoanalysis, with its practice of signifying reduction and the generalized equivalence of affects and representations. It is on this side of this slapdash race to deterritorialize and to retailor subjectivity that we must try to home in on the serious problem of the surprisingly perennial nature of psychoanalytic myths, the fact that they always manage to get back on the bandwagon – just as well as and perhaps better than the grand myths of monotheism.

Our schizoanalytic research will thus consider psychoanalysis as not so much a corpus of personological and inter-subjective representations (Oedipal triangulation) but as an activity for the meta-modelling of pragmatic models of submission to the modern systems of 'gentle' alienation and exploitation. In going beyond its elitarian exercise – the scene of the couch – in ceaselessly gaining more ground in the apparatuses of health, in the university, the media…, psychoanalysis has succeeded in requalifying the sacerdotal mission of its instituted chapels. These find themselves being progressively discharged of their old therapeutic responsibilities and put into a position, if not of direct supervision, at least of the theological overcoding of the functions of culpabilization and normalization that operate in the collective psyche through a multitude of molecular relays, in the manner of viral waves.

2 SEMIOTIC ENERGETICS

*It were better to follow the myths
about the gods than to become a slave
to the destiny of the natural philosophers'*

EPICURUS[1]

Before introducing my thoughts on the matter of 'schizoanalytic cartographies', I will briefly examine certain disabling effects of the importing of thermodynamic notions into the human and social sciences. I will also recall the stroke of genius, if not the touch of madness, that led Freud to invent a *semiotic energetics*, the first theorizations of which were, all things considered and despite their naively scientist character, less reductionist than those that he was later to develop in the context of the institutionalization of psychoanalysis.

The entropic superego

Marx wanted to weigh down social relations with the Flows of work, and Freud, psychic life with the Flows of sexual libido.[2] Certainly, it wasn't part of either's intention to establish a mechanistic causality between a base of energy and social or mental superstructures. Yet we know how their theories were to reinforce the most reductionist of conceptions and practices! It is evident that any rapprochement between their methods would be arbitrary and any conjectures about an influence of the first on the second even more so. On the other hand, it is perhaps justified to ask about a certain parallelism between their undertakings, which I will relate to one and the same *infrastructure complex*, a complex that has had damaging effects within the human and social sciences, to the extent that their role in industrial societies was asserted. 'In any domain whatever, give us a base that can be characterized in terms of energy and we will construct a genuine science from it'. It is on the basis of this paradigm that an entropic *Superego* was established, which had as its principal effect to make those who were afflicted by it incapable of perceiving a movement, a transformation, an alteration, anything 'experiencable' whatsoever, without relating it to a single economy of energy, founded on the two sacrosanct principles of thermodynamics. One can represent this parasitic instance as a sort of epistemological crab pulling apart the givens on which it feeds, always following the same ceremonial movement:

With one of its claws,

1 it places on one side those givens that it circumscribes as arising from the energy Capital in question, as the only reality susceptible of scientific consumption;[3]

2 it crushes these givens of energy so as to relieve them of their specific traits and confer on them a uniformly convertible character; with its other claw.

With its other claw,

3 it reduces the givens, which have resisted its enterprize of energeticisation, to the state of abstract equivalent, giving, for example, Capital, the Libido, Music, Scientificity…;

4 it prepares a super-equivalent (a 'capitalistic pulp') on the basis of all these regional equivalents, in such a way that the ensemble of singularities and intrinsic structures, the ensemble of representations and affects relating to them and, in certain extreme cases, the ensemble of energetic processes themselves find themselves totally dissolved and assimilated.

At its terminal point – I'm thinking here of structuralisms and systemisms – the disease of entropism may seem to evolve towards remission by the spontaneous lifting of the Infrastructure Complex. In effect, traditional dualisms of the matter-form type thus seem to be overcome because of a transfering of formalism, supposed to arise from superstructures, towards infrastructural levels.[4] Unfortunately this is not the case: the focus of reductionism is simply displaced towards a matter that is even more radically purged of its final specific traits, to the profit of an energetic hyle assimilated to a Flow of binary alternatives (despite multiple safeguards against the paralogism that consists in deducing the identity 'neg-information = energy' from the identity 'neg-entropy = information').[5]

By postulating a radical separation between the production of subjectivity and semiotic effectiveness, converted into a cult of information or of the signifier, the monotheisms of energy have led to an impasse regarding the dimensions of singularity, irreversibility and bifurcation of cognitive Assemblages and, in a more general fashion, regarding the relations of interdependence between the systemic given and structures of (observational, conceptual) expression.[6] That is probably what confers on them the place of choice that they occupy in the mega-machine of the production of culture, of science and of subjectivity that is constituted today by Integrated World Capitalism, which means to allow only those modes of expression and valorization that it can normalize and put into its service to subsist on this planet.

Freudian semiotic energetics

Without a doubt the scientific yoke that Freud never abandoned had as its principal function to protect him against the too brutal ruptures of sense to which listening to neurosis, but also his self-analysis, exposed him. Whatever the case may be – and although he did not maintain such direct interactions between Flows of energy and unconscious psychic life in his subsequent models – at the base of his diverse theoretical edifices one will continue to find apparatuses interlacing energy components and instances of mental representation in a more and more metaphorical, but also more and more insidious, way.

The so-called model of the 'first topography' will thus propose that the unconscious is engendered on the basis of a dynamic of the repression of representations linked to a curious type of drive, associating two levels:

1. one that is somatic, putting into play a drive energy – the nature of which is not defined in any other way but which seems to be of a biochemical order – finding its *source* in zones of excitation characterized as erogenous, and the *aim* of which responds to a principle of constancy tending to ensure a homeostasis of the tensions engendered by the aforementioned excitations;

2   another that is psychic, articulating language, object
representations, phantasms, inter-subjective relations with the
object of this apparatus and which constitutes its variable, of sorts.

Whilst being anchored in a physics of energy, unconscious psychic life
– such as Freud conceives it – doesn't fall into a total dependency
on a causality of drives. In reciprocity with the distortions that the
'primary process' makes it undergo (displacement, condensation, overdetermination, hallucination…), it is capable of imprinting a diverse range
of inhibitions, deviations and sublimations on the libido…In truth, at this
step in the theory, it is rather difficult to locate with precision the points at
which the somatic and psychic stages of the drive latch on to each other.
One doesn't know exactly if this curious missile is destined to remain fixed
to the soil of the somatic, restricting itself to emitting affects and pertur-
bations in the sky of representations or if, on the contrary, it is already an
integral part of the psychic world within which it is required to evolve.
But for Freud that is not the essential point. What mattered to him was to
furnish passages between the sexual libido and effects of sense. Even when
he came to seek a cosmological foundation for the unconscious on the
basis of the dualist paradigms Eros-Death, Love-Discord, Order-Disorder,
he never renounced his initial hypothesis of an energy whose effects would
be *at the same time* both physical and psychic.

With the Freudian 'second topography', in which the triad
Unconscious-Preconscious-Conscious found itself dethroned by the triad
Id-Ego-Superego, the energy metaphors fade, to the profit of more anthro-
pomorphic models,[7] and the psychoanalytic movement will subsequently
not stop making the concept of libidinal energy undergo the most diverse
treatments, to try to overcome the 'theoretical scandal' of which it is the
bearer. I will mention here only its final metamorphosis under the aegis
of Lacanian structuralism, for which it was a matter of nothing less than
its quasi-total 'liquidation', in the form of the signifying chain. From his
first writings, Lacan distanced himself from Freudian metapsychology.
He initially professed that the libido was nothing but a simple system for
the notation of energy.[8] Then, reducing thermodynamics to nothing more
than a play of the signifier,[9] he went as far as to deny it its character as a
Flow, making it an *organ* of the drive,[10] which for its part metamorphosed
into the *treasure trove of signifiers*.[11] However, this libido, the 'organ of the
incorporeal' (compared elsewhere to a flying lamella, immortal and asexual
like amoeba), which he also characterizes as a 'hommelette'[12] was not
completely deprived of its decidedly sacrosanct energy status. But evidently
it was no longer a question of anything other than a rather particular form

of energy, since, as Lacan notes, it was susceptible of 'a quantification which is all the easier to introduce into theory as it is useless, since only certain *quanta* of constancy are recognized therein'. He then specifies that 'its sexual colouring, so categorically maintained by Freud as its most central feature, is the colour of emptiness: suspended in the light of a gap.'[13] With terrain having been so radically cleared, one feels more relaxed about risking one's own conjectures!

The schizoanalytic unconscious

The term 'Unconscious' is only retained here for ease of use, as the field of schizoanalysis far exceeds that which psychoanalysts consider their own, that is: 1) an individual oral performance, generally centred on a certain familialist habitus of subjectivity, in the context of developed industrial societies; 2) affective manifestations circumscribed in the etiolated space of the cure. Schizoanalysis, on the contrary, endeavours to mobilize collective and/or individual, subjective and/or objective formations, becomings human and/or animal, vegetable, cosmic…It will be directly involved in a diversification of the means of semiotization and will refuse any centering of subjectification on the supposedly neutral and benevolent person of a psychoanalyst. It will thus quit the terrain of signifying interpretation for that of the exploration of *Assemblages of enunciation* that contribute to the production of subjective Affects and machinic Effects (I mean here everything that sets off a processual life, a problematic that deviates, if only slightly, from stratified redundancies, an evolutionary phylum, in whatever order that may be – biological, economic, social, religious, aesthetic, etc.).

Does this signify that every evaluative perspective and every scientific prescription in this domain is definitively put aside? Can one conceive the reconstitution of a model of the Unconscious which, whilst giving up a 'hidden' libidinal parameter (which in fact escaped from every conceivable test of 'falsifiability'), nonetheless confers full status on physical, biological, sexual, social, economic, etc. *energies* (in the plural, I emphasize)? In itself, the hypothesis of a flow of energy associated with each psychic operation wasn't in the slightest unreasonable. It was only legitimate to distrust it from the moment it induced the exporting of thermodynamic concepts outside their original domain of validity, which had been laid out in such a way that the incorporeal objects and dissipative processes proper to organic and psychic life were excluded from it. The universality of the principles of the convertibility of energies and the growth over the course of time of entropy that is correlative to it is only 'tenable' in the frame of well-specified Assemblages of techno-scientific enunciation. In any case, I don't imagine that anyone would doubt that in ordinary life, principally in the life of desire, 'discharges' of energy arise more from a principle of 'defence' than from a principle of equilibrium and constancy. For the conception of an unconscious founded on an economy of drive quantities and a dynamic of conflictual representations, I would thus substitute a transformational modelling such that, under certain conditions, Territories of the Self, Universes of alterity, Complexions of material Flows, machines of desire, semiotic, iconic Assemblages, Assemblages of intellection, etc. can engender one another. Also, it is no longer a matter here of sticking to the form of instances, but of acceding to the transmutations, the trans-ductions of their substance. Our psychophysics is separate from those to which Freud referred in that it refuses to give itself a univocal energetic and material substrate. It will not postulate a Manichean dualism between what could be called an undifferentiated 'energetic inertia' and a subjective 'anima' creative of differentiation. 'Prior' to the establishing of a matter and extension that can be located in the energetico-spatio-temporal dimensions of the physical world, it will begin with transformations that establish themselves 'straddling' the most heterogeneous of domains conceivable. It will presuppose diverse modalities of 'transversality' between: 1) Flows of matter and energy; 2) the abstract machinic Phyla that preside over objective laws and changes; 3) existential Territories, considered from the angle of their self-enjoyment (their 'for itself') and, finally, 4) incorporeal Universes, which escape from the energetic, legal, evolutionary and existential coordinates of the three preceding domains. Its problem will no longer be to make the soul enter into matter or energy into representation, or even to accept an unavoidable 'Popperization' of the Third World, but that of drawing all the consequences from the fact that if one has come to accept that life, mind, desire and truth today exist 'far from equilibrium', this is because they had to exist already, in the night of time, in the form of powdery metamorphic bifurcations at the heart of the most apparently amorphous of states.

On a methodological plane, what also distinguishes our project of a mapping of Effects and Affects from previous scientific points of view in this domain is that its quantification will be different from the traditional quantimetries of physics and quantifications of logic. It will no longer have as its object sets [ensembles] characterized in a univocal fashion, that is to say, for which the elements have been previously collected in an exhaustive fashion and in such a way that one can always know, without ambiguity, if one well-determined element amongst them is a part of the set or not. It will devote itself to Assemblages that can be subject to radical transformations, to schizzes or relinkages that change their configurations, to re-orderings through fluctuation, irrevocable implosions, etc. This ubiquity and this multivalence of schizoanalytic entities – an illustration of which can be found in dreams, but also in intellection in the nascent state – remain irreducible. Leibnizian monads, Michel Serres' myriads – such entities do not arise from simply belonging to 'fuzzy subsets' which might be homed in on by a probabilitarian or modal evaluation. They arise from a general Plane of immanence that implies them all in relations of presupposition that will be considered as so many *levels of consistency of energy*. But maybe it is preferable to take things the other way round and posit that it is the fracturing of the *Plane of Consistency* that each one of these entities makes happen which manifests specific levels of energy. Whatever the case may be, it will only be possible to 'discernibilize' these intensive entities and the quanta of energy relative to the consistency of their (actual and virtual) inter-relations through the complex Assemblages that semiotize them.

It will be noted that the semiotics of which it is a question is no longer an outer suburb of linguistics, as it is in the Saussurean tradition. Instead, from the perspective of its founder, it will be imagined as an encyclopedic science of the phenomena of expression, a 'phaneroscopy.'[14] It also borrows certain categories from Louis Hjelmslev's glossematics, which advocated a semiotic opening of linguistics that is all the more broad for being conceived from a fundamentally immanentist point of view.[15]

Non-separability, separation and quantification

The quanta of 'transversality', whose existence prior to material states of things and Universes of sense and value we are imagining, cannot be described in the framework of the spatio-temporal coordinates to which the physics of masses and energies habitually refers. But these pre-coordinates, these ante-coordinates do not for all that arise from pure arbitrariness, from a murky world of the aleatory and undifferentiated unless the aleatory is understood here in Van Gogh's sense, when he characterized himself as an 'aleatory colourist.' The exact contrary of an entropic drifting at the mercy of common colours! That the basic material of the schizoanalytic Unconscious is constituted by non-programmed potentialities (or programmed by discontinuous segments), by unforeseen smoothings and foldings of possibility, in no way requires that one fail to recognize the existence of libidinal stratifications, repetitive structures literally mimicking the homeostasis of systems of physical fluctuations at equilibrium (neurotic negotiations between narcissism and object investments, failure syndromes, repetition compulsion). It is simply that the energy balance corresponding to these systems of repetition will no longer be the foundation of subjectivity, as was the case with the Freudian death drive. The generalized energetics of schizoanalysis will accord it a place, as a case of a massive freezing up of inter-entitarian degrees of freedom.

Our model of the Unconscious rests on the circumscription of three types of energetico-semiotic quantum configuration: non-separability, separation and quantification.

Non-separability

I call non-separability the synchronic correlations at a distance that guarantee modes of compossibility between diverse entity states. This non-separability is established outside of any criterion of semiotic localization and its status as intrinsic reference can therefore not be called into question because of the intrusion of an 'observer' Assemblage. Tensors of non-separability are inscribed on the general Plane of consistency of inter-entitarian relations as a function of an axis of *deterritorialization* (ordinate axis in Figure 2.1). Later we will be led to distinguish two configurations

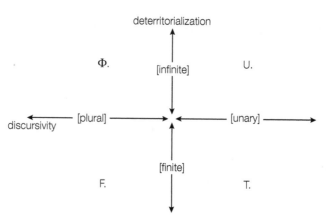

FIGURE 2.1 The axes of deterritorialization and relative discursivity

of intrinsic deterritorialization: Systems and Structures, and two configurations of extrinsic deterritorialization: semiotic Content and Expression.

Separation 2.

I call 'separation' the diachronic inter-entitarian transformations on the basis of which the components of semiotization are established. It manifests the propensity of the states of entities to exit, discursivize, delocalize or detotalize themselves. It is at this level that the complementary dimensions of time and becoming come into existence. Separation is neither a tracing nor the opposite of non-separability (such a symmetry would amount to reintroducing 'hidden' semiotic dimensions into non-separability that would confer on it either the classic status of a possibility awaiting its incarnation in a reality or the evolutionist status of a potentiality awaiting an actualization). Whatever processes of expression might occur, and although I relate it to a level of the Unconscious characterized as primary, non-separability knows nothing of such expectations! It suffices to itself. Separation is already in it and, reciprocally, it can pass entirely into separation without the autonomy of either the one or the other being affected. Separation is inscribed on the Plane of Consistency by vectorized tensors according to an axis of discursivity or detotalization (axis of abscissae, Figure 2.1).

There are two sorts of tensors of separation:

- *semiotic tensors* (continuous line, Figure 2.4), which engender sites of sense entities (sensible Territories, Diagrams, Noemas and machinic Propositions) in domains lateral to those of their point of origin;
- *tensors of surplus value of the possible* (ΔF, ΔT, $\Delta \Phi$, ΔU), which have the capacity to relay the sites of sense entities and to transfer them towards pragmatic Effects and subjective Affects.

Quantification

I call 'quantification' the inter-entitiarian relations established between non-separability and separation. Strictly speaking it is not a matter of an interaction between these two dimensions. In effect here we are only dealing with the establishing of sites of entities, that is to say, a level onto which will (or will not) come to be grafted instances that will be specified energetically from a thermodynamic, physico-chemical, biological, etc. angle. It is only in the context of such a taking consistency of Flows that notions like those of action and reaction will become pertinent. In other words, interactions can only be taken into account in our model (on an actual and/or virtual plane) in so far as Assemblages of enunciation have been constructed and in such a way that they have effectively become producers of quantification, that is to say, have acquired a sectorial 'point of view', a 'reading capacity', the state of entities as an economy of energetico-spatio-temporalized Flows. This paradoxical dimension of a quantification proper to the 'order of things', the fact of considering a 'point of view' as an energy charge rests on the same kind of petition of principle as those that inspire our whole 'metapsychology'. Here it leads us to postulate that if, at a molar level, there is numbered and numbering striation, grasped at the nth degree of redundancy of entity sites, this is because such a problematic was already posed at the most molecular levels. Besides its role in articulating the two primary quantum configurations, quantification will thus also have as its mission the retroactive and prospective projection onto the Plane of Consistency of the potentiality for the discernibilization of: 1) quanta of deterritorialization within non-separability; 2) quanta of discursivity within separation. It will be noted that this retroaction differs from the previously refused postulation of hidden semiotic parameters, to the extent that for these parameters there is no longer any possibility of an articulation that can do without this third level of quantification.

And yet, quantification is no more a pragmatic superstructure of separation than separation was a semiotic superstructure of non-separability. Its classification in third position doesn't imply any subordination in relation to the two other quantum configurations. It is neither their mimetic tracing, nor their duplication or dialectical synthesis.

Quantification is represented on the Plane of Consistency by *synaptic tensors* that, prolonging the tensors of surplus value of the possible, transfer the quanta of discursivity of synapses of Effect (Se) and Affect (Sa) towards entity sites polarized into Systems and Structures. Consequently, an aggregation can be brought about between the non-separability of intrinsic reference and the separation of extrinsic reference.

Because of the segmentation of the axes of deterritorialization and discursivity, to which I will return later, the Plane of Consistency finds itself divided into four domains of consistency:

- energetic-signaletic *Flows* (F), the entities of which are arranged in Complexions;

- abstract machinic *Phyla* (Φ), the entities of which are arranged in Rhizomes;

- existential *Territories* (T), the entities of which are arranged in Cutouts;
- incorporeal *Universes* (U), the entities of which are arranged in Constellations.

In the rest of this text, this quadripartition will be figured on a two-dimensional plane, although it would be more pertinent to represent it by a topological surface, layered or folded into four parallel subsets, traversed by a complex line of Assemblages, the discontinuities of which would correspond to the ruptures introduced by tensors of discursivity (Figure 2.2).

The cartography of Assemblages

The three constraints of the model

Our model of the Unconscious is torn by contradictory demands:

- it is based on an autonomous economy of each of its three levels, but
- the entities that constitute those levels do not cease to entertain relations of presupposition, to 'write themselves' through one another, to transform themselves into one another.

Under these conditions, how is one to avoid the model sinking into the same undifferentiated and aleatory continuum? I will endeavour to

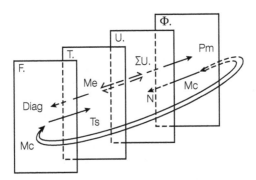

FIGURE 2.2 The layering of the four levels of intensive quantification

confront this question through the imposition of certain topographical constraints.

There are three such constraints:

1. a *principle of exclusion* that forbids direct tensorial relations between, on the one hand, the consistencies F and U and, on the other hand, the consistencies T and Φ;

2. a *principle of dyschrony* that differentiates these tensorial relations according to whether they are vectorized along the axis of deterritorialization (bijective-synchronic tensors) or along the axis of discursivity (projective-diachronic tensors). The distinction between level I of the Unconscious (where the sites of intensive entities will acquire a weight of intrinsic reference, a systemic or structural 'truth') and level II (where these same sites become ontologically precarious and are charged with risks and new potentialities for crystallization) follows from this last constraint;

3. a *principle of presupposition* between the levels, such that:
   - Level I (of intrinsic Reference) doesn't presuppose any other level;
   - Level II (Semiotic) presupposes level I;
   - Level III (Pragmatic and Subjective) presupposes levels I and II (Figure 2.3)

The four domains of the Plane of Consistency

The segmentation of the Plane of Consistency, from which the constitution of the four domains F, T, U and Φ results, rests on two basic arguments:

A. For discursivity: an *ontological argument* that is difficult to avoid, which can be stated thus: 'there is the Given, thus there is the Giving', from which it follows that there are:

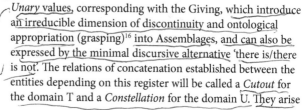

   - *Unary* values, corresponding with the Giving, which introduce an irreducible dimension of discontinuity and ontological appropriation (grasping)[16] into Assemblages, and can also be expressed by the minimal discursive alternative 'there is/there is not'. The relations of concatenation established between the entities depending on this register will be called a *Cutout* for the domain T and a *Constellation* for the domain U. They arise from an economy of *mixture* (in the Stoic sense of mixis)[17] conferring on them the possibility of a total inter-penetration, without direct interaction, that respects the heterogeneity of their components.

- *Plural* values corresponding to the Given, which introduce a dimension of continuity and processual multiplicity into Assemblages, and can be detected by the proliferation, which is in principle limitless, of kinds, species, differences, accidents and other attributes. The relations of concatenation established by the entities will be called *Complexion* for the domain F and *Rhizome* for the domain Φ. They arise from an economy of *fusion* (in the Stoic sense of synchisis),[18] conferring on them the possibility of secreting relative delimitations, remanences of being, trajectories of becoming.

There is the Given, there is the Giving, but neither the one nor the other should be considered as subjected to compartmentalized domains of consistency. If, under certain conditions, there are systems proper to the Given-non-Giving and structures proper to the Giving-non-Given, there is also an intersection between Given-Giving and Giving-Given (Figure 2.5), which constitutes what Hjelmslev calls the semiotic function (or Solidarity) and the two functives of which – Content [C] and Expression (E) – he refuses to oppose, unlike Saussure.[19] (From our point of view, it is their belonging to the same Plane of immanence that authorizes the translations, symmetries and reversions between these systems, structures and functives of semiotic solidarity.)

B For deterritorialization: a somewhat risky, but, on reflection, obvious enough *cosmological argument*, which postulates the

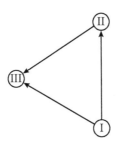

FIGURE 2.3 The relations of presupposition between the three unconscious levels

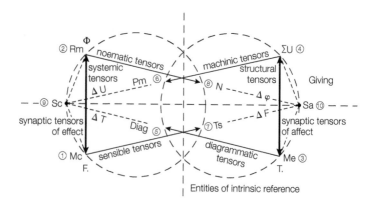

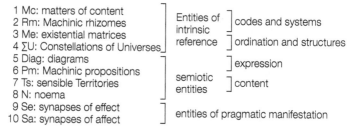

1 Mc: matters of content ⎤
2 Rm: Machinic rhizomes   ⎥ Entities of ⎤ codes and systems
3 Me: existential matrices ⎥ intrinsic   ⎥
4 ΣU: Constellations of Universes ⎦ reference ⎦ ordination and structures
5 Diag: diagrams   ⎤   ⎤ expression
6 Pm: Machinic propositions ⎥ semiotic   ⎥
7 Ts: sensible Territories ⎥ entities   ⎥ content
8 N: noema   ⎦   ⎦
9 Se: synapses of effect ⎤ entities of pragmatic manifestation
10 Sa: synapses of affect ⎦

FIGURE 2.4 Map of entities and tensors

existence of two domains of intrinsic reference, without immediate intersection, whose relations can only be mediatized by tensors of discursivity or by Assemblage synapses. This argument can be stated thus: 'An intrinsic systemic Referent corresponds to the Given (Rsy); an intrinsic structural Referent corresponds to the Giving (Rst)' (Figure 2.5).

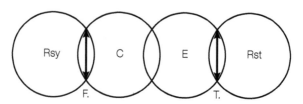

FIGURE 2.5 Intersection of the Given and the Giving

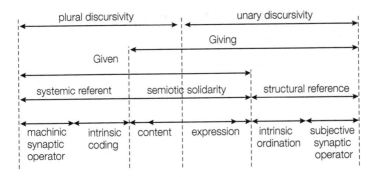

TABLE 2.1 Relationship between categories of discursivity

The axis of deterritorialization is in turn divided into two segments, corresponding to the two types of generic value that they can be attributed:

- finite values, for reversible relations of deterritorialization referenced around an equilibrium point;
- infinite values, for relations of deterritorialization drifting irreversibly outside of any equilibrium point (Figure 2.1).

		Discursivity	
		• plural • continuous • fusional	• unary • discontinuous • of mixtures
Deterritorialization	• Infinite • Irreversible • Far from equilibrium	Φ. Processual machinic *phyla* (Rhizomes)	U. Incorporeal *universes* (Constellations)
	• Finite • Reversible • Close to equilibrium	F. Energetico-signaletic *flows* (Complexions)	T. Existential *territories* (Cutouts)

TABLE 2.2 Values and characteristics of the four domains F, Φ, T, U

Structures and systems of the primary unconscious

The tensors at this level, called tensors of intrinsic reference, are represented (Figure 2.4) by bijective couples with a continuous line. When confronted (indirectly) at this level of the primary Unconscious – through the mediation of the secondary and tertiary levels – schizoanalysis has to surrender. It is even essential that this is the case, in other words that it knows how to recognize the domains on which it can get no hold.

Tensors of intrinsic reference can be classified into two categories:

1 *systemic tensors* ($\overrightarrow{12}$) that are established on the side of the Given, between sites of F entities and sites of Φ entities (for example, organic systems articulating, at an ontogenetic level, material and energetic Flows (Mc) on an abstract machinic nexus (Rm), itself philogenetically positioned);

2 *structural tensors* ($\overrightarrow{34}$) that are established on the side of the Giving, between sites of T entities and sites of U entities (for example, a musical structure crystallizing heterogeneous incorporeal Universes of a rhythmic, melodic, harmonic, contrapuntal, vocal, instrumental, etc. origin, unlocalizable in energetico-spatio-temporal and historical givens, whatever its manifest date).

The semiotic tensors of the secondary unconscious

The tensors at this level, called tensors of intrinsic reference, are represented (Figure 2.4) by projective vectors with a continuous line. Unlike the previous vectors, they are not reversible: the entity that is at their point of origin implies an entity at their point of arrival – called a semiotic entity – without the reverse being true. As a counterpart to their ambiguity, their ontological ambiguity, these semiotic entities are bearers of a surplus value of possibility susceptible of being actualized at the pragmatic level.

At this secondary level of the Unconscious, the labour of schizoanalysis bears on the components of semiotization. It may engage in a multiplication in, or reduction of, their number; an enhanced discernibilization or a globalization of their operations; an acceleration or a slowing down of their mode of temporalization; an enlargement or a shrinking of their object, an enrichment or a divesting of their matter of expression...

The four tensors of semiotic potentialization can be classified in four categories:

1 **Two tensors of persistence,** vectorized from Systems towards Structures:

   Sensible tensors ($\overrightarrow{17}$), which virtualize sensible contents within the domain T. Discursivity passes here

   From energetico-signaletic Complexions that are adjacent to intrinsically referred systems ($\overleftrightarrow{Mc} \quad \overrightarrow{Rm}$)

   To existential Cutouts (Ts), 'without guarantee' that are charged with a possibility-potential and are dependent on a duration with neither subject nor object, a pure existential turning-over, the entities of which have a null speed (for example, a totemic icon, in the context of an anthropological Assemblage, cut out on the basis of the most diverse Flows, or a territorialization refrain, in the context of an ethological Assemblage, or even of an 'imago' in the context of a fantasmatic Assemblage);

   Noematic tensors ($\overrightarrow{28}$) which virtualize noematic contents at the heart of the domain U. Discursivity passes here

   From abstract machinic Rhizomes adjacent to intrinsically referred systems ($\overleftrightarrow{Mc} \quad \overrightarrow{Rm}$)

   To incorporeal (or paradigmatic) noematic Constellations, 'without guarantee', charged with a potential for possibility dependent on an infinitely fragmented, 'multiplicitous' duration, the entities of which have an absolute speed, that is to say, a speed that cannot be related to EST coordinates (for example, the Cheshire cat's smile, which Whitehead tells us is encountered at all points in space without it being possible to localize it at any point in particular).

2 **Two tensors of transistence** vectorized from Structures to Systems:

   Diagrammatic tensors ($\overrightarrow{35}$), which actualize a diagrammatic Expression at the heart of the domain F. Discursivity passes here

   From existential Cutouts that are adjacent to intrinsically referred structures ($\overleftrightarrow{Me} \quad \overrightarrow{\Sigma U}$)

   To energetico-signaletic Complexions (Diag) 'without guarantee',

that are charged with a potential for possibilities, dependent
on a relative temporalization and whose entities are obliged to
respect the celebrated law which states that physical particles have
speeds that are less than or equal to that of light (for example,
the signaletic matter of a credit card, able to trigger an ATM,
depending on whether or not its PIN corresponds to what is typed
into the machine, whether or not the card or machine is damaged
and, I'm forgetting the essential point, whether or not one is in
France or abroad…);

- *Machinic tensors* ($\overrightarrow{46}$), which actualize an abstract propositional
expression at the heart of the domain. Discursivity passes here

  From incorporeal Constellations of Universes adjacent to
  intrinsically referred structures ($\overline{\overline{\Sigma U \quad Me}}$)

  To abstract machinic Rhizomes (Pm) 'without guarantee', charged
  with a potential for possibilities, dependent on a temporalization
  that ceases to impose on the entities that fall within their
  jurisdiction the need to maintain a speed less than that of the
  relative threshold of the speed of light. In effect, once they
  have manifested themselves, we know that they are capable of
  'overtaking' the matters of expression that were their messengers,
  so as to start existing immediately in the mode of having been
  always and everywhere *already there* (for example, the incorporeal
  faciality of Christ, which is projected onto all capitalist machinic
  Phyla, which traverses spaces before they have unfolded, which
  retroactively and projectively 'smoothes' the temporalities and
  epochs that they vampirize).

Persistence and transistence of the tertiary unconscious

Level III of the Unconscious is essentially constituted by pragmatic synapses
(Se) and subjective synapses (Sa), the function of which is to 'adjust' the
three types of quantum configuration of non-separability, separation and
quantification. Thus the past potentialities of the Systems and Structures of
level I and the surplus values of possibility of the semiotic concatenations
of level II, bearing the future, find themselves capitalized, put into action,
rendered present. The actualization of Effects and the virtualization of
Affects cannot be assimilated to mechanical causation or dialectical implication, because their occurrences are indissolubly linked to the contingent,

singular character of the Assemblages that effectuate it. The 'present' of schizoanalytic pragmatics doesn't imply any primacy of a clear, distinct, continuous, rational, capitalistic and symbolically castrated consciousness. The temporal schizzes and the dyschronies generated by fragmented becomings are inscribed in its register in their own right.

We have seen that the function of the tensors that were *afferent* to synapses was to relay the surplus value of risks and possibilities 'in waiting' in the semiotic entities arrived at in level II, and that of the *efferent* – pragmatic and subjective – tensors was to aggregate these surplus values at the systemic and structural sites of level I.

The 'canonical' model of the Assemblage in Figure 2.4 only constitutes a limiting case of schizoanalytic cartography, those 'on the ground' necessarily putting into play a much greater number of synapses, articulated within a complex network of Assemblages. (This limiting case would be worth going into more thoroughly as such because it represents the ideal type towards which the ensemble of capitalistic productions of subjectivity tend.)

Each synapse can have an indefinite number of valences depending on the number of tensors it puts into play.

Bivalent codings and orderings result from the conjunction of two afferent tensors of surplus value of possibility. When these have a:

- consistency F and Φ (ΔT and ΔU), one has an *Effect of extrinsic coding* (for example, a 'groundless' perception of the order of delirium or hallucination);

- consistency T and U (ΔF and Δ Φ), one has an *Affect of extrinsic ordering* (for example, a 'lived impression' on an aesthetic, oneiric or mystical plane).

Trivalent synapses result from the conjunction of two afferent tensors and one efferent synaptic tensor. When the latter has a:

- consistency F (91), one has a *systemically closed Effect*,[20] or an effect of enslavement in the cybernetic sense (for example, a conditioned reflex system);

- consistency Φ (92), one has a *systemically open Effect*, or a system far from equilibrium (for example, the micro-social systems in which family therapy and network practices endeavour to intervene)[21];

- consistency T (10, 3), one has a *structurally closed Affect* (for example, an ego, superego or ego ideal function…);

- consistency U $(\overrightarrow{10, 4})$, one has a *structurally open Affect* (for example, a 'becoming' animal, child, vegetable, cosmos…).

Tetravalent synapses associate either intrinsic coding Effects with systemic synapses that are at once both open and closed, or extrinsic ordering Affects with structural synapses that are at the same time open and closed.

Synapses Sa and Se always function in a coupled fashion. The constitutive threshold of an Assemblage of enunciation is only crossed when such an articulation effectively takes place. On this side of the threshold, one has to consider that the entities arise from other formations, which have to be searched for bit by bit.

We will say that whenever an Assemblage finds itself polarized according to a relation of persistence $\overrightarrow{Se\ Sa}$ there is the *virtualszation of an Affect* and that whenever it finds itself polarized according to a relation of transistence $\overrightarrow{Sa\ Se}$, there is the *actualization of an Effect*. This perpetual switching between persistantial virtual implosion and transistantial actual expansion never implies the total elimination of the two poles of Affect and Effect.

Everything here is a game of taking consistency. The more (intrinsic or acquired) consistency an Affect possesses at the degree zero of discursivity, the more consistency the differentiated Effect, with which it is assembled, is in a position to acquire. And inversely. Virtual affectation and actual affectation come face to face with and envelop one another. They have the same ontological status. It is no longer a question of making a mimetic double of the virtual, an attenuated reflection of the real or a crystal of possibility on which actualization would confer the weight of existence. The virtual

	F	Φ	T	U
F	Complexion (Mc)	Open systemic effect (Se)	Sensible tensor	
Φ	Closed structural effect (Se)	Rhizome (Rm)		Noemic Tensor
T	Diagrammatic Tensor		Cutout (Me)	Open structural affect (Sa)
U		Machinic tensor	Closed systemic affect (Sa)	Constellation (U)

TABLE 2.3 Intra- and inter-domain transformations

charges of the Unconscious are potential energies in the same way that the actual charges that physicists concern themselves with.

One last remark: this double movement of the affectation and effectuation of consistencies implies the calling into question of the hierarchy of types according to which logics have been constructed since Bertrand Russell, because as has been seen in the course of the development of our argument, the same instances found themselves successively and simultaneously in the positions of elementary quanta of 'pre-energetic' correlation, semiotic operator and Assemblage quantification. It is a dream logic, then? A logic of archaic intensities?[22] And perhaps also the logic of an era to come of sign-particles?

3 THE CYCLE OF ASSEMBLAGES (FIRST GLOBAL APPROACH)

Preamble: Why start from four entities?

Axiomatics with two terms (of the Being/Nothingness type) necessarily result in an 'depotentialized' representation and an inaccessible 'grund', whilst dialectics with three terms lead to pyramidal, arborescent determinations…It is only with 3 + n entities that one can establish: 1) a trans-entitarian (matricial) generativity, without any essential priority of one essence over another (without the infrastructure – superstructure relation, for example); 2) a principle of self-affirmation, auto-retroaction, a self-transcending (Jean-Pierre Dupuy) or auto-poietic (Francisco Varela) foundation.

Exo-referred modelling systems can be modelled perfectly well on the basis of two types of notion:

- F notions of discontinuous discursivity;
- Φ notions of continuous 'intercalary' discursivity.

It is not the same with *endo-referred* meta-models, which call for a heterogeneous multiplicity of categories, or more exactly, for which the meta-modelling categories must account for fundamentally heterogeneous dimensions, specific processes of heterogenesis and problematics of singularization. The unary discontinuity of contingency T cannot be simply articulated to intensive incorporeal (non-discursive) multiplicities

U. Between (finite discursive) contingency and (intensive continuous) auto-transcendence, heterogeneous operators must of necessity intercalate synaptic operators resulting from another use of machinic relations Φ.

	Discursive	Non-discursive
I continuous	Φ	U
II discontinuous	F	T
	Exo-referred modelling	Endo-referred meta-modelling

FIGURE 3.1 Matrix of four modelling and meta-modelling entities

Level I of Φ and incorporeal U represents the deterritorialized integral of the territorialized ('contingent') F and T of level II.

Φ is a category of discursivity

The phenomenological approach to discursivity appears easier than that of non-discursivity. It seems to go without saying that there is a *discursive Given*. Philosophy was constituted around the meta-modelling of non-discursive *Giving*, whilst on the side of the sciences, the degree of deterritorialization of the Given remains marked by a lack of elucidation of the Assemblages of enunciation of the Giving and of logics of non-discursive intensities.

Continuous discursivity Φ marks the infinite multiplicity of a state of fact or a state of things which, in any case, is only given in 'contingenced' (territorialized) Assemblages.

Discursivity is synonymous with sequential order exo-referred to EST coordinates. This sequential order can be presented in two modalities:

- rhizomatic ($Φ^r$);
- parallel linear chains ($Φ^l$).

The rhizomatic organization of chains of discursivity includes knots, cross-roads and implies a networked machinic consistency.

Linearized organization separates machinic clusters and agglomerations, it heterogenizes them. Its general consistency implies the erection of changes of level, the crossing of thresholds of deterritorialization.

Operators of trans-deterritorialization then open up onto Constellations of Universes of reference that refer us to the logic of bodies without organs (TU).

With the rhizomatic formula, we will speak of *immanent machinic relations*; with the formula for multiple linearities and multiple articulations, we will speak of *transcendent machinic relations*. At the junction of n machinic articulations *problematics* are established that may be open to:

- an interlinear composition (a polyphonic multiplicity, in Bakhtin's sense);
- enunciative mutations of a harmonic order;

(Machinic (rhizomatic) sequences do not imply any synaptic openings: UT.)

Questions left in suspense

- How is machinism in rhizomatic clusters and trans-linear machinism to be articulated?
- How does enunciative intrusion (UT) pose itself in the case of figures of linearized consistency?
- Can the machinics of immanence do without the quadrant FΦTU?

Φ is a category of exo-reference or allo-reference

Discursivity is not pure succession without memory. Memories themselves are not simple passive recordings. All memories are machines. All machines are memories.

Φ is constituted of chains of machine-memories inhabited by potential surplus values. Here surplus value signifies that the concatenation of Phyla is able to produce something more than a simple addition of the components put to work. Integrals of memory [ΦU] are grafted onto the Flows F of pure discursivity (break-Flow of Flows). Not only memories of actual potentiality (Φ), but also memories of virtual potentiality (U) (= the point of view of all potential enunciators).

Example: under the conditions of actual variable potentials Φ, all the potential experiences in other contexts of virtual Universes U are added to the interaction between two particles (in a cosmological black hole at instant $\theta = 10^{-36}$ of Big Bang, etc.).

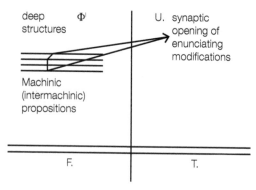

FIGURE 3.2 Deep structures Φⁱ and synaptic opening

	Discursive actualization	Enunciative virtualization
Possible occurrences	Φ	U
Contingenced (real) occurrences	F	T

FIGURE 3.3 Matrix of the Possible, Real, Actual and Virtual

The exo-reference of Flows operates in the framework of logics of finite dis-continuous discursive sets, whilst those of Phyla Φ operate in the framework of logics of infinite continuous algorithmic discursive sets. This gets us out of the framework of relations of the type *Figure/Ground* (cutting out of a Figure/discontinuous referential Ground) and establishes a framework of relations:

Machinic knots/continuous systemic Ground

The mode of discursivity particular to machinic Propositions rests on the metabolism of Universes of reference.

Φ is a category of continuity

Φ expresses all possible pro-positions and trans-positions with regard to 'contingenced' states of Flow.

A particularly difficult leap will consist in passing from this register of the multiplicity of possibilities, which can be pinpointed by its effects to that of the powers of virtual affect (enunciative virtualization).

Φ is a proto-energetic category

The continuum Φ of possibilities harbours every possible entry for transfers of effect. To introduce the idea of an equivalence:

availability of Effect = potential energy

Impact: these transfers of Effect not only comprise charges of material potentiality caught in EST coordinates but also charges of semiotic potentiality (of code, moulding, catalysis…). Hence the necessity of a general theory of signaletic-diagrammatic charges establishing that a semiotic effect (the impact of a sign-particle) can be the bearer of real energy effects.

From a general point of view, we will consider that all discursivity (territorialized or deterritorialized, material or semiotic…) has energy consequences.

Energy expresses the consistency of transfers between deterritorialized levels. In sum it is a matter of a deterritorialization to the nth degree (the integral of deterritorializations of all discursivity of Flows).

Remark: The turning of semiotic energies into material energies can only be understood on condition that one maintains the reversibility of the positions of entities. What was Φ can become F; what was T can become U, etc.

Machinic diachrony and synchrony

Our first apprehension of machinic Phyla was inscribed in a double point of view.

A A machinic evolutionism (the mechanosphere) comprising:

a diachronic dimension
Each technical or semiotic machine is inseparable from the machines for which it is substituted and from the machine that it prepares for the future (the tree, or, rather, rhizome of machinic implication);

a synchronic dimension

As planetary machinic integration proceeds, each machine is inseparable from its overall environment. At the limit, there is just one machine on the horizon. Not as the science-fiction of yesteryear imagined, in the form of a tyrannical mega-machine, but as a powdery molecular machinic multiplicity.

B The older view of an opposition between machine and structure. The machine is conceived as being the bearer of a machinic surplus value, of a 'possibilistic' life, whilst structure is exo-determined, passive. There is never any innocent feedback. The slightest feedback is the bearer of Universes of self-reference, and when it turns back on itself in a feedback loop, it knots together a proto-subjectivity. It is necessary to think these proto-durations at very heterogeneous levels: that of the cell, for example, the organ, neurological integration, corporeal memories, the ego, domestic memories, etc. Hence the question of Assemblages.

But the consistency of machinic regions doesn't only rest on an extrinsic determination: it also arises from a self-consistency that is transistential, that is to say, is established at problematic deterritorialized levels. Hence the question of Φ in their relations with self-consistent U.

The machinic Plane of consistency (Φ) thus finds itself doubled by a Plane of immanence (U) or Plane of self-reference. The question gets more complicated in that this Plane of immanence is not a universal frame but the locus for the generation (the heterogenesis) of singular positions of existence.

Universes and paradigms

What is missing in Kuhn's paradigms is that they only exist in Phyla and are not linked by Constellations of Universes.

Problems live in the same way as do other, living beings, with the difference that they do not move about in the same coordinates. Ultimately, we will distinguish: extrinsic EST coordinates and intrinsic intensive coordinates.

With the first generation of 'desiring machines' it was a matter of making a bridge between the diagrammatic effectiveness of signaletic matters and the most deterritorialized of subjective operations. It was appropriate to presuppose abstract machines traversing the most deterritorialized orders.

Process, the processual line of deterritorialization capable of carrying out this traversal, became the category of desire. These questions of desire are now reframed in terms of problematics of the production of enunciation.

Flows and Phyla

An attempt to go back up to the starting point: there are Flows; the world presents itself in the form of fluctuation.

Let us note some traits relating to these Flows, which we will come across again during their later evolution into machinic Phyla.

Flows are:

- smooth: the 'identitarianizing' repetition of forms which, in this way, find themselves identified = linearization;
- cut into discrete figures;
- They are only given in a finite approach that circumscribes their delimitations in time and space, more generally in EST coordinates.
- bearers of feedback, a memory of smoothing;
- Whilst the antecedent characteristic of discretized smoothing called for that of proto-enunciation (T), the characteristic of feedback calls for a category of proto-machinism.

Flows only exist as intensive fluctuation. This leads us to pose a first *relation of territorialized discursivity* indexed on three characteristics:

1 a *primary material continuum*, or *primary matter* (or primarized matter) which will subsequently be specified as:
- energetico-spatio-temporal matter (EST);
- signaletic matter;
2 a *repetition of divisible and smoothed forms*, on the basis of this continuum or *proto-machinic form*;
3 *mediative operators* for the position-retention of proto-machinic forms, capitalizing a memory of being (persistence) or *proto-enunciative substance* (T).

Fluctuation (or the relation of territorialized discursivity) can be represented by the following figure:

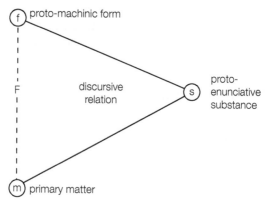

FIGURE 3.4 Matter, substance, form

Let us now underline the reversibility between the dimensions of the primary matter of a Flow and its proto-machinic form.

This relation of territorialized discursivity corresponds to a first stasis of deterritorialization, *substantial deterritorialization.*

We are now led to characterize a second stasis of deterritorialization: the *relations of expression* that will result from the bipolar concatenation of 'n' fluctuations F. Each fluctuation of substantial deterritorialization can be subject to two functional modalities:

1 The 'autistic' *closure* of proto-machinic figures, prohibiting any interaction, any communication with what they are not (of the cosmological black hole type). With nothing new occurring during the repetition of figures of Flow, proto-machinic form continually falls back onto primary matter. The continuity of Flow thus only manifests a formal reiteration.

We have

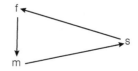

That we could write

2 Dialectical *exhaustion,* which follows from the putting into relation of the diverse forms borne by proto-machinic figures. Effects that were not included in any of the smoothings of Flow in presence result from this (expressive surplus value or existential supplement, which will be noted ∆F.: the elementary concatenation of a surplus value of Flow).

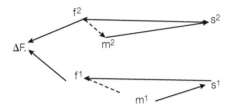

The set $\overline{\Phi Te}$ – constitutes an existential *basic module.* This dialectical exhaustion leads to a *bipolar regrouping* of smooth components around a function of Content (ΔF^c) and a function of expression (ΔF^e). The articulation of these two functions is brought about via a new type of entity: chains of expressions of *machinic Phyla* (Φ) in the register of enunciative virtualization, accompanied by the putting in place of a new type of territorial encompasser Te (*existential Territories* or graspings).

This relation of expression corresponds to a second stasis of deterritorialization, *expressive deterritorialization.*

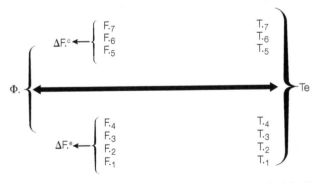

FIGURE 3.5 The bipolar arrangement of an expressive deterritorialization (with seven Flow components)

Assemblages of enunciation

We can try to situate the different categories of deterritorialization (substantial, expressive and others to come) in relation to the quadrant FTΦU.

The first objective is to pass from the proto-machinic smoothing of Flows to the deterritorialized machinic Phyla. But the resolution of this problem will take us further and will lead to us envisaging more general functions of smoothing and striation that are established in the ensemble of intra- and inter-entitarian relations. This will result in us considering that:

1 every heterogeneity developed in an entitarian register is a *striation*;

2 every inter-entitarian transformation of the neighbourhood between two registers is a *smoothing*.

In the first case, it is on the basis of the homogeneity of an entity that a heterogeneity circumscribed in the same register results. In the second case, it is on the basis of the heterogeneity of register that a new trans-entitarian homogeneity results.

For example, the concatenation of Flows in the register F is correlative to a striation, a heterogeneization (or hetero-genesis) of the sensible world, whereas the bipolarization of Flows into semiotic Flows and EST Flows is inseparable from the putting into play of smooth machinic Phyla in the neighbouring register Φ.

To restrict ourselves to this corner of the quadrant (to which we will later return in more detail), we have:

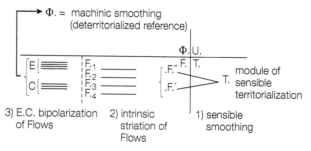

FIGURE 3.6 The three modalities of fluctuation

I now propose to describe the processual cycle of relations of striation/ smoothing, on the basis of Figure 3.7.

It is to be noted here that each striation, internal to a domain of entities, is the junction-operator of two smoothings:

- a vertical smoothing of deterritorialization;
- a horizontal smoothing of discursivization.

Starting from the domains of manifestation FT, the smoothing of deterritorialization engages in the constitution of processual and prospective levels operating via continuous fields of the possible and the virtual (domains Φ and U).

For its part, starting from the domains TU, the smoothing of discursivization constitutes the entities of the domains F and Φ at the crossroads of extrinsic coordinates.

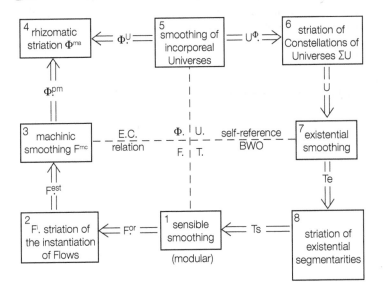

F^i	instantiated Flows	Φ^{ma}	Rhizome of abstract machines
F^{est}	energetico-spatio-temporal Flows	U^V	virtual Universes
F^{or}	Flows of relative ordination	ΣU	Constellations of Universes
F^{mc}	concrete machines	Te	existential Territories
Φ^{pm}	Phylum of machinic propositions	Ts	sensible Territories

FIGURE 3.7 Cycle of the Assemblages of enunciation

One can now see a problematic of energy emerging at the junction of the instances of striated Flows. It is in correlation with the fact that Flows of Expression (F^{est}) 'extract themselves' from sensible fluctuations (machinic deterritorialization) that an energetic smoothing of Flows occurs. That is to say, energetic discursivity is a function of the status of the (concrete and abstract) machines that articulate it.

Description of the first four phases of the cycle of the Assemblages of enunciation

An initial remark: Figure 3.7 presents a closed cycle. But it is still only a matter of a first approach, because subsequently we will see that a continuous expansion of deterritorializations and reterritorializations leads to the constant grafting of new loops in the domains of manifestation and fields of possibility (Figure 3.8).

Sensible smoothing: Sub-position

We will start from an initial state of the 'Brownian' dispersion of redundancies of entity, the extension (the amplitude) of regularities only arising with the appearance of stochastic series.

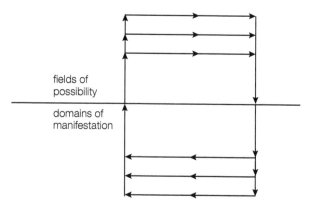

FIGURE 3.8 Expansion of the fields of the Possible

```
O-OOO-OO- -OO
OO- -OOOO--OO-
O- -O O- - -O-O-
O-O- - - -O-O-O
-O-OO--OO--O
OO-OO- -O- -OO
```

This 'first' level of the smoothing of flows proceeds by modules of the *linearization of redundancies.*

What is in question here is the transformation of aleatory chains of the 'primitive soup', or redundancies, into smoothed, proto-machinic sequences that have been brought under control.

Certainly it is not possible to determine a clear frontier between 'spontaneous' chains and crystalline, proto-vital, proto-machinic forms of organization. But this passage is only envisaged here in a speculative fashion so as to bring to light certain constitutive steps in machinic processes.

At its most elementary level, a redundancy requires the putting into play of three simultaneous series of operations:

- segmentation;
- identification of the segment generated;
- the retention in memory of the two preceding operations, guaranteeing their possible reproduction.

With the linearization considered here, these operations will cross a supplementary threshold of consistency of manifestation (persistantial consistency) characterized by a particular structure of the process of identification and by a change in the nature of the memory of redundancy.

The identification of redundancies is henceforth accomplished in relation to a system of relative ordinates, whilst their memory ceases to be proximal and is organized on two levels. On the level of 'internal' memories of concatenation, one passes from a memory of redundancies with an extension of two – synonymous with a systematic forgetting of the engendered chains – to a memory with an extension of greater than two. This enlarging authorizes the establishment of a second 'external' memory, the indispensible condition for operations of calibration and reproduction of deterritorialized forms. It is advisable to note that the terminal state of the smoothing of Flows does not abolish the unformed character of the input Flows (F^m). As in wave-particle physics, the output Flows of the module (F^{or}) associate, in an apparently contradictory fashion, memorized

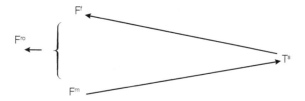

F^m material Flow = initial unformed state of redundancies
T^s substantial (or sensible) Territory = non-discursive operator
F^f Flow-form = formed state of redundancies
F^{ro} Flow with relative ordinates = end state of smoothing of Flows

FIGURE 3.9 Module of the sensible smoothing of Flows

and controlled states of discursivity with virgin states of 'matter', available for other reshufflings of form. We see here that the matter-substance-form triangulation does not have a classically dialectical character. The thesis subsists under the synthesis like a residue that can reaffirm new potentialities and re-orient the formal processes started up.

The instantial striation of Flows: Dis-position

Now the promotion of the category of heterogeneity finds itself called into question. From the endo-ordination of sensible smoothing one moves on to an in-stantiation by trans-ordination, itself announcing the expressive coordination of machinic smoothing.

With endo-ordination, segmentary identification and its memory were finalized on the linear taking consistency of Flows. But they did not 'take off' from the segmentary processes; they remained parasitic on them like pilot fish. With the trans-ordination of the striation of Flows, the situation changes: evaluation crosses a threshold of existential consistency. We are no longer dealing with a simple calibration of internal ordination (F^{or}) but also with a differential pinpointing that I will call in-stantiation or the marking of difference.

The striation of Flows is illustrated in Figure 3.10 by a numerical difference bearing on binary sequences of signs. But this representation is not sufficient to account for the category of the heterogeneity of Flows, which puts into play something rather different to quantifiable differences, that is to say, sensible and abstract qualities that are both fundamentally resistant to being reduced in the form of a 'digitalized' message.

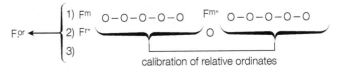

FIGURE 3.10 Pseudo-synthesis of the sub-position of Flows (endo-ordination)

We must remember here that, as Figure 3.7 indicates, the striation of Flows is situated at the junction of two types of smoothing:

- discursive smoothing along the axis FT, which has as its function the calibration and articulation of sensible qualities;
- deterritorializing smoothing along the machinic axis FΦ, which positions it in the register of abstract qualities inherent to machinic propositions.

Whilst sensible qualities enclose striation in a discontinuous finitude (endo-ordination), abstract qualities, on the contrary, open it onto a continuous and transfinite evaluation (trans-ordination).

Consequently, we will distinguish two heterogeneities: a sensible one of positioning, which is nevertheless amorphous, with proximal references only, and the other which is 'charged' with processual potentialities and which is, as we will see, proto-genetic. We will note here that if, in this last modality, heterogeneity succeeds in opening up, in charging itself with possibilities, this is so only on condition that it mobilizes the ensemble of the four domains of entities (FTΦU) represented in Figure 3.7. In any case, it is the same with all the other categories described here. But we must go further: not only is

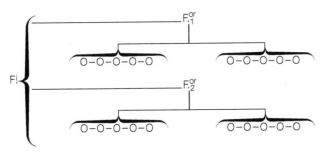

FIGURE 3.11 The in-stantiation of Flows

each category supported by the ensemble of striations and smoothings of the cycle of Assemblages but in addition, each particular positioning of an entity draws into its wake the requalification of all the others. The instantiation of a Flow, for example, leads to the requalification of material Flows and the Flows of endo-ordination, and the passage of machinic Flows in turn entails the requalification of instantiated Flows…The decisive turning point, with the surplus value of possibility generated by the instantiation of Flows, is that it is no longer only the manifest being-there, the attested locality of a figure of redundancy, that is taken into account, but also the integral of its possible dis-positions, before, after, next to and beyond its actual manifestations.

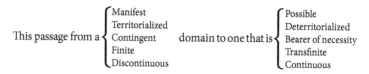

corresponds to a first static mutation of its of consistency, which will be essential to the subsequent stasis, which will sweep them, smooth them, not into Flows, but into fields of possibility (machinic Phyla).

Machinic smoothing: Pro-position

Machines and machinic fields are engendered on the basis of striated Flows. A particle accelerator, for example, is established at the meeting point of Flows of algorithms, concrete, steel, glass, energy, monetary signs and, finally, particles. On the other hand, the striation of ploughing – Flows of earth, of grains, of water, of seasons…– results from the intervention of technical human and celestial machines…In other words, having the machine follow the smoothing and the striation of Flows is a presentational choice. The inverse would have been equally legitimate.

The striation of Flows passes on a static instantiation of possibility. It will pertain to machinic smoothing to make this legacy bear fruit by dynamicizing its Capital of heterogeneity well beyond the elementary operations of calibration or transordination of Flows. To succeed in this, it will not be enough to work the raw mass of Flows globally; machinic smoothing will select certain of their interactions in the framework of a regrouping and a bipolar disposition that, by convention, but also for good reasons, I will characterize as relations of Expression-Content (abbreviated as EC). Let us specify straightaway that this EC function does not in any way imply that Expression and Content are anchored, once and for all, in a transcendent reference. These

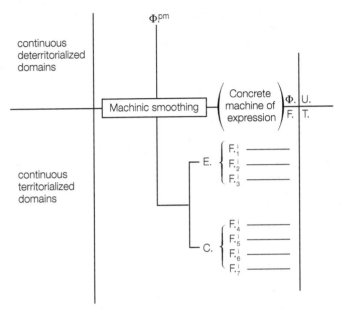

FIGURE 3.12 Double articulation of machinic smoothing: the EC function (repeated from Figure 3.5)

two positions are capable of every turnaround, of every reversal. They are only there so as to manifest a principle of the expression or extraction of traits of machinic effectiveness (machinic pro-positions composed of sign-particles).

Machinic expression has three principal functions:

1   to confer a specific consistency on the differences between instantiated Flows, allowing them, if one will accept this image, to acquire a language that is proper to them;

2   to release the new continuum of possibility whose sudden appearance was authorized by the dividing up between the poles E and C, which this time abstracts from the originary contingency of instantiated Flows on which they rest (their discrete and finite 'contingencing' at the heart of the quadrant F);

3   to confer a pragmatic effectiveness on the machinic pro-positions (Φ^{mp}) thus promoted, or, in a more general fashion, a machinic power implying an energetic requalification of Flows previously considered (the retro-active smoothing of Flows).

This pragmatic taking consistency is inscribed in the most general logic (one ought to say 'machinic') of the cycle of Assemblages, which makes inter-entitarian intervals exist for themselves by engaging them without respite in new (evaluative, expressive, machinic...) constructions. This 'headlong flight', which results in these intervals being processed to the first, the second, the third, the nth degree, leads to a sort of continuous expansion of discursive domains, of fields of potentiality and of Universes of virtuality.

However these domains, fields and Universes will not bring about their generic mutations directly through this flight: it is through rupture and the rearrangement of their ontological texture as well as through procedures of the inflation-integration of basic entities. It pertains to the operators of substantial smoothing (corresponding to the summits s of the triangulations of matter-substance-form) to trigger these ontological mutations. In order to better situate the particular position of expressive-machinic smoothing, let us enumerate the three mediators of substantiation called into question in the cycle as a whole.

1 *The substantiation of Flows*
   We have already noted that sensible smoothing ruptured with existential endo-reference and that it 'secreted' linearized discursive sequences, the calibration of which was based on a principle of immanence.

2 *The substantiation of machinic Phyla*
   For its part, machinic smoothing, carried out by the EC function, breaks with the uniquely proximal type of discursivity specific to Flows, so as to introduce a caesura, a completely new opening of 'possibilization' and to authorize pragmatics (machinics) that are creative of temporalization and spatialization, energy conversions, putting to work of encodings and diverse modes of semiotization.

3 *The substantiation of incorporeal Universes*
   Further on, with the smoothing of Universes, we will see a generalized and infinite opening appear, escaping radically from discursive coordinates, whatever their nature might be, preparing the promotion of monads of substantial self-referencing of the type matter-substance-form (m.s.f.).

Before finishing with this anticipatory detour, the following figure will position these three modes of substantiation on the cycle of Assemblages in relation to the four triangles m.s.f.

The double triangulation of the smoothing of Universes will be examined later.

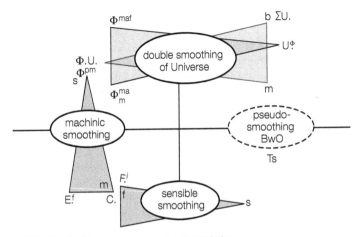

FIGURE 3.13 The three modes of substantiation

The absence of a mediating triangle for the smoothing of bodies without organs (the existential pseudo-smoothing of self-reference) translates the fact that there are no longer any extrinsic relations,which arise from the logic of discursive sets, between the Universes of incorporeal multiplicities and the 'unary' existential Territories,

Let us now return to the question of the energetic requalification of Flows brought about by expressive-machinic smoothing. The bipolarization EC radically changes the points of view on being-there and the scope of fluctuations. It goes beyond the effects consecutive to proximal heterogeneity. It explores an a-topographical and trans-temporal heterogeneity – which I call pro-positional or trans-positional – not only at a distance but also outside the field of enacted spaces and durations. To change a point of view, in these conditions, is like changing your Kelton – it can change your life![1] But it is not only a question of local 'look', of a treatment of environmental ordinates; it results in the putting into play of coordinates of a general order, prospective coordinates, original problematics; it permits the intervention of statistically unpredictable components in the initial context.

We need to untangle the sign-machine-energy complex. Our problem is to try to understand how the machine converts the continuous integral of points of view into a potential energy. But, for the moment, we are still only dealing with machinic smoothing, the proto-energetic taking consistency of the differential interval, of the 'heterogeneification' carried out by the EC function. It is only subsequently that machine time properly so-called will come.

Let us follow the steps that mark out our access to it once again. With the EC function, heterogeneity ceases to be something simply registered: it becomes productive of Effects, although it is true that a simple registration [constat][2] is already an effect, a way out from the pure adequacy to itself of the identity of being, the fusional, narcissistic expression of a radical impotence.

Let us say that the EC function brings about a change of state that consists of passing from a state without any registering of heterogeneity, or with its passive registration, folded back on itself, to a state indexed by active registering. What does that imply? A passive registration remains without any external reference, whereas an active registering is framed by a reference capable of situating it, prolonging it, enriching it and capitalizing on its implications. Except that whoever says 'change of state', or even the simple modification of anything whatsoever, also says 'work of energy'. No physicist would agree to depart from this fundamental principle! In these conditions, one has to admit that the passage from an evaluative registering of the calibration or striation of heterogeneity to an active registering (due to the rearrangement EC) implies the beginning of a reference to energy. Signaletics or the indices of encoding, afferent to evaluation, are charged with energy. And this charge has to lead retroactively to a requalification of the neutral Flows implied in the affair.

If in the course of analysis one arrives at the conclusion that complex Assemblages of semiotization succeed in having effects with a great scope – such as putting a man on the moon – it is necessary to admit the existence of minimal quantum thresholds, pragmatic machinic Effects, at the most elementary levels of a signal expression or encoding.

The basic idea is that prior to any categorisation in terms of objectivity and subjectivity, *a 'point of view' is an act,* an interaction. The heterogeneity of EC is an amplification and multiplication of this basic heterogeneity of action. It capitalizes it, aggravates it, opens up other paths for it. One rediscovers the function of arbitrariness (I would like to say 'arbitrarization') between signifying chains and their corresponding signifieds, described by structural linguistics. But, in our semiotic-machinic perspective, one cannot, like Ferdinand de Saussure, remain content with the substantial independence of signaletic form in relation to its referent. In machinic Assemblages, it may happen that formalism meshes directly with the realities of reference (diagrammatism). Thus passive figures of expression are transformed into active *sign-particles* and the question of semiotic energies can no longer be avoided.

We must draw all the consequences of Hjelmslev's analyses, which led him to posit that the form of figures of Expression is identical to the form of figures of Content. This assertion of the existence of the same deterritorialized machinism where Content and Expression overlap (correlative to their always possible reversibility as semiotic functors) tends definitively to invalidate any structuralist dualism. That machinic functions imply the putting into play of Assemblages of signs shouldn't astonish anyone in the era of informatics and artificial intelligence! That Flows of energy are intimately mixed with signaletic Flows is an everyday experience (one need only think of the use of bank cards, which trigger the physical effect of distributing money, or the connection with P and T.) But what is more difficult to admit is that it is the formalism as such that is the bearer of a certain type of energetic potentiality, independently of the fact that the signs and the figures that it animates are or are not magnetized, electronized, 'cerebralized'…

Let us consider the set of profiles that ordinary metal keys can have. This constitutes a continuum of forms within which each particular key cuts out a specific zone of effectiveness for the opening of the lock to which it corresponds. This zone is bordered by two limit-profiles – two diagrams that can be ciphered, digitized – defining the thresholds of tolerable 'error' beyond which the opening effect ceases. This infinitesimal passage (which can be characterized as a signaletic catalysis) from incorrect to correct form has mechanical-dynamic implications that have no common measure with the energy 'stake' necessary to set it off. Let us note that, as in the case of chemical catalysis, this energy 'stake', despite itself being infinitesimal, is not null. When it enters a phase of signaletic catalysis (or of encoding), the sign or the elementary figure of expression no longer just refers to similar forms: it bites into matter, that is to say, into energy. In these phases of activity (of EC machinic smoothing productive of Phyla $\Phi.^{\text{Pm}}$), signaletic matters pass into the sign-particle state. The portion of territorialized Flows (striated Flows) that finds itself implicated here, is requalified, charged with power. This power derives from the putting into play of effective forms come from elsewhere, imported from deterritorialized machinic propositions ($\Phi.^{\text{Pm}}$) and abstract machines ($\Phi.^{\text{ma}}$), of which it will be a question later. Thus there will be machinic or signaletic catalysis when the relation of Expression and Content allows forms to go exploring, far from their original striations, becoming multilocal. Here, for example, one can see that the correct form belongs to: 1) the key; 2) the lock; and 3) the effective zone of the continuum between the two limit profiles at the same time. Thus the form has changed ontological texture. It can be assimilated to a crystal of heterogeneity. The correct form of the key gathers together:

1   the heterogeneity between the concretized (dimensional) form
    in the key and the concretized form in the lock, which can never

completely coincide but whose variations are required to remain within the typical interval;

2   the heterogeneity between this type of singularly incarnated form and the possibilistic form of the sweep between the two limit profiles.

This association of a manifest heterogeneity and a possibilistic heterogeneity is characteristic of smooth machinic Flows. That is what gives it a new consistency with inter-entitarian dimensions. In becoming coherent, extensive coordinates charged with potential, the old endo-ordinates and relative ordinates describe in their wake new possibilistic fields and open the floodgates to the entry of new energies. The category of energy then tends to be substituted for that of identity. Being loses its fidelity to itself; endo-reference fades away in face of the principles of deterritorialized constancy and consistency.

Rhizomatic striation: Trans-position

Machinic smoothing leads us to postulate that the codes and signs that catalyse the molar economy of Flows ought to be the bearers of molecular and infinitesimal (deterritorialized) charges of energy. But these same smoothings can equally become the object of striations that valorize their heterogeneity and potentialize them in another mode. One then passes on to a different stasis in the cycle of Assemblages of enunciation: that of machines properly so-called.

The continuum of possibility (Φ) deployed by the figure of the correct key remained of a relatively restricted scope; it corresponded to the paradigm weighing over the set of effective profiles. It is true that this paradigm, in turn, furnished other openings onto the multiple Universes that can be discovered behind a door! Except the springing up of Universes always remains unforeseeable, even aleatory. With the abstract machine, on the contrary, these openings of Universes will be coordinated; there will be a systematic management of possibility considered in the diversity of its degrees of deterritorialization. Whilst a machinic Phylum $\Phi.^{pm}$ (a Phylum of machinic Propositions) resulted from a dis-position of Flows into fields bipolarized over EC, now it is a Rhizome of the multipolar trans-position of the possible to the nth degree that will be produced by the interaction $\Phi.^{ma}$ of the Phyla of abstract machines. Let us take the example of the complex sexual machine that results from the 'marriage' of the wasp and the orchid (it works to the benefit of the reproduction of the orchid, but it plays an equally important role in the biological economy of the wasp.) This machine, which associates very heterogeneous components and whose model is crystallized deep in the genetic codes present, traverses not only the individuals but also the evolution of the species in question. We will note here that it no longer arises solely from a bipolarity of the EC type, to the extent that it implies evolutionary dimensions that are inseparable from multiple environmental components relative to the ecological niche considered. We will call this putting into interaction of possibilistic Phyla $\Phi.^{pm}$ at the most deterritorialized levels, 'rhizomatic striation'. For their part, the operators of this selection will be called 'abstract machines'.

Heidegger insisted on the fact that the Being of being should not be reduced to the reality of the real but should be enlarged to the possibility of the possible and the necessity of the necessary.[3] On this point, machinic operators, such as we conceive them, require that one not restrict oneself to such general considerations, because their function is precisely to convert fields of possibility into *effects of necessity*. In this respect one can consider machines as instances of ontological production. In so far as it is a crystallization of the real, the possible and the necessary, Being is essentially a machinic product. This ontological mutation, which makes us pass from the possible to the necessary, is correlative to the establishing of a caesura that is generative of a new smoothing: that of the substantiation of incorporeal Universes. Let's note from the outset that this caesura is no longer of the same nature as the preceding two caesura, i.e.:

- the caesura that 'extracted' the exo-ordination of instantiated Flows $F.^i$ on the basis of the endo-ordination of $F.^o$,[4] and which proceeded by a sort of layering of the Flows $F.^{or}$, without the sub-positional evaluating instance $F.^i$ detaching itself from them entirely and becoming autonomous;

- the caesura of the relation EC, which operated on striated Flows and which presupposed a complete making explicit of the ordination process by way of the linearized dis-position of Flows, guarenteeing their heterogeneity.

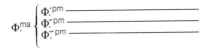

$$\Phi.^{ma} \begin{cases} \Phi.'^{pm} \text{———————} \\ \Phi.''^{pm} \text{———————} \\ \Phi.'''^{pm} \text{———————} \end{cases}$$

FIGURE 3.14 Abstract machines

With the caesura that engenders the machinic pro-positions Φ^{pm}, the evaluative instance proper to the second model of smoothing, we leave the terrain of extrinsic ordering bearing on autonomized Flows regrouped according to the poles of Expression and Content. We pass from the register of the *expressive* to that of the *intensive* or, if one prefers, from traits of extensity (the signaletic part of sign-particles) to traits of intensity. This caesura no longer has as its mission the capitalization of a base of heterogeneity for the production/prospecting of fields of possible points of view. Machinic striation as such is the operational integration of heterogeneous points of view. With machinic striation, it is the very idea of an external point of view that disappears.

The operator of this caesura no longer proceeds either by the peeling apart of the layering of redundancies or by the bipolarization of sheaves of Flows, but by the molecular secretion of Universes of reference 'parallel' to the molar worlds of manifest Flows. Unlike Flows, deterritorialized machinic Phyla are multipolar; they proliferate in every direction and in all dimensions, they overlap in Rhizomes, are transposed, bud in knots of effectiveness. Such a striation confers on them a hyper-continuous character that will allow them to be established in the subsequent stasis, in a, let us say, volumic manner, through the fitting together of incorporeal Universes of possibilities, themselves entertaining relations of compossibility.

The immanence of evaluation implied by this striation of machinic propositions leads to a general requalification of the redundancies that, during previous stases, found themselves in a position of semi-transcendence with regard to Flows, which itself conferred on them a specific ontological consistency. Let us not forget that it is always the same 'basic' entities that find themselves tirelessly taken up again throughout this cycle of positionings and requalifications by stases. Now, the requalification of machinic Propositions Φ^{pm} as abstract machines Φ^{ma} will lead the former to lose certain of the characteristics that they had inherited during their 'passage' through the state of Flow and, primarily, a certain model of identity and of identification. Let us recall that in this regard the preceding configurations of *sign-particles* (constitutive of $\Phi.^{pm}$) still played a double game:

1 in the register of the smoothing of sensible qualities, by their extrinsic circumscription by means of coordinates of the spatio-temporal type (traits of extensity);

2 in the register of the smoothing of abstract machinic qualities, through an 'invisible' positioning of their pragmatic-machinic

effects resting potentially on systems of invariants, constants, formulae, laws, statistical regularities and other algorithmic compositions inseparable, in the final analysis, from an energetic computation.

Now, the _traits of intensity_ constitutive of abstract machines cease to be pro-positional so as to become trans-positional. They sweep across their paradigmatic Phylum of origin and can, at any moment, leap from one Phylum to another.

So, exit the manifest configurations of Flows: only the deep structures of abstract machinic Phyla remain. Consequently, the landscape changes radically because these deep structures no longer respond to the logic of clearly and distinctly exo-referred sets of objects. One will not be able to arrange them in the manner of the arborescent diagrams of Chomskyan generative grammar, each articulation of which is duly hierarchized[5] and even less assimilate them to mathematical statements supported by an axiomatic foundation. They are constituted by abstract machines without any fixed identity, which – although expressed through formulae and laws – nevertheless escape from any transcendent coding inscribed on a bedrock of scientificity, as hard as the diorite stelae of King Hammurabi.

These abstract machines ceaselessly explore and work the variations-derivations-integrations proper to the fields of possibility (operations characterized here as trans-positional), outside of any testifiable tempo-rality. But if nothing, neither God nor structure, can impose its law on laws, then is not our striation of machinic Phyla condemned to sink into anarchy and powerlessness, each machinic monad interfering with everything and nothing only to close up on itself in the last instance? By examining the subsequent stasis, we will see that this is not the case because abstract machinism is, on the contrary, the instance par excellence of the capitalization of processual powers. This machinism responds to other principles, not those of the endo-ordination of sensible Flows or the relative ordination of instantiated Flows, but a processual trans-ordination, because it is through its intermediation that enrichments of complexity, re-orderings far from territorialized equilibria and singularizing bifurca-tions pass. Each supplementary degree of deterritorialization of an abstract machine thus corresponds to an increase in its power of effect, which will no longer be expressed in terms of a quantity of energy but in terms of a reinforcing of the potentiality for singularization, or, in other words, a reduction of entropy.

Example: in parallel to the deterritorialization of the concepts of mathematical physics, applied nuclear physics found itself in a position to liberate more and more powerful quantities of energy. One will never be done with machinic deterritorialization! It escapes from ordinary laws, hierarchies and metrics. There is no initial state or terminal state with it. And consequently, there is no zero time of Big Bang, nor any rebounding on itself of the expansion of the cosmos. It is becoming processual-izing itself, the heterogeneous in the process of differentiating itself. The incessant relaunching of new givens by the coming into play of original Constellations of Universes of reference. In short, process! We will have to describe how the processuality of hypercomplexification is articulated with the 'passage into being' of existential singularization. But we are still only at the phase of the possibilization of processes and we must stop and look back so as to try to elucidate the relations between deterritorialized abstract machines and the concrete machines of machinic smoothing that manifest themselves in the domain of territorialized Flows.

Abstract machine and concrete machine

At first sight, a concrete machine appears to be a clearly defined object, closed in on itself, only opening onto the outside in so far as functional imperatives impose this on it (input of a Flow of primary matter; output of a Flow of 'machined' products…). In fact, that is only an appearance, the concrete cutting out of machines always being more or less arbitrary. Is it legitimate, for example, to consider a locomotive independently of the track on which it has to run, or the professional bodies able to manage its functioning? Social machines of this kind are equally inseparable from one another. That is why the Apollo rocket, which allowed men to walk on the moon, cannot be separated from either the NASA team that built it nor from the political machine that supported Kennedy when he approved the project. Little by little, all machines can be connected to one another by a multitude of trees of implication with innumerable branches. But to the extent that the essence of the concrete machine no more resides in its visible delimitation than in its internal organs or in its status at the level of the factory, the branch or field of industry concerned, where does one grasp it if not in a machinic functionality that traverses all these segmentary stratas? Unlike the interactions that are produced between non-machined natural elements, this functionality is inseparable from signaletic systems of which machines are the incarnation at the heart of Flows.

Here two difficulties await us. First, one has to admit that it matters little if such systems are designed by the brains of humans, or produced, encoded and transmitted genetically by living structures in the course of a long and complex evolution. The signaletic soul and/or encoding of the machine is not peculiar to man. All one can say about it is that it implies the exhaustion of a more or less autonomized expressive stratum. All sorts of physico-chemical and organo-chemical Assemblages can also do this. The second difficulty resides in the fact that one evidently ends up going round in a circle here. We previously posited that expression EC was generated on the basis of the smoothing and instantiation of Flows and here we are now with this same smoothing and this same instantiation appearing to result from systems of expression acquiring a machinic function. So, is this a vicious circle or feedback, a feedback loop? I have already said that my description of the cycle of Assemblages started from Flows so as to pass on to machines, incorporeals and existentials, but in the last part of this text I will turn around and go in the opposite direction. At the moment nothing prevents the smoothing and instantiation of Flows from appearing to be carried out essentially by machinic entities (material, living, social, abstract machines…). In truth it is the concrete machines themselves are in a double position. Traversed by Flows, they relay each other so as to smooth the Flows in different ways, although they are themselves a tissue, a junction, a knot of Flows. In whatever way one considers them, their ontological formula is mutant. They are essentially a mixture of territorialized Flows and deterritorialized Phyla. Thus, the soul of code, of the sign, language, catalysis, the imprint, the image, the tracing, the plane, the programme of concrete machines, what I call *their diagrammatic function*, associates two modalities of evaluation. One is exo-referred and attached to the materiality of process; the other, endo-referred, confers on it its complexity, its singularity, its existential consistency. Let us try to determine this double belonging more closely by starting again from the elementary example of the lock and key machine. We saw that it implies the conjoint putting to work of two types of forms with different ontological textures:

- contingent, concrete, discrete forms whose singularity is self-enclosed, incarnated respectively in the profile of the lock F^l and that of the key F^k;

- Possibilistic forms constituting a band of continuous variation Φ, expressing a processual singularization, of which the principle traits are the following:

    - It is limited, without that prohibiting its infinite character, which results from its continuist texture;

- This characteristic of infinity is the index of its belonging to an incorporeal Universe – a Universe of virtual alterity, as it happens – subsuming here the set of profiles, whether or not they are authorized;

- It constitutes a reference for the pragmatic calibration of the system under consideration, that is to say, in this particular case, the set of states in which the truth of the statement 'in this case, it works' is sanctioned.

It is essentially because there is a conjunction between the two types of concrete and possibilistic form that a machine exists. With such an association of simple heterogeneity and heterogeneity of heterogeneity, we have one possible definition of the machinic function. In effect, the passage from manifest heterogeneity, carried by $F_.^k$ or $F_.^l$, to the intrinsic heterogeneity of the band between A and B allows the character of *reproductiveness* (or of repetition) proper to every machine to be guaranteed. Let us explain this: a singularity of the type $F_.^k$ or $F_.^l$ is never done singularizing itself: one can always add an extra decimal point so as to specify more rigourously its extrinsic coordinates of time, space and energy:

It is only asymptotically, where $n = \infty$, that it would be licit to hypostasize the possibility of a rigourous reproduction. Repetition thus only becomes possible ideally, at an infinitesimal scale as it can only be apprehended by signaletic means of the sign-particle type. It is completely different on the band Φ, where singularity becomes relative to the margin of 'error'. Between A and B, the intervals $F_.^{k'}$ -$F_.^{k''}$ or $F_.^{l'}$ -$F_.^{l''}$ can play out. 'Mechanics is play' is a well-known maxim of professors of technology. The machine

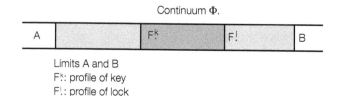

Continuum Φ.

Limits A and B
$F_.^k$: profile of key
$F_.^l$: profile of lock

FIGURE 3.15 The band of continuous variation of the lock and key machine

is also a play of margins that delimit reproducible – relatively reproducible – forms, at an ontogenetic level. At a phylogenetic level, it is even this play that authorizes evolutionary variations. One then passes from a concept of absolute, solipsistic heterogeneity to a concept of relative, reproducible, evolutionary heterogeneity. Once again it is in the domain of molecular differences, where the passages from dis-position (F^{i}) to the pro-position (Φ^{pm}) then to trans-position (Φ^{ma}) are played out, that the new register of meta-positions U are elaborated. The infinite no longer folds back on itself, in a sort of backwards flight past the decimal point in pursuit of an extreme limit of singularization. It makes itself extraneous, it 'extraneates' itself on the continuum Φ between the limits A, B. It becomes productive of the possible and the virtual.

Let us summarize this point:

- At each position F^{k} F^{l} there is an *instantial striation* of a dis-positional form.

- Via the biunivocal relationship between F^{k} and F^{l} there is a *pro-positional smoothing* of a ubiquitarian (deterritorialized) machinic form that synchronically 'inhabits' the two manifest positions previously mentioned.

- Beyond the limited Phylum between A and B there is the possibility of the *transpositional striation* of general formula for a concrete machine with a coded closure (the lock and key machine).

A question left hanging: what is the nature of the relation between the play of the machinic margin just mentioned and the infinitesimal energies put to work through the catalysis of sign-particles? Signaletic machines correspond to a limit state of machinism, to a maximal abstractification of the supporting Flows and existential Territories. They start processes of virtual deterritorialization starting from signaletic singularities for which the referents are solely categorial. By contrast, concrete machinism implies the putting into function of Flows and existential Territories. Consequently, machinic catalysis exits its solely infinitesimal circuit; it contaminates the molar fields that are instituted as Content in relation to the molecular fields of Expression. One can now see that the ontological status of concrete machines implies not only the entry of abstract machinic functions but equally existential operators allowing them to be aggregated with the incorporeal Universes and existential Territories that confer on them a self-consistency, a necessary character which in fact requires a complete looping and inversion of the cycle of Assemblages.

Before finishing with the rhizomatic striation that is the bearer of abstract machinisms, it remains for us to consider the categorial requalifications that are correlative to it. I will not come back to the general movement of ontological requalifications that made us pass from the manifest character of instantiated Flows to the possibilistic character of smoothed Phyla, then from the characteristic of effectiveness, proper to abstract machinisms, which leads us to the necessary character of the following stasis, that is, the smoothing of incorporeal Universes, if not just to propose a provisional summary (Figure 3.16)

Remark: Whilst smoothing previously appeared to us as essentially having a function of ontological conversion (the substantiation of manifest Flows; the substantiation of machinic Phyla, the substantiation of incorporeal Universes…), striation reveals itself to be synonymous with processes of the enrichment of the possible and the virtual. Smoothing passively takes note of the *state* resulting from an ontological mutation/caesura; it equalizes-legalizes-capitalizes this state, whereas striation develops it, 'stuffs' it with new potentialities, processualizes it, intensifies it.

We will now have to linger a bit longer on the requalification of extensive coordinates (traits of extensity EST) as intensive ordinates/traits of intensity (Figure 3.17).

What gives body to the machine thus no longer arises from exo-referential coordinates but from endo-referential traits. What was enunciation by discursive spatialization, temporalization and energization finds itself requalified in traits of non-discursive self-enunciation. Here the paradox of a non-discursive complexity, arising from incorporeal Universes of reference, must be maintained. It can only be accounted for by the transfer of existential affects and meta-modellings of singularities and processes that are, in any case, fundamentally un-modellable. Extensity imposed the framing of an inside and an outside on each entitarian circumscription, it established an exclusive dual relationship between the intended object and its reference, its obligatory figuring on an undifferentiated ground. Now, the sequential body of the abstract machine no longer knows of any such delimitation; it carries away the entirety of its universe of reference in the mode of a continuous variation rearranging its dis-positions and pragmatic affectations as a function of its temporal positioning. In coming back to the same place, one doesn't necessarily return to the same extensive situs. Whilst the extrinsic coordinates were reversible, that is to say, autonomous in relation to the objects referring to them, intensive ordinates make us enter into the register of irreversibility. However, there is no brute solution of continuity between exo-reference and endo-reference.

	Stasis of Assemblage	Entities	Topos	Enunciation	Operators	Ontological modalizations
F.	1. Sensible smoothing of Flows	$F.^{or}$ (Flow of relative ordering)	Sub-position $F.^{or}$ { F^{b}, F^{s} } → Ts	Endo-ordination	Modules of territorialization	Substantiation
F.	2. Striation of instantiation of Flows	$F.^{i}$ (Instantiated Flow)	Dis-position $F.^{i}$ { $F.^{or}$ }	Exo-ordination	Concrete machines: Traits of molar extensity	Manifestation
Φ.	3. Machinic smoothing of Phyla	Φ.pm (Phylum of machinic propositions)	Pro-position $\Phi.^{pm}$ { E. }	Coordination	Concrete machines: Sign-particles	Possibilization
Φ.	4. Rhizomatic striation of Phyla	Φ.ma (Phylum of abstract machines)	Trans-position $\Phi.^{pm}$ — $\Phi.^{ma}$ — $\Phi.^{pm}$	Trans-ordination	Concrete machines: Traits of molecular intensity	Effectuation

FIGURE 3.16 Ontological requalifications of the four primary stases

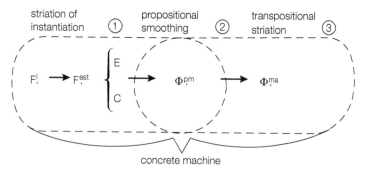

FIGURE 3.17 The concrete machine or the extensity/intensity transformation

The transition between them is worked, negotiated – the way a racing car driver negotiates bends in the road – via the concrete machines. Before breaking free from manifest Flows and giving themselves unreservedly to exclusive self-reference, deterritorialized machinisms proceed by a relative confining of the powers of self-reference. Although no longer falling under the signaletics of quantification, self-reference is only produced as quantities of intensity through the intermediary of non-oppositional, non-discursive traits (which is what separates them from the signifying traits dear to structuralists, which they substituted for libidinal energy). Concrete machines thus find themselves to be the bearers of qualifying traits organized according to specific rhythmic sequences (for example, 'refrainized' spatio-temporal sequences). Between the start and finish of these sequential rhythms, a *state function* plays itself out, in the course of a time that produces a partial opening and is relative to possibilistic Phyla and virtual Universes that were not implied in the raw givens of the flows existing at the start.

One can quite clearly see what the spatio-temporal sequentiality of a combustion engine is, for example. One is less prepared to consider the phylo-genetic line on which this sequence is inscribed, the historicity of this motor, its position on the trees of machinic implication, the actual and virtual mutations entailed by the occurrence of its machinic generation...

The question of a general translateability of energy – which is equally a requalification of energetic discursivity during its integration into the new machinic sequencing – could only be posed for stratas territorialized separately from one another. At the level of deterritorialized machinic knots sweeping the entirety of a pragmatic-possibilistic field in the mode of continuous variation, the question changes nature. One is no longer dealing with testifiable differences of potential. The quantitative difference inherent in this type of potential could only subsist, in effect, in the frame of an economy of discursive and properly contingenced Flows. The molar play of large stratified differences now finds itself subjugated (in its original sense of enslavement) by the molecular play of charges proper to sign-particles. Negentropic charges that escape from exo-referential measures, because they are charges of self-consistency of a certain batch of hyper-complexity (traits of intensity).

In sum, the charges of pragmatic-possibilistic effect differ from undifferentiated energetic charges, such as they are dealt with in the diverse domains of physics, in two principal ways:

1 From a quantitative point of view, the energy charges associated with molecular chips of negentropic hypercomplexity are incommensurably smaller than the molar charges whose Assemblages they pilot. However, despite this incommensurability, there exist differences between them, relative degrees of deterritorialization. Moreover, it seems that there is an inversely proportional relation between the deterritorialization of molecular machinic mediators and their potential for molar effect. We know, for example, that the implementation of thermonuclear weapons was only possible when, correlative to the 'maturing' of the necessary technical means, the signaletic machines of mathematical physics had reached a sufficient degree of 'takeoff' in relation to the concepts of classical physics. And tomorrow, nuclear fusion will doubtless only be domesticated in parallel to the consolidation of the theory of the unification of four fundamental interactions. It is something of this order that I am aiming at in speaking of differential degrees of signaletic deterritorialization.

2 From an ontological-qualitative point of view, it is no longer a question, with the molecular charges of sign-particles, of a transfer of undifferentiated charges of energy but of a transfer of charges of potential pragmatic effects. On the one hand then, one has charges of energy that are quantifiable in extrinsic coordinates and, on the other, charges of effect that are qualifiable in fields of possibility. (We will see that these transfers of possibilistic-potentiality will find themselves relayed by other charges of existential necessitation.)

But how is one to account for the operative differences between degrees of deterritorialization, once it is said and repeated that they arise neither from the logic of discursive sets nor from any possible quantification? It is certainly appropriate to maintain a strong link between the quantitative dimensions of energy and its qualitative-possibilistic aspects, and, as consequence, to be a little wary of the hegemonic pretentions of approaches founded solely on general postulates of the equivalence and translateability of diverse forms of energy. The negentropic 'reasons' of the Phyla Φ^{pm} and $\Phi^{ma}_.$ function as reservoirs of potential effectuation, the intensive power of which is expressed in terms of the more or less great richness of Constellations of Universes of reference that they imply (or, if one prefers, in terms of the optimization of qualitative openings of the machinic monads they put into play). Thus ordinates of intensity control the entry and adjustment of Phyla bearing (potential then necessary) effects on the scene of Assemblages. Traits of deterritorialization, irreversibility, self-consistency, self-evaluation, self-enunciation, associated to varying degrees and in varying modalities, confer on them their relative capacity to be established transversally to heterogeneous, exo-referred strata. These specific traits of abstract machinic requalification could be called *traits of inherence* in opposition to the *traits of disherence* proper to the previous stases, which implied the dis-junction of the coordinates of space, time and energy with regard to each effect, and the exhaustion of autonomized and powerless discursive chains of expression.

4 REFERENCE AND CONSISTENCY

The chaotic Plane of immanence

In the first place it is worth retaining a certain mistrust of overly static representations of chaos, especially those which would try to illustrate it in the form of a mixture, of holes, caverns, dust, even of fractal objects. What is particular about the chaos of the 'primordial soup' of the Plane of immanence is that it can only exist in and as the process of 'chaotizing' and in such a way that it is impossible to circumscribe a stable configuration in it and to maintain its consistency. Each of the configurations that it can outline has the gift of dissolving, at an infinite, if not absolute, speed. In its essence, chaos is rigourously ungraspable. As it cannot be assigned any subset, it can be considered to escape the logic of discursive sets.

Is this to say that chaos is a very simple, binary and aleatory thing? Certainly not, because the process of proto-fractalization that works it generates as much disorder as it does complex virtual compositions: the very same compositions that I just said appear and disappear at infinite speed. (Let us note in passing that from such a point of view, the status of the virtual for an entity would consist in finding itself caught between two infinities: that of an absolute existential intensification and that of its immediate abolition.)

So, we will start from the idea that the actual powers of disorder vary concurrently with virtual potentials of complexification. Chaos thus becomes the primary matter of virtuality, the inexhaustible reserve of an infinite determinability. This implies that in returning to it, it will always be possible to rediscover in it matter for the complexification of the state of things. Thus each ordering finds itself doubled by entropic tensions, whereas symmetrically, each aleatory sequence is susceptible of bifurcating towards virtual attractors of processual complexification.

But perhaps it would be preferable to say that chaos is the bearer of *hyper-complexity*, thereby underlining that it not only harbours the discursive complexity proper to states of things but that it is equally capable of self-generating instances of discursivization of this same complexity – instances that will be characterized here as *filters*. In other words, surplus to the programmed arrangements [déclinaisons logicielles] of order and disorder, we will have to accept that chaos is the reservoir of existential operators and the optional matters of their manifestation.

Once it has been stated that chaotic hyper-complexity (virtual, non-discursive and constantly on the way to dissolution) is distinct from ordinary complexity (which is proper to real Flows and possibilistic Phyla), it would be a good idea not to confuse chaos and catastrophe, because what specifies a catastrophe is precisely the subsiding of the 'enunciative' dimension of the Assemblages that find themselves implicated in it, and the abandoning of their discursivization filters. Chaos is not only the bearer of 'pre-programmed' morphogenetic potentials, it harbours the processual embryos that enable mutant morphogeneses to be brought to light. It is seeded with 'bifurcation points', with 'mutant filters' for which no calculation can predict the position or the potentialities.

Let us note for the moment that it is only by starting from a virtual non-discursive state of 'chaotic' matter that what will later be called the relation of endo-consistency between existential Territories and their Universes of reference is constituted.

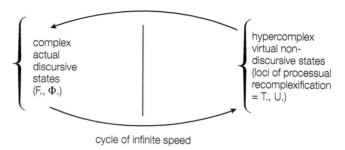

cycle of infinite speed

FIGURE 4.1 The two states of chaos

The crossover of entitarian dimensions

Two types of relations can be established at the heart of the 'primordial soup' of the chaotic Plane of immanence: relations of reference and relations of consistency.

Considered at this first level of self-referencing, reference is still only the pure passive connectivity of instances of being-there – whether they are territorialized or deterritorialized. It thus functions in the mode of 'holding together' – it being clear that there is no-one, no subject, to hold together anything at all! There is the dis-position of a 'there is' *and* of a 'there is' *and* of a 'there is' etc, without it ever being possible to decide if it is a matter of the same 'there is' or another. Reference here is repetition, iteration, in which something stays in its place by returning to it incessantly, finding itself constituted in such a way that the existential glue oozing from chaos becomes the correlate of an ex-position of a proto-spatial order. Space is essentially glischroidic, without limit, without contour, without any possible internal displacement or division into subsets. Existence here is still only co-existence, trans-existence, existential transitivity, trans-versality. In order not to miss its specific characteristics, it is necessary radically to uncouple the idea of reference from that of interaction. It is accepted that in order for there to be action or reaction, an object-context relation or, at the very least, a multipolar structure must be established – none of which can happen here. Unlike the case of perception or conscious realization, nothing is transmitted, nothing 'passes' between the referring and the referred. This movement of reference, as a grasping of being, an existential self-affirmation, forces us to accept the double aporia of changes of state brought about:

- without any transfer of energy (by virtue of the fact that we are confronted with the very state of change, with the processualizing of process);
- at an infinite speed of transformation $[+\infty]$, transgressing the sacrosanct principle of contemporary physics based on the speed of light, which consists in fixing a threshold limiting the size of the ensemble of possible speeds.

It is on the basis of the notion of a reference speed that we will try to redefine consistency, which will be affected by two fundamentally different types of iteration: that of infinite speed and that of 'decelerated' speed. 'Deceleration' (or reterritorialization), which leads us to draw out consistency as a fundamental new dimension of Assemblages, whose operations begin in chaos, should allow us to better support the previously mentioned categorizations of referential Universes (U), possibilistic Phyla (Φ), existential Territories and material and/or semiotic Flows (F).

1   Infinite speeds of reference [+∞], which have already been mentioned in relation to the 'principle of evanescence' that presides over the destinies of chaos, will now find themselves converted into transfers of complexity and hyper-complexity between the domains Φ and U. This infinite speed is synonymous with the absolute lability of iteration and, as a consequence, with zero consistency. As the reiteration sequences here are infinitely short, we will say of the entitarian arrangements under consideration that they have an infinitely weak measuring capacity.

2   From another point of view, decelerated and modulated reference speeds will be at work in the modules of territorialization associating T and F. This modular structure derives from the existence of thresholds of discontinuity in phenomena of the deceleration of existential 'grasping' (or self-referential agglutination). A striation of reterritorialization is somehow produced whilst distinct zones of being-already-well-and-truly-there are constituted. Consequently, these 'decelerated' speeds are synonymous with an intensification of consistency. When they fall to a quasi-null speed [−∞], the sequences of opening back up can become of a quasi-infinite length. We will then say that the measuring capacity of such arrangements acquires a strong value.

Of a more temporal order, consistency expresses the fragility and precariousness of connective processes, their relative density, but also their finitude, their transitional, sequential character – which derives, I repeat, from the fact that their existential distinctiveness is essentially tributary to contingent arrangements at heterogeneous levels. Under certain conditions – which we will return to when it is a question of Assemblage synapses – entitarian apparatuses owe their capacity for opening up to other formulae for arrangement, other axiomatics, other abstract machinisms, their capacity, in short, for quitting a regime of connective passivity so as to attain an active and processual conjunctivity, to fractures of consistency.

An association of this sort between the concept of existence and that of consistency[1] as the bearer of heterogeneity and precariousness, implies giving up massive binary oppositions of the type essence/existence,

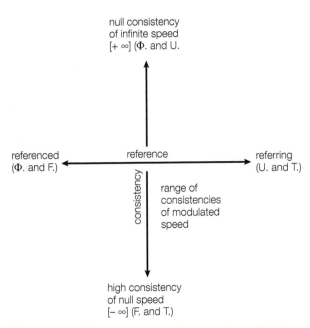

FIGURE 4.2 Intersecting dimensions of reference and consistency

Being/Nothingness, etc. (Whilst in Sartre's ontology, for example, detotalization remained indissociable from nihilation, here, on the contrary, it is inscribed on a referential axis of proto-spatial modular reference (TF) that is fundamentally heterogeneous to the axis of proto-temporal consistencies on which the levels of deterritorialization are established (fractal Expression FΦ). Thus an open range of existential intensities is substituted for the brutal caesura Being/Nothingness.) In another manner, it leads to us freeing ourselves from ancestral myths relating to the perenniality of being, or to those more recent and more tenacious myths of the conservation of energy. There isn't any brute form of being, rooted there, once and for all, independent of the Assemblages that apprehend it, so as to undergo its effects or inflect its trajectory of destiny. Being is the modulation of consistency, the rhythm of putting together and dismantling [montage et démontage]. Its cohesion, if not its coherence, arises neither from an internal principle of eternity nor from an extrinsic causalist framing that would hold existents together at the heart of the same world. Rather, it results from the conjugation of processualities of intrinsic consistency, themselves engaging in generalized relations of existential transversality. In part, it is this requirement of transversality that calls for the recourse to infinite speeds of reference, a sweeping of all spaces and a recursive smoothing of all possible temporalities, but this processual character also imposes the striation of relative speeds of reference.

In order to illustrate this question of reference speeds, let us consider for a moment what it is that separates an ordinary catalyser in inorganic chemistry from an enzymatic catalyser in organic chemistry: essentially, the speed of the catalysed reaction, its specificity and what I will call its processual implications. Enzymes can speed up reactions by considerable factors, of the order of between 10^9 to 10^{15} in moderate conditions (aqueous milieu, temperate and ambient pressure). For example, one molecule of a specific enzyme can hydrate 100,000 molecules of carbon dioxide, whereas it would have required 10 million seconds to obtain the same result without recourse to the genius of the enzyme. Besides, each enzyme catalyses one type of reaction expressed on a precise point of the substrate molecule and constitutes a stereospecific filter that selectively 'recognizes' one molecule amongst many others, even those with a very similar structure (as with optical isomers). For example, nickel or palladium can catalyse the hydrogenation of the double bonds of very different molecules, whilst an enzyme like thrombin can only bring about this same reaction on an extremely specific substrate.[2] We could multiply to infinity the illustrations of this kind of association between the three functions of smoothing, acceleration and specificity of effect, consequent to the putting to work of operators of catalysis, polarization, etc., (grouped together here under the generic term of 'filtering'). From our point of view, these three functions are the correlate of a loss of ontological consistency that is synonymous with a deterritorializing opening onto new possibilistic Phyla: in the occurrence, here, through enzymatic deterritorialization, access to nothing less than the fields of the possible (Φ) and mutations of virtuality (U) proper to living matter.

Filters

The 'primordial soup' of the Plane of immanence is thus populated by two types of entitarian state:

- chaotic multiplicities composing and decomposing complex arrangements at infinite speeds;

- existential filters selecting relatively homogeneous sets of arrangements characterized by the iteration of local and localizing decelerations.

Filters thus present themselves in the first instance as hooks for chaotic multiplicities. Engendering one another in a continuous fashion, these two states ensure the crossing and uncrossing of the dimensions of reference and consistency previously described.[3] Conferring a relative stability on the sequences of taking consistency pertains to filters whereas, during stases of uncrossing, the task of multiplicities is to 'recharge' the Assemblages considered with hypercomplexity. As long as one remains in a regime of uncrossing the filters return ceaselessly to chaos, whilst in a regime of crossing over marriages are carried out, new entitarian compositions can proliferate to infinity. That being so, one must never lose sight of the fact that crossed and uncrossed regimes envelop each other constantly, such that the supremacy of crossing makes us enter the domain of the possible, whilst inversely the supremacy of uncrossing keeps us in the domain of the virtual. In the form of filters, barriers, moulds, modules, punctual, circular or strange (or fractal) attractors, catalysers, enzymes, genetic codings, gestaltist perceptions, mnemotechnical props, poetic constraints, cognitive procedures, but also financial institutions, institutions of publicity, etc. Everywhere, in every register, in the form of barriers, moulds, modules, punctual, circular or strange (or fractal) attractors, catalysers, enzymes, genetic codings, gestaltist perceptions, mnemotechnical props, poetic constraints, cognitive procedures, but also financial institutions, institutions of publicity, etc., filters are constituted as interfaces between: 1) the virulent virtualities of chaos, stochastic proliferations; and 2) actual potentialities that can be listed and consolidated.

It is thus only under the regime of crossing over that the dimensions of reference and consistency will manage to acquire their respective identities. Reference only acquires a 'scope', only conquers a vital space, and 'consistantiation' only manifests its stances (substance supporting qualities and trans-stance or transistance 'transversalizing' these same qualities) on condition that the crossing over of entitarian dimensions begins as an inaugural step in the cycle of Assemblages. But we have to insist that the striation of immanent Planes of reference by values of consistency doesn't proceed by exclusive binary alternatives, nor even by distinctive oppositions of a systemic character. Existential consistency arises instead from the pathic categories that Viktor von Weizsäcker opposes to ontic categories. The first – which are relative to willing, to power and the diverse modalities of duty – mask one another by mutual disguising, and the second – relative to relations of time, space, numbers and causality – cut out non-dialectisable entities. In von Weizsäcker's idea of subjectivity as the movement of a relation to the ground (Grundverhältnis) one also finds the beginnings of a theory of existential appropriation and of generalized existential transference such as we are proposing here, with our categories of non-discursive reference – existential Territory and Universe of reference.[4]

Not only can the same concatenation of entities engage in consistencies with antagonistic definitions, but it is the way that infinitely 'rapid' and absolutely deterritorialized, null consistencies are twinned with and adjacent to tardy and relatively deterritorialized consistencies that characterizes what will later be defined as a collective Assemblage of enunciation. Once again, another series of paradoxes from contemporary physics – when the same quantum of energy is incarnated in forms that are simultaneously wave *and* particle, discontinuous *and* continuous, separable *and* inseparable – come to mind. In their way, schizoanalyses will also put themselves in a position to map the components that disjunct in a psychosis, in apparently contradictory forms:

- a corporeal ego Territory with a 'slow' consistency;
- deterritorialized Universes associated with this Territory as 'referent' and yet with a 'rapid' consistency, which could possibly be expressed by the truth charges that delirium might harbour.

As in quantum physics, for the purposes of observation, measurement and inter-action, it will be impossible to apprehend the exo-referred dimensions of consistency (Flow and Phyla) and its endo-referred dimensions of existential auto-agglutination (Territories and Universes).

Discursive determinability occults the fractures that generate existential intensification and, as a counterpart, processes of fractalization break up certified circumscriptions in such a way that one will never be able to grasp in a single block its:

- exo-referred *propositions* embedded in dis-stanced coordinates of potentiality;
- endo-referred virtual *dis-positions* incarnated in ordinates of in-stantiation.

In combination (1) a proposition is given on a background of stable coordinates, but the Universes of enunciation remain fuzzy (loss of qualitative intensities). In combination (2) it is, on the contrary, the proposition that

	1) Potential	2) Virtual
	proposition (Φ.)	dis-position (U.)
	dis-stance (F.)	in-stance (T.)

becomes fuzzy and the figure/background relation that blurs whilst the existential instance of reference becomes the primary given in existential transference.

Proto-enunciative processes

The work of filtering, on the basis of which the striation of reference speeds into heterogeneous components of consistency would become possible, cannot be summed up as the simple passive smoothing of powdery diversity. It also leads to the release of an existential surplus value, the scope and capitalization of which we will follow later by examining in more detail the cycle of Assemblages of enunciation. We will then see that the relations between the domains of Flow, existential Territory, possibilistic Phylum and Universe of reference are not only linear but also matrix-like and, consequently, put into play a more complex range of operators and filters for trans-entitarian transformation. In anticipation, Figure 4.4 presents the complete form of the crossover between reference and consistency.

The line φ^{nm} of exo-consistency is composed of all the points of bifurcation proper to fields of possibility. The lines φ compose Rhizomes of abstract machinic possibility. The line in Figure 4.7 authorizes the passage from an arrangement of order n to an arrangement of order m.

Each series s^{n}, s^{m}, etc. possesses an enunciative guarantor t^{n}, t^{m}, etc. in the domain T of endo-consistent-endo-reference. But the deterritorialized lines of the type φ^{nm}, which are entwined with these series so as to lay down the law, code them, situate them in fields of possibility and assign them a differential consistency, also have enunciative guarantors in this same domain of endo-reference, except that they are of an entirely different nature.

The territorialized guarantors of the series (and Flows) were modular and thus their existential operators were attached to being-there like

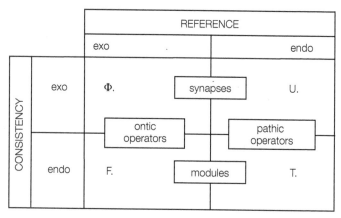

FIGURE 4.4 Matrix of reference/consistency crossover, in the context of an Assemblage

limpets on a rock, whilst the deterritorialized guarantors of the abstract Phyla inhabit everywhere and nowhere. Their 'existentialization', produced by mutational filters, ceases to be territorially framed so as to become tributary to processual ordinates, which confer on them a character of ubiquity and absolute translateability. Their contingency is no longer of the order of the contingencing of a being-already-legitimately-there, but arises from a 'return-there where it could be', an artificially processual repetition. We will come back to this question later, when we will have to substitute the pseudo-transcendence of the a-signifying ruptures of formulae and laws, which can be of the greatest complexity, for modular immanence. But the Phyla Φ of deterritorialized consistency nonetheless remain consubstantial with the series and Flows F. The whole question consequently becomes one of making the speeds of infinite redundancy of the first hold together with the absolute decelerations of the second, whilst rendering possible discontinuous intensive striations at the crossover between the two entitarian dimensions. Once again, one comes back to the paradox of the continuous that envelops the discontinuous and the intensive, the discursive.

Before advancing any further on this terrain, we must return to the previous considerations in order to try to better specify, with a series of schemas, the genesis of proto-enunciative processes during their release in the very first steps of the composition of entitarian redundancies in the 'primordial soup'.

Exo-reference/endo-reference

Take a multiplicity of order n. We will call 'exo-reference' the serial arrangement resulting from the putting into discursive connection of n terms of the multiplicity. We will call 'endo-reference' the intensive, that is to say, non-discursive, proto-existential operator from which the preceding arrangement results.

Exo-consistency/endo-consistency

We have seen that the existential glue proper to the exo/endo-reference relation can be one of cold consistency, or pure passive territorialized connectivity, or of a hot, deterritorialized consistency implying, in addition, regularities, algorithms. We will thus distinguish between:

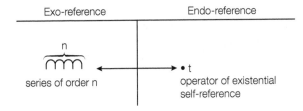

FIGURE 4.5 Exo-reference and endo-reference

Domain	Exo-reference	Endo-reference
1) exo-consistency (null and hot)	Φ.	U. intensive operators of absolute speed
2) processual transistency (intermediary and striated)	φⁿ	T. U. machinic striations of consistencies of mixed and relative speeds
3) endo-consistency (maximal and cold)	n´ n˝ (series of order n)	t intensive operators of infinitely decelerated speed

FIGURE 4.6 Exo-consistency and endo-consistency

1   *exo-consistent* domains, characterized by their capacity to open up new fields of possibility Φ, consequent to the enacting of new Constellations of Universes of reference (ΣU);

2   *trans-consistent* (or transistent) domains within which processes of filtering and striation are at work (of the mixture, crossing-over, moulding, catalysis, fusion, etc. types);

3   *endo-consistent* domains composed of 'decelerated' series of Flows.

As a consequence, existential surplus values will only succeed in being capitalized in incorporeal Universes of reference by the aleatory and contingent mutation of mutational filters (synapses). I will recall that this type of deterritorialized referencing only operates at infinite speed, that is to say, with no ontological consistency, although according to a principle of irreversible necessitation (the pathic mode of referencing).

During the crossover time from arrangement n to arrangement m, it is as if the line of exo-consistency φ^{nm} was cast back into the soup of chaotic consistencies, the better to set off again in new processual directions. This theoretical montage, presupposing an always latent relapse into matters of expression in a chaotic hyper-complex state, appears necessary to me if

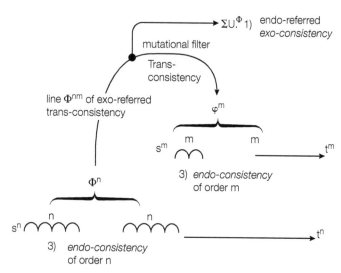

FIGURE 4.7 Levels of consistency

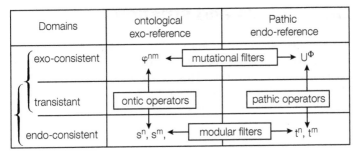

FIGURE 4.8 Ontological exo-reference and pathic endo-reference

one wishes to account in a worthwhile way for what Freud designated as 'primary process', or 'fecund moments' – remanences of being that are both labile and dazzling and which punctuate early childhood, schizophrenic catastrophe, the experience of drugs, archaic fusional trances or creative inspiration.

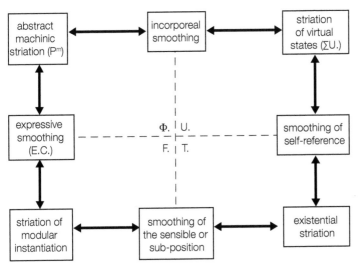

FIGURE 4.9 The smoothing and striation of Assemblages of enunciation

Smoothings and striations

The entitarian arrangements examined so far principally put into play the relations of proximity between the four domains FTΦU. With the Assemblages of enunciation, which we are going to tackle in the next chapter, each entitarian positioning will henceforth engage in the economy of these four domains in a synchronic fashion.

5 THE DOMAIN OF FLOWS F

Between the domain of Flows and that of existential Territories a territorialized smoothing is established, variously characterized as 'grasping', as manifestation or as 'putting into being'. By virtue of this smoothing, a sort of existential homogenization – in some cases indexed with intentionality – operates in a way that is immanent to modular 'experientiations' (sensible as well as cognitive, memorial, affective, imaginary, etc.). Between this same domain of Flow and that of deterritorialized Phyla, a form of smoothing that opens onto the possible is established. In a different way, this also subsumes the diversity and heterogeneity of entitarian compositions.

The striation of Flows is at the junction of the two previous smoothings; in sum, it derives from them starting to bud in two antagonistic directions, in the context of an Assemblage of enunciation:

- that of the discontinuous, on the side of territorialized references on the axis FT, which must be conceived as the vertigo of an absolute slowing down of determinability ($d^{-\infty}$);
- that of the continuous and its absolutely accelerated speeds of reference of determinability ($d^{+\infty}$), on the side of deterritorialized consistencies, which is associated with another sort of vertigo, this time correlated to an always imminent alternative: either latching on to new Constellations of Universes of reference or returning to the soup of chaotic redundancies (Figure 5.1).

As a first approximation, we can say of the domains Φ and T, crossing over in Universes of reference in the particular conditions of the Assemblage, that real-actual Flows find themselves 'doubled' by incorporeal-virtual components.

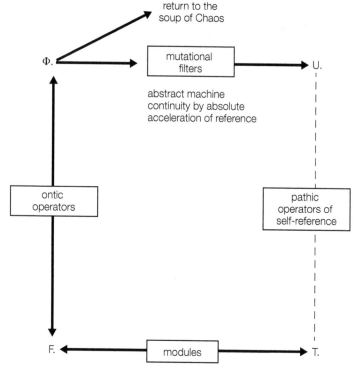

FIGURE 5.1 Ontic and pathic operators

However, our meta-modelling instruments should protect us against any temptation to consider that such components might acquire an eternity and universality by being anchored in Platonic Ideas (even if they have come back into fashion in Réné Thom's theory of elementary 'catastrophes'!). Rather, the adjacency of incorporeals to sensible and semiotic realities arises here from an ontological pragmatics implying the *necessitation* that I have already signalled, which will turn out to be simultaneously contingent, singularizing and irreversible. But, in order to be sustained, this somewhat paradoxical characterization will call for the conjoined enacting of:

- modules of territorialized proto-enunciation;
- deterritorialized ontic operators (concrete machines);

- mutational filters (abstract machines);
- pathic operators of self-consistency.

It will thus call for the mobilization of the entire cycle of Assemblages. But at this point on our trajectory, our cartographic horizon essentially remains turned towards the preparation of an enlarged framework within which the three following orders of paradoxes and aporia can coexist:

- those concerning relations of exclusion and yet of co-occurrence in the domain of physics, between the continuous and the discontinuous, the wave and the particle, the aleatory and the determined;
- those relative to the relations between Expression and Content, the Semiotic and the 'material', the contingent and the universal, the immanent and the transcendent;
- those of aesthetic and religious a-signifiance, such as are at work in the 'existentializing function' inhabiting diverse forms of discursivity.

The Rhizome of laws and codes of the domain Φ hangs over the domain F of material and/or semiotic Flows but it also inhabits its most molecular pores.

Being tributary to no God, no absolute alterity, no law of the Father, of the son or of the signifier, this domain of Flows forces us to conceive relative levels of transcendence, a transcendence that is in some way contingent, or 'contingenced' by way of diverse operators – let's call it an operational contingency.

Let us now re-examine in more detail the linking of the smoothing-striation-smoothing sequence operating in the domain of Flows.

Sensible smoothing or sub-position

A The 'originary' state of *'Brownian' dispersion* of redundancies of entity placed us at a paradoxical level of reference, a place in which nothing referred to anything so as to refer to everything, at such a speed that nothing remains of these references. One might say that the memory m of the arrangements of the soup of chaos equals zero.

```
O \ O  O  O  O \
O   \ O   O  O  O \
O  /  O \ O | O _ O / O —
—  —  — O _   _ O  —
O  O _ \  O \  O  \
```

FIGURE 5.2 The 'soup' of redundancies: m = 0

B From there we arrived at a first type of smoothing of linearization
carried out by filters that are alone able to memorize the passage
from one entity to another by making them unwind, by aligning
them without retaining anything from them. The memory of
these filters could thus be said to be equal to one. This unary
linearization, the vital minimum of consistency, might recall
the activity of an amnesiac saying his rosary: what it affirms
through repetition is not the discursivized figure but only itself, as
principle of repetition. The filter in the preceding case of Brownian
dispersion dissolved before even constituting itself! Now it
sustains itself as an empty form of existentialization, without, as a
consequence, being the support of any content relation.

C With *stochastic linearization* we passed to memories greater
than zero. Filters are no longer only the minimal memories
of themselves but initiate the retention of formal relations of

FIGURE 5.3 Persistence of a filtering t, content unspecified (m = 1)

		t_1	t_2	t_3	t_4	t_5	t_6	t_7
Domain		– – –		O O		–		O O O O O
Domain		3		2		1		5
Domain			x		x		x	

FIGURE 5.4 Stochastic linearization: m > 1

symmetry, homology and disparity, which I propose to call durations of alterity.

Let us note that memory still sticks here to the most basal discursivity. It can only register two types of given: qualitative ruptures and the more or less lengthy durations of alterity. Apart from that it remains incapable of discerning figural Constellations.

D *Serial smoothing* is constituted once the filters find themselves implicated in a system of evaluation – a system which for all that is very different from the previous quantitative evaluation and which now arises from the non-discursive enunciative intensities of the domain T. This leads us to postulate the existence of memories of memories, of memories to the nth degree, which aggregate with one another without, for all that, accumulating, but somehow 'possessing' one another (it being possible to understand this term in the sense that one speaks of dances of possession).

Here the filters no longer proceed by the simple passive registration of the existence of regularities that are already there. They actively re-produce, re-engender, 're-exist' these regularities, by making them come alive within their own paradigmatic stagings. In this way, a multiplicity of memory series, the non-discursive repetition of filtering or traits of enunciative intensity, find themselves superposed on the preceding stochastic chains.

The accidental repetition of, for example, the occurrence twice in a row of the sequence (– 000) under conditions of random emission,

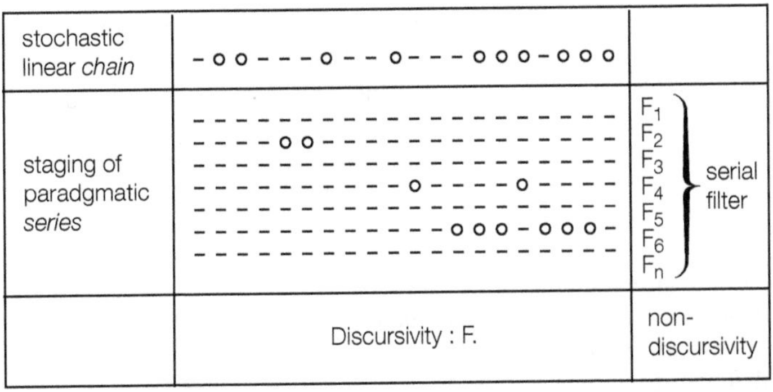

FIGURE 5.5 Serial smoothing

can be predicted on the basis of the calculus of probabilities. But such a prediction, and the very status of the couplet 'random-determined', presupposes that, through material smoothing, iteration-memories are in play, and a correlative persistence of the filtering of traits t_1, t_2, t_3.

Whereas the chaotic filter dissolved instantaneously in the Universe of virtuality, and unary stochastic connectivity only slowed the reference iteration down for long enough to deploy an ungraspable persistence of being like a stroboscopic afterimage, serial memory thickens and is weighed down with more and more 'givens'. It is furnished with rhythms and refrains, the declension of which will mobilize more and more 'heavy' temporalities in the register of discursivity.

E *The sensible smoothing of Flows*

Serial filters did nothing more than 'layer' linear stochastic chains. However, they did not confer on them a consistency of their own. The economy of Flows only begins at the moment when the enunciative traits t_1, t_2, t_3 start to function together within a process of self-consistantiation (or process of territorialization). This consistantiation is effectuated on the basis of a double process of the internal coalescence of series and of the heterogeneification (or heterogenesis) of finite serial groups. But a third moment, of the regrouping and intrication of series through the exchange and permutation of their traits of enunciation, is added to those of processionary linearization[1] and paradigmatic memory already mentioned (Figure 5.6).

With this regime of the heterogenesis of Flows, not only is inter-entitarian difference no longer abolished but it consolidates its existence, which it 'shares' with the diverse serial operators of reference t_1, t_2, t_n…that memorize it. The serial taking of consistency that results is instantaneous and continuous with regard to the 'previous' operations of self-concatenation for each series m (Figure 5.6b), as well as with the supports for interserial layering n (Figure 5.6c).

All referential and consistantial occurrences are engendered simultaneously – once again this presupposes the existence of infinite speeds of determinability (noted $d^{+\infty}$) for all the operations of transmission that concern them. In other words, the following formula can be established:

a) processionary linearization with memory m = 1

$$S_1 \ S_2 \ S_3 \ S^n$$

b) paradigmatic coalescence with memory m = 5

$$S_1 \ S_2 \ S_3 \ S_4 \ S_5$$

c) heterogenesis of Flows

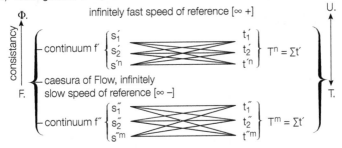

FIGURE 5.6 The serial coalescence and the heterogenesis of Flows

$$d^{+\infty} = \text{continuity}$$

On the other hand, with the stopping of the layering of determination into s^n, s^m, etc., a series of finite points of view (of the thickness, or order, of r) is constituted. Every relation of reference that could subsequently be presented is infinitely deferred. But we prefer to say that their return will take infinitely long, or that their determinability is infinitely slow (which we will note $d^{-\infty}$ and which will introduce the status of virtuality). We will thus have the complimentary formula:

$$d^{-\infty} = \text{discontinuity}$$

Hence, as these two operations of coalescence and heterogenesis can be reduced to one – the halting of the process of serial determination (Figure

5.6), coming up against a finite term s^n or s^m – Flow properly so-called can be redefined as the product of a modular component of enunciation associating continuous references and discontinuous consistencies.

Let us note that the process of determinability will not for all that find itself definitively interrupted. It is only suspended, deferred and constrained to pass via the Phyla and deterritorialized Universes of the cycle of Assemblages.

The striation of the in-stantiation of Flows

Flows only subsist if supported by the modulation of an immanent 'point of view' that 'finitizes' or 'contingences' their determinability. That this gives their intrinsic memory a boundary of undecidability must not be credited to a deficiency, a passivity inherent in their territorialization. On the contrary, finitude and contingency are the obligatory seat, the launchpads of processes of the enrichment of possibility likely to come to light in the domains of machinic Phyla and their non-discursive self-enunciative correlates (U).

In other words, although from the point of view of its modular composition along the axis FT the striation of Flows remained passively determinist, now, from the point of view of its possibilistic deterritorializations along the axis FΦ, it opens up to a logic that generates molecular intervals, amplifications, bifurcations and infinite fractalization (incorporeal heterogenesis).

We must press on with our theoretical montage now to provide a suitable place for the components of intermediary reference that proceed by relative temporalization. The amorphous for-itself of territorialized distinctiveness and the evanescent for-others of pure deterritorialized reference find themselves in some way associated by the same incapacity to open up to an ad-vent [ad-venir]. We do not get out of this symmetrical impasse through the dialectical exhaustion of these two statuses but rather through their criss-crossing – a sort of frantic slalom to escape the double threat of petrification and dissolution that they represent.

The instantiation of Flows results here from: 1) the agglomeration in a finite bundle (n, m,...) of referential series of infinite speeds (this agglomeration is characterized as a module of territorialization); 2) the existence of an attractor φ (or phase space) with an indefinable contour, between these modules, which unifypotential series of determinations. Although their number is presumed finite, it remains indeterminable. This stopping zone, this zone of the suspension of determinability, is one of null speed ($d^{-\infty}$).

We will note that certain series can belong to several modular agglomerations (for example, the series s in Figure 5.7a).

The traits of potential determination of the attractor φ enter from two sides: 1) from the non-discursive side TU, corresponding to a possible existential agglomeration T^{nmo}, by the Assemblage of a new module T^o, which confers a territorialized incarnation on the serial determinations $d'^{-\infty}$ that had remained virtual (for example, the series s_5 in Figure 5.7). This re-agglomeration will be characterized in terms of existential self-consistency; 2) from the discursive side F, φ, Φ, where it corresponds to the opening of new fields of possibility (machinic smoothing), the 'pre-possible' φ, which still only skirted mutely the modules t^n and t^m that found themselves rendered partially present by virtue of the existential co-optation of the module t^n.

The latter henceforth incarnates certain serial traits $d^{+\infty}$ that had hitherto

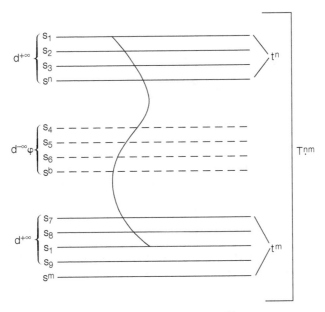

FIGURE 5.7 The two sequences of the striation of Flows
a) The module passive sequence

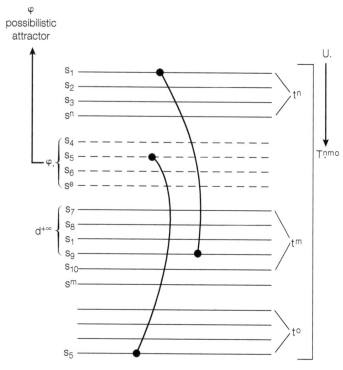

φ
possibilistic
attractor

b) The active processual sequence

remained outside of memory (Figure 5.7b). The 'durations of alterity' of the stochastic linearization of Flows, it will be recalled, had been schematically quantified (Figure 5.4) whereas the paradigmatic series of serial smoothing had been the object of a finite numbering (Figure 5.5). But we see here the insufficiency of such a mode of representation at this stage of striation. In effect, if the sensible heterogenesis of Flows truly arises – on its FT base – from quantifiable categories,[2] on its flank φ it calls for a description of qualities of possibility that are fundamentally recalcitrant to any reduction in the form of digitalized messages, that is to say, to being fixed once and for all, as faithful and incapable of deception. This is the 'revenge of the figure on the calculations', in the felicitous expression of Ivar Ekeland,[3] the return of cartographies, perhaps, much more than of geometries and topologies…The striation of Flows is established at the junction of two types of smoothing:

- a territorialized discursive smoothing on the axis FT that has as its correlate the articulation and virtual calibration of sensible qualities;
- a deterritorializing smoothing of positioning, on the axis FΦ, in the register of abstract qualities inherent in machinic Propositions. Whilst sensible qualities close striation onto a discontinuous finitude, manifested by endo-ordination filters, abstract qualities, on the contrary, open it onto continuous and transfinite evaluative instances (trans-ordering).

From here, two types of heterogeneity can be distinguished: a sensible one of amorphous positioning, with uniquely proximal and 'digital' references, and another which is 'charged' with processual and – we will come back to this – proto-genetic potentialities. We cannot emphasize enough that this last modality of heterogeneity only succeeds in changing possibility on condition that the four domains of entity FTΦU are mobilized. It is this putting into play of the complete cycle of Assemblages and this permanent requalification of each entity by the overdetermination of its ad-vent through the ensemble of smoothings and striations that gets us out of the limited determinism of quantification. In effect, the ad-vent of a possibility can remain indefinitely fixed, awaiting a rare break/cut, a hypercomplex singularization that will authorize its existential coagulation. The surplus value of possibilities generated by the in-stantiation of Flows is thus necessarily correlated to a-signifying ruptures that are no longer entirely of the aleatory and stochastic order. It isn't just the contingency of being-there, the certified localization of its redundant figures, that gets taken into account but, in addition, the integral of its dis-positions, transpositions, catastrophes and possible accidents, before, after, to the side of, beyond its actual manifestations.

6 THE DOMAIN OF PHYLA ⌽

What does our problem come down to? To trying to construct ordinary consistencies and temporalities from infinitely slow speeds of separability and infinitely rapid speeds of continuity. The montage of the cycle of Assemblages should allow us to achieve this. But, for the moment we have to free ourselves from the modular striation of Flows, which – we have posited in general terms – was established at the overlapping of two smoothings:

1   of the series $d^{-\infty}$, on the side of existential Territories;
2   of the series $d^{+\infty}$, on the side of possibilistic Phyla.

The spatio-temporal coordinates proper to modular discursivity are strictly subjected to principles of neighbourhood and rules of distribution that guarantee it a certain compactness. In the domain of Phyla, this compactness will cease to exist because we will be dealing with other types of relations of contiguity and succession. Traits of determinability will no longer have to remain stuck to one another to be related: they can also be infinitely dispersed in a generalized regime of separability. Idem with relations of duration: the chains will no longer be chronological but sequential and algorithmic. In other words, what happens here and now can be related to events that are infinitely remote in times before and times after (problematics of the retroactive smoothing of time referred to by Réné Thom).

Perhaps we finally have here the means to rid ourselves of the territorialized affectations proper to the modules of fluxion? Are the instruments of 'transversalization', which will allow us to cross spatial and temporal distances, to be sought on the side of these series $d^{+\infty}$ and $d^{-\infty}$, which can exist both in a state of layering, within molar-modular concretions in the domains F and T, and in a state of incorporeal molecular dispersion, in the domains Φ and U?

Let us call intrinsic determinability, D^i, the determinability that proceeds by the modular fixation of serial references $d^{+\infty}$ and $d^{-\infty}$ and extrinsic determinability, D^e, the determinability that allows serial traits to migrate into the deterritorialized spaces and durations of the domain of possibilistic Phyla and incorporeal Universes (U). In fact, it is a matter of more than a simple affair of compactness. We find ourselves faced with two complementary forms of putting into relationship of entitarian systems. The relation of modular reference D^i consists in holding together entities with an identical ontological status (this is the case, for example, with the linearization or indeed the entitarian coalesence represented in Figure 5.6). The consistency of the entities concerned is not damaged by 'additions' or 'subtractions'. Separation remains essentially connective, contiguist. That being the case, no delay is tolerated when the modular ensemble takes shape: all its sequences of determination are immediately consecutive. This is perfectly compatible with the existence of traits of determinability $d^{+\infty}$, but it implies a considerable aporia as well, if one considers that the structure of modular fluxion also comprises caesuras $d^{-\infty}$. The landscape changes radically with the relation of extrinsic determinability D^e, in so far as it initiates a genesis of consistencies putting into play entitarian ensembles with a heterogeneous ontological status: besides modular components, discursive phase spaces, non-discursive enunciative basins, etc. With this relation, the more and the less are no longer inscribed 'between' entities, but incrusted in their very being. It is no longer a matter of an extensive but of an intensive relation, and separation ceases to be passively connective so as to become actively disjunctive, that is to say, generative of processes of complexification.

The smoothing of extrinsic determinability

Modular striation endeavours to fabricate a sensible Territory on the basis of serial aggregates of speed $d^{+\infty}$ (Figure 6.1). With expressive smoothing, serial aggregates of speed $d^{-\infty}$ of a completely different nature find themselves taken into account as a matter of urgency.

$D^{-\infty}$ separations are no longer confused in the same undifferentiated vacuum. The phase space φ orders the rhythms of stopping and starting of 'negative' determinability.

Let us now superimpose Figures 6.1 and 6.2 so as to produce the simplified Figure 6.3, re-baptizing the apexes of the two triangles considered: m for matter, s for substance and f for form. (We can, in effect, consider that the cycle of Assemblages is constituted by diverse mediators of substantializing mediation transforming states of non-formed matter m into formed states f.)

In Figure 6.3, the modular striation of Figure 6.1 is schematized by the triangle m^{ts} s^{ts} f^{ts} and the expressive smoothing of Figure 6.2 by the triangle m^e s^e f^e. The unformed matter m^{ts} takes on the consistency of formed Flow f^s by the substantializing modular mediation s^{ts} (the proto-enunciative function). But the whole question of expressive smoothing will be played out around the 'takeoff' of the summit s^e (belonging to the triangle m^e s^e f^e) starting from f^s (the point of 'arrival' of the module m^{ts} s^{ts} f^{ts}). A passive form here will take on an active value of existential transmutation. We will examine successively the fractal nature of this takeoff and then the putting to work of the two functions that are consecutive to it, that is, the expressive function f(exp) and the existential function f(exi).

It is worth first conceptualizing the position of formed Flow f^s as being in a tense co-incidence with that of unformed modular matter m^{ts}. You can't have one without the other and yet their association cannnot be assumed either! It can break down: the play of a little difference, the intrusion of an infinitesimal deterritorialization – symbolized in Figure 6.3 by ∂^e – can functionally detach an entitarian position s^e that ruptures consistantial solidarity with m^{ts} so as to work for itself somehow and engender a new type of Flow: *signaletic Flows*. By losing their territorialized coordinates, by freeing themselves up from modular confinement, the referential series $d^{+\infty}$ and their traits of separability

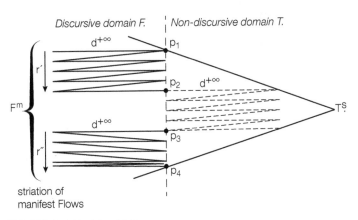

FIGURE 6.1 Modular striation

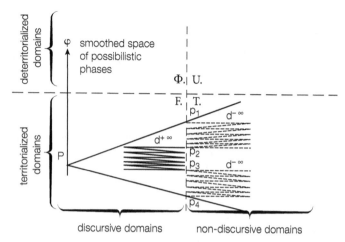

FIGURE 6.2 Expressive smoothing

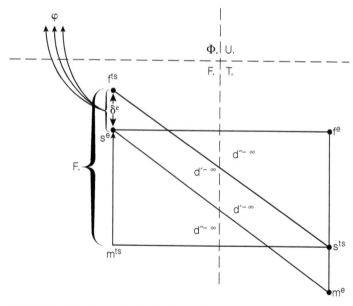

FIGURE 6.3 The take-off of machinic surplus value

d$^{-\infty}$ rupture the matter-form tensor, which obliges their manifestations to remain under the regime of sensible striation, and acquire a 'charge' of arbitrariness correlative to the aleatory openings. Thus, once the elastic m^{ts} – f^{fs} is stretched, it is the whole of the modular economy that collapses, whilst determinability deserts the register of extensivity and of extrinsic coordinates to invest itself elsewhere in the smoothing of molecular intensities.

Everything plays out around the springing up of the rupture s^e, the point of emergence of expressive fractalization, from which the conversion of certain material Flows into signaletic Flows will make itself felt. No longer held in a modular framing, determinability at the same time turns in on itself like a molecular ball and starts to proliferate like a Chinese paper flower that is thrown into water – the first entity constitutive of s^e doesn't even have the time to try to put itself into relation with another entity before the line that separates them starts to bud in a multiplicity of entitarian choices, optional junctions, generating so many lines of flight of possibility. Caught in this sort of on-the-spot commotion of inter-entitarian relations, determinability can no longer stabilize itself by means of the extrinsic procedures which had to that point circumscribed it. Its series enter into an infinite process of imploding, their old, crumpled compositions constantly attempting, throughout this vertiginous implosion, to hang onto a homothety or to a differential foundation that itself is always becoming more infinitesimal. The image that may be proposed here is that of a 'baker transformation' each fold of which would equally have as its effect a diminution of the total surface of the dough. However, although it develops aleatory aspects, this fractal-implosive deconstruction is not, for all that, synonymous with anarchy, because, in effect, it proceeds by equally infinitesimal thresholds, the 'decelerations' d$^{-\infty}$ of which are no longer regulated by a modular striation but by the specific instances of deterritorialized domains of Phyla and of Universes, namely the phase spaces (φ) and enunciative basins (ΣU).

The two types of Flow

	Striation of sensible Flows	Smoothing of signaletic Flows
Level	molar	molecular
Element	serial traits	fractal folds
Reference	extensive coordinates	intensive ordinates
Regime of discursivity	separability	non-separability
Consistency	territorialized	deterritorialized
Symmetry	reversible	relative irreversibility
Ontic status	contingency	singularity

The expressive function: f(exp)

What is most important to bring out is this survival, through a processual headlong flight, of a form that, having lost its sensible support and its material 'base', one might have thought was condemned to abolishing itself. Instead of that, it persists in reproducing the modular references from which it stemmed, and, more importantly, it enriches them by inserting them into an infinitely proliferating phase space of possibility. Concretely, it is a question here of all the expressive matters open to the facets of mutation and creation: genetic, ethological, semiotic codes, semiologies and the ensemble of situations in which a 'constructivist' Expression is grafted onto material – phonic, scriptural, organic – chains, by starting to play the double game of being-for-itself what it is, through the modular relations that articulate it, and of being-for-something-else, elsewhere and after, as a function of a variety of memorial and possibilistic pro-positions (P^m).

From the moment that there is a fractal unsticking of a signaletic fluctuation (or a fluctuation of code), two distinct elements must be taken into account:

- a fractal proliferation properly so-called, the base of the expressive function f(exp), which will evolve within abstract machinic Phyla Φ^{am} and, correlatively, incorporeal Universes of reference;
- residual discursive forms that remain there, in place, collapse, stretched, ruptured from the sense woven by matter-form relations which, nevertheless play a key role in the constitution of the existential function f(exi), as will be seen in the following chapter.

Generated by the deterritorialized fractal process, the expressive function f(exp) intervenes in two registers. On the one hand, it repeats and echoes indefinitely the formulae of symmetry proper to the sensible module that served as its support (it repeats them whilst deforming, twisting and miniaturizing them to infinity). On the other hand, it reframes this same formula in a set of references – or phase space (φ) of possibility – that throws light on the ensemble of imaginable and unimaginable angles of approach. Expressive fractalization is not just repetition; it produces an added value, it secretes a surplus value of code. It is always ready to pull something new out of its pocket. Thus φ represents the integral of possibilities adjacent to F. As an illustration, let us arbitrarily represent the definition of the Point of Contingency P^c (by which the expressive function EC will find support) by the figure 225. The phase space φ relative to this figure is constituted by all the procedures that can engender the figure 225, upstream as well as downstream (by having recourse to whole numbers, fractions, irrational numbers, imaginary numbers, etc.).

The space φ envelops the ensemble of possible geneses of P^c. But this illustration still remains too 'flat'. Let us come back instead to our magic skin baker transformation.[1] Let us call the different operations that contribute to positioning P^c *folds of contingencing* – p_1 representing the last operation before arriving at $\overline{P^c}$, p_2 the penultimate, etc. As in the baker transformation, the folds are both 'necessary' and generative of aleatory aspects.[2] Hence the ambiguous character of the entitarian position P^c. On the one hand, it is only one illustration among an infinity of others from a range of possible procedures; but on the other hand, it constitutes the contingent and necessary hook without which the aforesaid procedures would not be in the slightest position to start up and be deployed.

One can also imagine more qualitative examples. This plant on the windowsill makes a sensible Territory present, one of the reference traits of which is the colour green. At the modular level of intrinsic determinability, one must admit that this green is encysted in the contingent being-there of the plant, in one way or another. But at the same time, it offers itself to us through many facets from the multiple points of view that one can have on it. Certain folds of contingency will be relative to the distance of the observer, others to gradations of colour, to relations of contrast or complementarity, yet others will be modulated as a function of the various possible intensities of light and temperature, etc. Little by little, an infinity of points of view will be unfolded that all result in the same 'terminal' that this green being constitutes here at this moment. That being so, the set φ_1 of these points of view does not constitute an indifferent jumble; it is organized on the basis of certain constraints, assembled in such a way that the reddish glimmer of the fire must be related to φ_2, a different phase space from φ_1, that is to say, one that is generated by different sequences of fractal folding. Unless of course a third phase space φ_3 encompassing the previous two,

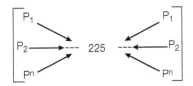

FIGURE 6.4 Space φ of P^c

were to set about associating the green of the plant and the reddish glow of the fire, as in the composition of a pastel drawing.

We will start from the principle that if a knowledge of forms and their interactions 'finally' happens one day, with the appearance of life, it is because in one way or another and doubtless according to very different modalities, it already exists at other ontological levels. This proto-knowledge must be an intrinsic part of every existential taking consistency, every constitution of a structural Territory or deterritorialized system. The articulation of the Point of Contingencing P^c to the Space of representative phases φ is the cornerstone of this conjunction between being-there, closed on itself and proto-alterity, which links together the things of the world and life. Henceforth, we will (re-)characterize this articulation: the Expression-Content relation (contingent Expression E^c, phase Content C^φ).

C^φ is the place where the traits of intrinsic formal determinability (D^i) (which were knotted together in territorialized modules) are focused and deterritorialized, now encountering extrinsic determinability D^e so as to be concatenated with it. In fact there is no reason here to distinguish D^i and D^e traits. The same serial traits $d^{+\infty}$ and $d^{-\infty}$ coexist in two states: 1) the modular state D^i; 2) the state D^e, which migrates across the cycle of extrinsic deter-minability, according to different consistencies and regimes of functioning.

Thus the same serial trait – the 'green' – can be circumscribed in a modular relation mf or circulate in φ in an 'atmospheric', fractal state, in an infinitesimal discursive form or in U in a non-discursive incorporeal form. Being-green-there, clinging on to the plant, is certainly not nothing! But being green by a detour through the Virtual Universe of colours or through algorithms and technico-scientific procedures capable of presiding over the wavelengths of luminous Flows is something completely different! But is it really necessary to repeat that the one does not happen without the other?

So, must it be inferred that the two worlds – of contingent territorialities and of transversal, fractal and deterritorialized entities – overlap and inter-penetrate? That would be a little too simple! Doubtless one cannot avoid postulating the existence of a level of pure abstract incorporeal reference, which we will call the Plane of Consistency (PoC), traversing the ensemble of states of things. But from a cartographic point of view it will be much more profitable to link the two extreme zones of contingency FT and of virtuality ΦU together in a zone of intersection E^cC^φ, also called an Assemblage of intermediary temporalities.

So, one will never encounter FT contingency in the pure state and even less so ΦU transcendence, but only degrees of contingencing and degrees of deterritorialization, associated within expressive Assemblages E^cC^φ. And yet an indirect access to these extreme states is sometimes given to

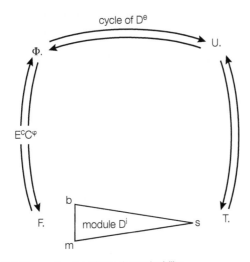

FIGURE 6.5 The cycle of extrinsic determinability

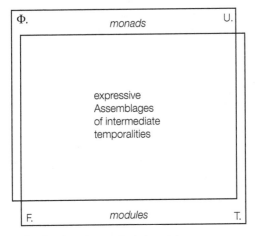

FIGURE 6.6 Overlapping of monads and modules

us, through a sort of divinatory hysteria, in the nauseous experience of Sartrean facticity, or in mystic experience. Even as a mirage, these strange outskirts of ordinary enunciation nonetheless remain indispensible components in the preparation of speculative maps relative to the production of subjectivity, whether they are of the ritual, initiatic or mythical order (when, for example, they turn around incarnation or symbolic castration). Before some final remarks about expressive smoothing, let us keep in mind that we now have three different kinds of enunciation of discursivity at our disposal:

- modules of finite contingencing (which the next chapter will be devoted to redefining);
- monads of infinite determinability, which will be tackled with incorporeal smoothing φU;
- the Assemblages of relative contingency-transcendence, which, it must be said, we are a long way from having finished considering, as they constitute the principal basis for the cycle of Assemblages.

From our point of view, Expression has thus become essentially correlated to a deterritorialized and fractal smoothing of the set of striations of Flows. Machines of Expression somehow have the function of making the possible ooze out of all the encysted modular forms that harbour it. Their work of smoothing consists of decompartmentalizing it, of spreading it out from within the diverse immaterial, atopographical, unlocalizable fields of possibility where Content originates. But in this sense, there is no univocal register of Expression articulated to another, equally univocal, register of Content. We are never in the presence of a homogeneous order of Content articulated to a hegemonic order of Expression, and still less the massive structuralist opposition of Signifier/Signified. One only ever deals with degrees of smoothing of Content on the basis of the conjoint intervention of:

1 heterogeneous components of Expression;
2 diverse substantial consistencies relative to the multiple incorporeal referents on which it [Expression] is inscribed.

One must therefore admit the existence of different incorporeal *qualities*, heterogeneous deterritorialized materials. The same abstract formula treated in the referential texture of baroque music does not bathe in the same field of possibility if, at another time, it finds itself incarnated in a tissue of mathematical idealities...For all its generality, the transversality of deterritorialized forms of Content nonetheless knows thresholds, decelerations, detours. And as we note once again, the cycle of Assemblages functions perfectly well in both directions: modular contingency (D^i) here provides its certainties at the same time as those of non-discursive and extrinsic determinability (D^e).

As Figure 6.7 illustrates, these thresholds constitute potential junctions for the branching of new components of extrinsically modalized possibility D^e through the debut of adventitious Universes of reference that had hitherto remained 'in reserve'.

Between E_1^c and C_2^φ, fractal folding functions autarchically. It stops at C_2^φ when the constituted phase surface is compatible with the basin of virtuality of a new Universe of reference.

Fractal folding will only be able to start up again on condition that this basin interferes with the previous basin, which implies that new components of expression E_2^c, E_3^c, E_4^c...make their appearance. Consequently the importing of an extrinsic determinability D^e will once again become possible. Let us note that the successive constitution of phase surfaces that results must not be assimilated to a striation, because each new formation

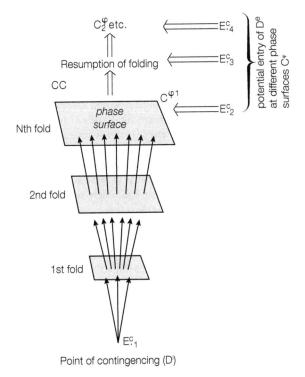

FIGURE 6.7 The entry of Universes of reference

φ substitutes itself for and effaces the previous in such a way that they are engendered continuously. However, it must be emphasized that their advent can be deferred in various ways because of the 'delaying' of the entry of a Universe of reference. It is the play of these 'différances' that generates the variety of stochastic incidences of bifurcation and confers a rhizomatic development of contents rather than an arborescent one (such as that of generative semantics). It is important to insist on the fact that if fractalization can start up again and lead through new deterritorializing foldings to another phase surface, at the end of each pause on Content, such a triggering is only possible to the extent that it is accompanied by the recomposition of referential enunciation. In these conditions, the paradigmatic interlocking of contents never develops according to purely formal principles of composition: at each taking consistency of an E^c, C^φ relation, the question of the singular and singularizing – in short, the irreversible – entry of a new enunciative basin (a Constellation of Universes of reference ΣU) is posed again.

Semiotic geneses are localized and unlocalizable at the same time. They are localized when they proceed by extensive molar coordinates in order to establish an extensive-intrinsic determinability (D^i). They are unlocalized when they proceed by intensive molecular ordinates in order to establish an intensive-extrinsic determinability (D^e). In the latter case, one might ask if there is any need to assign speeds to the traits $d^{+\infty}$ and $d^{-\infty}$, given that there is no longer any length of trajectory nor any time to travel across it. Extraverted spatio-temporal coordinates are converted into deterritorialized categories of measurement that include a dissymmetry between $d^{+\infty}$ and $d^{-\infty}$ and, above all, infinitely small quanta of energy that constitute a puzzle that is at least as maddening as that of the coexistence of infinitely fast and infinitely slow speeds! The only point in all this that seems unavoidable is that to be in a position to have a catalytic hold on the in-stantiation of material processes, the signaletic Flows put into play by the expressive function really must, in one way or another, have a charge of energy, however minimal it may be! This is the only way in which one can hope to think the relations between this expressive function and the conversions of energy. To place potentials for action and effect that are isolated in separate basins into communication, the expressive function must initiate minimal transfers of energy that are capable of triggering amplifying processes. And determinability as such already constitutes a principle of energy equivalence. In effect, to be in a position to exit from their ontological confinement, to interact amongst themselves, entities charged with a potential for action and effect are obliged, in their manner, to 'make signs' to each other, to recognize each other, to mutually apprehend each other. This signaletics within the materiality of Flows is in itself energetic in the sense that the possibilities for molecular action are rooted within this signaletics. These possibilities can redraw entitarian compositions, displace the traits of separability $d^{-\infty}$, trigger the fractal faults that, in the last analysis, pilot the molar order. Without having an energy charge, the entities in question would avoid each other or pass through each other without consequence. One must thus accept that it is necessary to make a basic principle – that of the expressive apprehension of entities and relations arising from the same phase spaces, the same basins of Universes of reference – prevail at the deepest point of the constituents of physics. These ways of being-outside-self for a particular species of alterity ought to be conceived as so many levels of energy. I underline the plural, because we are not in the presence of an Energy that would traverse the entirety of states of things without batting an eyelid, identical to itself, holding hands with its companion Information (or the Signifier, which amounts to more or less the same thing) – which for its part would traverse the entirety of states of sense with the same serenity! One must admit instead that expressive energies are converted, by way of an abstract (in the sense of extraction) equivalent, into entitarian potentials for action and effect, to then be transferred to the heart of the modular tensions that link matter and form.

Such would be the vital minimum of consistency, tangential to a chaos that offers neither stopping point nor last resort for any effect whatsoever. However, one ought not to lose sight of the fact that the module tensions in question result from a memorial taking consistency of Flows. One will recall, in effect, that the order r of the serial layering of Flows was directly dependent on their extensional memory m (Figure 5.6d). But now, the situation has changed, because by disarticulating the linearity of Flows on which they are based, expressive fractal rupture has liberated their traits of determinability – those of possible affirmation $d^{+\infty}$, as well as those of virtual separability $d^{-\infty}$. We have also seen that forms henceforth worked in deterritorialized and immaterial registers on their own count. Although they have thus become powdery, atmospheric, molecular...these latter have not for all that become free to invest themselves no matter where or to refer to no matter what! They now find themselves *assigned* to enunciative basins that are also deterritorialized (U), which can equally liberate themselves and invest themselves in other basins, at the behest of their own mutations, to the rhythm of the foldings of Phyla and due to other singularization factors that we will come back to later.

The existential function f(exi) and the diagrammatic function f(diag)

We must now examine the impact of expressive smoothing (EC) on the structures of modular – I would be tempted to say medullary – reference. It is impossible to go in one direction without taking into account the counter-effect of that movement on the point one has just left! Because of the fractal unfolding of fields of possibility, this incidence of Expression on territorialized modules will not take place brutally but by thresholds, to the extent that new attractors of Content C^φ will acquire consistency. When Leonoardo da Vinci dreams of flying machines, he sketches them out, he makes plans of them, but everything stays there. The representation bubbling away in his head has got no bite on the techno-scientific state of things of his epoch. But since then, the affair has taken on consistency, it has acquired a collective enunciation. Across chains of researchers, inventors, Phyla of algorithms and diagrams that have proliferated in technological programmes, books, teaching, forms of know-how, immense Capitals of knowledge have accumulated within institutions and apparatuses of every kind, now assisted with a formidable efficiency by computers. Today, the repercussions of the content 'flying machine' have become innumerable, to the point that their 'trees of implication' constitute a veritable forest! At successive levels, its diagramming has taken off from its initial domain as a dream, and then from the domain of the fantasy of slightly mad inventors, so as finally to be incarnated in the vital drives of modern societies.

That is where one must stop: just at the point where expressive discursivity no longer just refers to itself through the mechanisms of paradigmatic commutation, where it puts its relationship of neutrality and arbitrariness with regard to the referent into suspense so as to engage forcefully with reality, I mean with the modular stratifications of the everyday world. A passage of Expression to a pragmatic effectiveness, then, that can no longer just be added to the components of denotation and signification like a lifejacket in the way that linguists do! The only effect of doing that is to enclose linguistics in a specific axiomatization that Hjelmslev, for his part, vehemently refused (for different reasons to ours, it is true).[3] In truth, Expression doesn't just produce pragmatic drives, it also engenders existential mutations. It will have been understood that from our point of view, enunciation and existence arise from the same apparatuses of Expression and are even similar expressions, literally. It is through the continually restarted promotion of expressive functions f(exp) that the existential requalification f(exi) of territorialized sensible modules f(mod) is brought about. Figure 6.8, which completes Figures 6.1, 6.2 and 6.3 shows this inversion of the trajectory of the deterritorialization of forms, when they converge on a phase of attraction C^φ. (Let us note that this reversal of the form of Expression/form of Content relation also conforms with one of the fundamental intuitions of Hjelmslev.) At the end of this toing and froing and after an enrichment of their potentialities, the old modular sensible Territories Ts find themselves converted into a new species of existential Territory Te.

How has the phase space C^φ managed to affirm itself, to dance the dance, to requalify anterior referential modalities? We will have to come back to the extrinsic conditions of such a taking consistency of deterritorialized contents, in the form of Machinic propositions (P^m) redefined as a Capital of possibility, originating in part against the grain of actual Flows in the virtual domain of Universes of reference. But for now everything still seems to play around the extraordinary conversions of which the zone of Expression E is only the seat. We have seen this zone successively requalified as:

1 the formal endpoint f^s of the matter-form tensor of the modular function f(mod);

2 the Point of Contingencing P^c of the expressive tensor EC of the expressive function f(exp);

3 the point of substantiation s^e of the existential function.

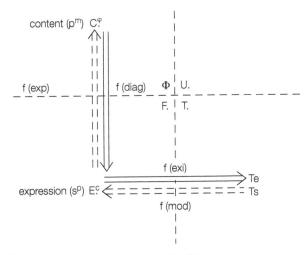

FIGURE 6.8 The inversion of deterritorialization

'Conversion' conjures up hysteria and this is perhaps not far off the mark, because the way in which discursive chains in s^e suspend their denotative function, adjunct to modules of being-there, and their expressive function – in so far as it opens onto trans-finite Phyla of content – does indeed seem to be similar to hysteria. One can see that these chains now incarnate, corporealize – I will dare to say 'somatize' – a non-discursive existentiality anchored in finitude. A delegation of being, an ontological simulation, the representation of an unrepresentable that is very different from the Vorstellungrepräsentanz of the Freudian drive. Through it, an existential-body-without-organs with neither distinct parts nor discernabilized external referent finds itself conferred with a proxy organicity, a borrowed soma.

Examples of these discursive chains serving as 'scene shifters', pragmatic stagehands or enunciative operators of existential *dis-position*: faciality traits, emblems and signatures, which I would happily regroup under the generic rubric of *existential refrains*.[4] Faciality traits are what they are first because of the modular structures that constitute the human face at the end of the deterritorializing drift that 'extracted' them from the animal muzzle. It goes without saying that subsequently they are expressive because of the modulation of basic terms in a code with theoretically unlimited potentialities. Theoretically – because practically their capacity for innovation is strictly marked out by the grid of dominant significations. (Excessive laughter makes one think of madness, the overly seductive traits of a female television presenter will make a part of the audience flood back.) But in the third place they are the diagrammatic key and the facialitarian signature of a particular individual or of a group which 'recognizes' itself in its leader, its media star. They catalyse a cultural effusion without any precise limits, as was the case during the High Middle Ages with the face of Christ Pantocrator, which began literally to haunt the multiple horizons of Christianity. It will be the same with the emblem and the signature, which, beyond their modular denotational function and the significant relations that they are able to trigger, 'existentialize' and at the same time responsibilize, 'ethico-politicize' an enacted subjectivity.

With this coiling back of Expression onto Existence we have returned from the fractal-molecular register to the molar-modular register. But we have not, for all that, gone back to the beginning! The new existential dis-position is not passively striated like the modules of sensible Flows were; it is worked by semiotic potentials, potentials of code, moulding, catalysis, etc. which themselves come from far off, in the still quasi-unexplored continents of possibilistic Phyla and Universes of virtuality. Let us follow this return to contingency a little more closely.

We said previously that the residual forms of fractalization stayed in place, collapsed, distended. This was only true from the point of view of intra- and inter-modular tensions, because the existential requalification generative of refrains imposes an entirely different way of seeing things. In effect, these shrivelled, serial stratifications, cut off from their old matter-form relations, nevertheless constitute a new, virulent, hyper-active memory of being, in parallel to the old modular striations of Flows, by virtue of its openness to the inputs capitalized as φ. Consequently one can consider that when an existential requalification f(exi) happens to succeed an expressive fractal rupture f(exp), the question of the existence of an operation of intermediary reterritorialization is posed. This operation is like the reverse side of the expressive function and I will characterize it as a *diagrammatic function* f(diag) (Figure 6.8).[5] This intermediary diagram in some way folds up all the potentialities that expressive fractalization had unfolded except that as a supplement it brings a surplus value of possibility δ to the sensible surface. This surplus value is inherited from the detour via the attractor $C^φ$ composed of non-stratified doublets of the traits $d^{+∞}$ and $d^{-∞}$ which one will see at work in the enunciative catalyses carried out by the existential refrains and synapses. But before getting to that, let us underline again the differences between this diagrammatic 'return' to the Point of Contingency and the previous expressive 'ascent'. The deterritorializing expression of f(exp) had something irresistible about it, it developed a fractalism everywhere, in an expansive mode within the phase spaces of the domain φ. On the other hand, the status of f(diag) is always precarious, aleatory, problematic, confined, contingenced by the margin of manoeuvre that is authored by existential refrains. In effect, the latter are obliged to ensure that the possibilistic quanta $d^{-∞}$ of the rearranging of modular striations borne by δ really do correspond to an existential (ex)tension of enunciation on the side of the Universe T and U, so as to allow the putting to work of said quanta. Once again, this imposes a detour via the complete cycle of extrinsic determinability. Only then will we be able to establish that it is in 'turning back' into a diagrammatic function that the expressive function energetically charges itself, putting into circulation *Sign-particles* (S^p) at the point P^c (Figure 6.8).

Existential refrains

The first refrains given as examples – faciality, signatures, emblems – did not sufficiently clarify the fact that they are established at the junction of two existential and diagrammatic functions or, in other words, that processual, active, aspects, imported via diagrammatic determination f(diag) could come to be added to the passive, 'hysterical' aspects of existential grasping f(exi). However, refrains of a 'psy' origin would show us the two states in which they are led to manifest themselves in a more suggestive way. Their symptomatic insistence through obsessive rituals or systematized delirium, for example, always presents two faces:

- one of the partial recomposition, made in any old way, of a more or less damaged existential Territory;
- the other of a processual nucleus, a line of flight, a 'fugue of sense', charged with a desire which, although neurotic-psychotic, is nonetheless intense and authentic.

In a general way, two states of the refrain can be distinguished:

- *An atonic state,* where it carries out a simple existential indexing and autonomization of a discursive residue that has become a dead memory, the witness-remnant of an old modular tension m-f which no longer has any other function than that of designating the being-previously-there of the pole S^{ts} of the defunct modular enunciator (Figure 6.9);
- *An excited state* where it additionally puts to use the surplus values of possibility δ'' 'conveyed' by f(diag) within modular striations, by bringing about original morpho-genetic catalyses, which could never have been imposed on them without its intervention (Figure 6.10).

The differential zone δ' proper to the atonic state of the refrain (Figure 6.9) represented an infinitesimal cracking intrinsic to the module. It

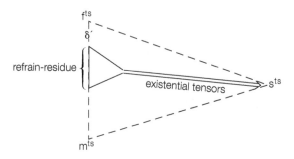

FIGURE 6.9 Refrain-residue and existential tensors

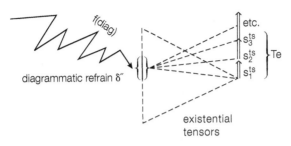

diagrammatic refrain δ″

f(diag)

etc.
s_3^{ts}
s_2^{ts} } Te
s_1^{ts}

existential
tensors

FIGURE 6.10 Diagrammatic refrain and existential tensors

was just enough to break the tension m-f. In contrast, the difference δ″ in the excited state (Figure 6.10) that results from the introduction of an infinitesimal slipping of the extrinsic point of view, which originates in f(diag), entails entirely different consequences. It is effectively the bearer of a positive determinability $d^{+\infty}$ twinned with a negative determinability $d^{-\infty}$ that constitutes as if a charge of a free and virtual valence of enunciative rearrangement. This time things get serious: the old modular structure is not only constrained to exit its dead autonomy but is constrained to open up to other enunciative Assemblages (Te). The refrain thus constitutes a sort of selector of choices, an option machine, for the treatment of the bifurcations around which the degrees of freedom of a system, the aleatory putting on hold of the enacting of heterogeneous components, will play…The different figures of the Assemblage with regard to charges of possibility are sketched out at this ethico-micro-political junction:

1   Either the contingent status quo: the cycle of Assemblages stays put. This is the reign of the emblem, of the signature (for its part, faciality can close up on itself like an institutional stamp, but it also opens itself up to creative fields again)[6]

2   Or the situation of unstable equilibrium: the refrain is then like the messenger-bird that taps on the window with its beak, so as to announce the existence of other virtual Universes of reference that can modify the actual state of enunciative dispositions profoundly. That is how I conceive the 'function' of the forgetting, slips of the tongue, oneiric gesticulations, etc. that were the fortune of the 'savage horde' of psychoanalysis. It is also the principal legacy of the Dadaists and Surrealists, with their *technical* utilization of aleatory caesura and their recourse to objective chance in their

montages, collages, etc. To my mind, all these psychoanalytic and aesthetic operations flow from an active utilization of existential refrains. These practices of putting into refrain don't just shake up encysted references and certainties. They indicate the potential lines of a many-headed fractalization, a multidirectional and transversalist fractalization that can carry its effects to the heart of fundamentally heterogeneous domains.

3 Or, finally, straightforward processual mutation, the standard reference for all time being 'the refrains of lost Time'.[7] First, it is the wobbly paving stone in the courtyard of the Hôtel de Guermantes that triggers the effective passage to writing in the 'Search', then, recursively, Vinteuil's little phrase, the bells of Martinville…not forgetting the madeleine that is now munched by everyone.

Later we will encounter another essential avatar of the refrain, in the form of concrete machines. But we will only be able to deal with them after having tackled the questions of the striation of Phyla and of the smoothing of Universes, because they result from a requalification – one more requalification – of this same junction zone, brought about on the basis of these two operations proper to deterritorialized domains.

That a practice of existential refrains is possible, that one is not necessarily condemned to remaining passive in the face of their springing up (an attitude arising from a general function of capitalistic-monotheism) is something that the ritual procedures of 'animist' societies in particular teach us. It is also what psychoanalysis missed somewhat: initially, with

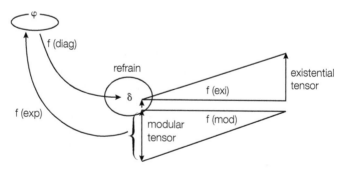

FIGURE 6.11 Existential refrains (repetition of Figure 6.8 as a function of Figure 6.10)

its overly energistic propping of unconscious complexes, then with its overly structuralist approach via part objects (which it would be better to call partialized, fractalized object-refrains). Equally a possible practice of institutional objects: in this domain, if one wants to escape from the weight of bureaucracy, Statist entropy, all the cogs are to be worked, artificialized, 'baroquized'. Taking into account the repetition-refrain, which insists for no reason, gets in the way of the 'normal' order of things and is synonymous with the casting off of paradigmatic moorings of technoscience, and a re-mooring to social and analytical practices on the side of ethico-aesthetic paradigms, the programme for an analysis of refrains, a refrain-analysis could be productive of a different subjectivity, other enunciative modalities that dis-pose existence differently.

The striation of Phyla

A map of Flows is only 'tenable' if it is established adjacent to a body of regularities, rules, legal regulations, principles, etc, something that is itself only viable if this body is the slightest able to stand up by itself. Such is the stake of the striation of Phyla: to confer a texture, a relative ontological autonomy on the corpus of abstract propositions that, whilst cohabiting with the sensible world, nonetheless escape from its existential 'framings' and its EST coordinates.

It is the same with this ontological striation as it is with that of the other domains: it is established at the junction of two smoothings and – in this instance – between the deterritorialized-fractal-expressive smoothing (EC) and the smoothing of incorporeal Universes of reference. But a difficulty in the exposition arises here that derives from the particular relations existing between incorporeal Universes and possibilistic Phyla. They cannot really be distinguished from each other; they entertain relations of com-possibility. There was a real distinctiveness between Existential Territories and Flows, such that the separative traits of determinability $d^{-\infty}$ found themselves confined to T, whilst the aggregative traits of determinability $d^{+\infty}$ found themselves stratified in F. In these conditions specific modes of the regrouping and exhaustion of each category of determinability became possible – and thus the smoothing and the striation of Flows turned out to be different to those of Territories. But, as will be seen further on, the fact that a radical mixing of the traits $d^{+\infty}$ and $d^{-\infty}$ exists between φ and U consequently renders their phases of smoothing and striation rigourously synchronic and homothetic.

That being so, before we can describe the striation of Phyla – that is to say, the requalification of passive phases Spaces – as active machinic Propositions and, consecutive to this the fourth requalification of the Point of Contingency P^c as a concrete machine, we will have to explore the domain of incorporeal Universes.

7 THE DOMAIN OF UNIVERSES ∪

The smoothing of Universes

Universes are the enunciative instances of the phase surfaces of possibility φ. But these phase surfaces constitute objects that no longer respond to the criteria of an actualized distinctiveness. In relation to one another they are distinct and indistinct at the same time. A phase space represents a certain state of possibility at a point θ of the duration of the fractal unfolding that originates in a fracture of contingency P^c. But it also represents, virtually, the other fractal unfoldings susceptible of succeeding it at the times θ_1, θ_2, θ_n. At the 'end' of an infinite process of fractal unfolding θ_∞, the phase space becomes identical to the general Plane of Consistency (PoC), or chaosmos, which itself corresponds to a state of infinite determinability (Figure 7.1).

Thus all the fractal processes of possibilistic determinability converge on the PoC. What 'stops' determinability at a phase θ is its putting into suspense by the intrusion of an infinitely decelerated determinability $d^{-\infty}$. But the situation now is very different from what it was with the modules. One recalls that with the latter, separability remained circumscribed and circumscribing at the same time. Here it becomes floating, diffuse, atmospheric.

A phase φ_1 is separated from another phase φ_2, which it skirts in a fashion that can be simultaneous, but at the same time it includes this phase φ_2 virtually, because in the final analysis both are 'required' to find themselves again at the heart of the same Plane of Consistency (Figure 7.2).

Let us accept that the phase φ_1 is separated by δ from the phase φ_2. This separation δ is effectuated at a speed of determinability $d^{-\infty}$. But at the same time, on the paradigmatic axis that leads them to the PoC, φ_1 and φ_2

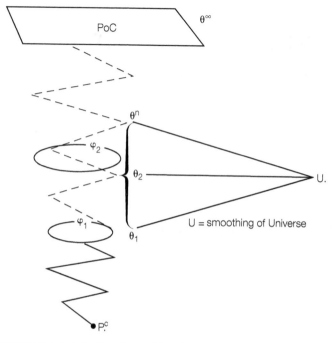

FIGURE 7.1 Arrival of the Plane of Consistency

are related to one another at a speed $d^{+\infty}$. As a consequence, the relations between the phases (or *phase transition*) are effectuated at a speed that is at the same time both infinitely rapid and infinitely slow and which will be notated: $d^{\pm\infty}$.

φ_1 and φ_2 represent a vibratory state of the same process. In the state represented by the shaded ovals in Figure 7.3, they exist in a regime of separability $\delta^{-\infty}$. In the state represented by the shaded intersection in the same figure, they exist in the state of phase transition communicating at an infinite speed $d^{+\infty}$. That is what happens on the side of continuist-fractal-molecular discursivity. But how are things on the side of non-discursive enunciation: U? Evidently it also finds itself totally delocalized, infinitely broken up, 'atmospherized'. The enunciation U of φ_1 φ_2 is at the same time both localized and contingenced, when φ_1 and φ_2 are 'dated' by an explicit fractal separation, but it is at the same time migrant, throughout the phase mutations spreading from φ_1 φ_2 φ_n to the PoC. U must be considered as the

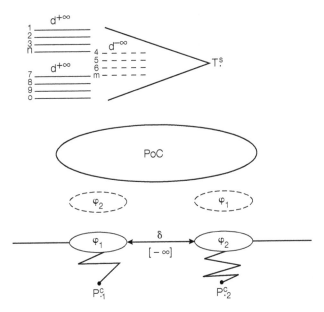

FIGURE 7.2 Phase spaces

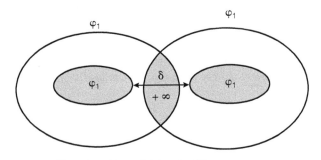

FIGURE 7.3 Phase transitions of determinability

integral of: 1) a contingent position of separability, φ_1 φ_2; and 2) the set of possible positions of fractal unfolding. It is at the same time both the locus of an actualized enunciation and of an infinity of virtual enunciations.

If determinability $d^{+\infty}$ and $d^{-\infty}$ is unlocalizable at the heart of the respective domains of Φ and U due to the fact that it is no longer graspable in a distinct aggregate, by contrast, each enunciation articulating a minimal determinability $d^{+\infty}$ is haunted by a virtual divisibility $d^{-\infty}$ (virtuality of a Universe). It is enunciative intentionality that, at its very root, sets off a process of continuous fractalization: a sort of race on the spot in which discernability tries desperately to catch its own tail. But by emptying out the intervals that separate them from the target at each median point in this way, the arrow will never reach its target! Constantly constrained to defer the grasping of a unary determination, this process of generalized intercalation is the daily bread of what one might call the obsessional condition.

Between the phases of actual possibility, that is to say, with each potential fractal fold, a virtual enunciation builds up which, by its infinitesimal proximity, succeeds in capitalizing the set of traits of determinability that had, until then, escaped from: 1) territorialized modular stratification; and 2) the hold of the deterritorialized, fractal phase. Returning to the previous illustrations, we can consider that enunciation U smoothes-gathers-integrates:

- intrinsic traits of determinability s_4, s_5, s_6, s^e, of the passive modular sequence (Figures 5.7a and 5.7b);
- extrinsic traits of determinability imported from phases of Content: C_1^φ, C_2^φ, etc.;
- the infinite set of enunciative traits $d^{-\infty}$ susceptible virtually of plugging into the process of continuous determinability en route.

It is, then, the coexistence of an infinite fractal process and of a contingent determination that, in some way, snags, fixes, ballasts it.

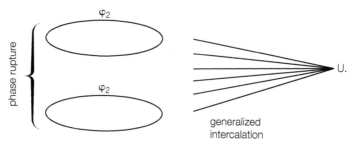

FIGURE 7.4 Virtual enunciation

The chaosmosis of the continuum

We are now in a position to take stock of three different kinds of enunciation:

- Modules of contingency;
- Monads of absolute determinability;
- Mixed Assemblages, the determinability of which is at the same time both infinite and convergent.

Modules of contingency make reference series ($d^{+\infty}$) converge on sensible Territories ($d^{-\infty}$), which they encounter as their finite term. Grasped as a sequence in the cycle of Assemblages, this finitude must be considered as an active finitization, a processual contingencing of a particularized point of view.

On the other hand, one is never finished with traits of determinability scattered by monadic enunciation, which always finds something to repeat. Each one of its actualized objectal apprehensions in turn channels the infinite set of virtual determinations relative to everything that could, for it, start to exist on its arrival from the rest of the world. The slightest serial positioning $d^{+\infty}$ scarcely has the time to assert itself, to hold out its hand towards a sister entity before it finds itself threatened with the interposition, between itself and others, even between itself and itself, of an enunciative filter ($d^{-\infty}$). But one might take things differently and estimate that the absolute, osmotic mixture of $d^{+\infty}$ and $d^{-\infty}$ also coincides with their total separation. Everything happens as if the virtual division and extraction of the ensemble of $d^{+\infty}$ and the ensemble of $d^{-\infty}$ was on the surface of possibility. However that may be, the seriality $d^{-\infty}$ finds itself conferred with an ontological plenitude, from the fact that it henceforth entertains relations of intensive polarity with this latter and in such a way that one can no longer say that it closes, segments or striates determinability $d^{-\infty}$, as was still the case in the epoch of intrinsic and finite modular determinability. Determinability $d^{\pm\infty}$ no longer has either positioning or separational function, properly speaking. Like an aerosol, its stays in a state of suspension at the heart of the 'chaosmic' Plane of Consistency, which constitutes primitive redundancies (the ensemble of neg-entropic virtualities that haunt the entropic tensions inherent to chaos) as a sort of paradoxical other side of chaos. Entirely separated and yet pairing up unceasingly, these two chaotic and chaosmotic poles of determinability promote new modalities of proximity: 1) of a spatial order, which can be infinitely distanced at the heart of the same infinitesimal circumscription; 2) of a temporal order, by the smoothing of infinitely remote future and past times; 3) of an energetic order, with 'capitals of effects' caught in fundamentally heterogeneous basins. By virtue of the passages from extensity ($d^{+\infty}$ separated by $d^{-\infty}$) to intensity ($d^{\pm\infty}$), the 'original' stochasticity finding itself as if hollowed and loaded with new transversalist virtues: it establishes and reinforces symmetries and gestaltist relations between apparently heteroclite situations. In short, it constructs new modalities of circumstance. These monads of absolute determinability seem dominated by a bulimic drive that leads them to devour their own limits without respite. Without any fixed contour, each one of them makes the same journeys, marked out by the other monads, indefinitely. An eternal repetition nevertheless secreting an inexhaustible surplus value of sense and existence. In fact, it is the very notion of alterity that collapses here, to the profit of a generalized enunciative transfer, a hegemonic transitivity and transversality.

Phenomenologically, we have access to this limit state of incorporeal enunciation, through the non-thetic apprehension of existential affects, that is to say, at the vertiginous level at which consciousness posits itself as founding the outside world, alterity and one's self all at once. Megalomania mixed with a disgust for all things, because of the fact that such a passion of/for absolute determinability is condemned to turn round in circles, since it is unable to encounter the caesuras and external intrusions that would bring it out of itself. A Sartrean experience of nausea, resulting from the invasion of an inexhaustible facticity. But also a general hint of capitalistic consciousnesses obsessed with a principle of generalized equivalence that gnaws away at and empties out everything in its passage.

I have already mentioned Assemblages mixing infinite determinability (D^e) and contingent determinability (D^i). I will not say much more about them here, as it is only ever a question of them at every step in the cycle of Assemblages. How should one conceptualize hooks for contingency that preserve the creational capacities of Assemblages? How can degrees of contingency, as well as the symbiosis of incorporeal Universes with sensible modules, be established? How is one to conceive intermediary temporalizations between $d^{+\infty}$ and $d^{-\infty}$ being established with the solutions of continuity that one already knows (points of rupture of contingency, refrains) and those that have been announced (machinic synapses and existential auto-consistency)? Always the same questions! That being so, we have perhaps advanced a little with certain of them, the status of the continuum in particular. Henceforth, we will no longer have to consider that the continuous and the discontinuous are passively given, but that they participate in processes of continuation-discontinuation that are implanted at the heart of the same molecular-fractal chaosmos, that is to say, the same Universe of determinability in the free state. Thus, the enunciation of absolute determinability haunts, sweeps and smoothes its basins of virtual determinability of all modular circumscriptions of contingent determinability. Inversely, this smoothing by the incorporeal enunciators U finds its diagrammatic grasp, its root of singularization (the fact that it is not a matter of Platonic Universals cut off from every sensible hook) in the points of contingencing, P^c, where the expressive foldings originate and where the diagrammatic foldings-up are snagged (Figure 6.8). It is perhaps also possible to advance just a little on another question, that of the different modalities of symmetry.

Symmetries

A particular type of symmetry corresponds to the striation of each of the three domains already examined:

- reversible extensional symmetries for Flows;
- relatively reversible fractal symmetries for Phyla;
- irreversible internal symmetries for Universes.

In F, the domain of spatio-temporal striations, the entitarian positions A, B, C, etc. imply the existence, in relation to one another, of common entitarian compositions traversing each in a sort of silent translation of their respective di-stances. Thus, to position A there will correspond the composition that will be found virtually in B, C, etc. in such a fashion as to constitute a series of extensional symmetries:

The series ensured an intrinsic contiguity between A, B, C.... But one could develop series of extensional symmetries, b, c..., on the basis of B, C...; the relations of translation that it is possible to establish on the basis of no matter what position of an entity of Flow will be characterized as reversible. They have no origin, one can always take them in the opposite

FIGURE 7.5 Extensional symmetries

direction. That is how they differ from the relatively irreversible relations proper to processual Phyla, for which each fractal step is 'dated' by an aleatory 'figure' that doesn't necessarily return.

The forms that traverse the fractal symmetries of the striation of Phyla lose their character of spatio-temporal identity so as to undergo infinite topological deformations and a deterritorialization that makes them topple over into an infinitesimal molecular register. The possibilistic smoothing brought about by this fractal deconstruction allows an extrinsic contiguity to be established between the 'visible' molar levels and the 'invisible' molecular levels. What a paradox this infinite contiguity is, constantly feeding on an equally infinite separability beyond contingency, at the heart of a milieu of infinitesimal implosion! Because – and I repeat – it is effectively a matter of an essentially proliferating contiguity in the making, which continuously secretes a virtual and unlocalizable separability. To say here that each series of trans-entitarian determination, of the type a, b, c,… (a variety of infinitely accelerated determinability $d^{+\infty}$) now corresponds to an enunciative anti-series $d^{-\infty}$ does not signify that one finds oneself faced with a simple change in sign of the same corpus of entitarian discursivity (infinitely decelerated instead of infinitely accelerated), or indeed the marking of a polar symmetry (its sequential links having been inverted, for example). An infinite multiplicity of series $d^{-\infty}$ corresponds to each trans-serial trait. Thus each signaletic element finds itself doubled by a multitude of 'freeze-frames', which have the capacity to blur this image. In other words, the $d^{-\infty}$ 'points of view' stop being purely observational – as was the case with modular determination: they intervene so as to transform the texture of determinability. The symmetry that is conveyed by the fractal folding of the Expression-function does not arise from algorithms closed on themselves, born by a Signifier that remains indifferent to the diversity of matters in which it happens to be incarnated. This symmetry lies in the encounter of machinic Propositions ('rising' towards φ with f(exp)) and particle-signs ('descending' towards F with f(diag)),[1] through which they transfer activated formulae, virulent abstract machinisms – I'm tempted to say 'abstract viruses' – that establish transverse, evolving, creative bridges between the different levels of biological, organic, cognitive, psychic, historical, but also physico-chemical, particulate, infra-particulate Assemblages. This is to say that its development is inseparable from the third mode of symmetry, which, for its part, works flush with the enunciative, deterritorialized, non-discursive and virtual matters. Which matters I have, once again, in distant reference to a category of contemporary physics, called 'internal irreversible dissymmetry',[2] immediately putting us under the aegis of the striation of Universes.

The striation of virtual Universes

Something that repeats, that affirms itself, that is neither localized, finite nor discursive but is nevertheless singular or, rather, irreversibly singularizing: this is what constitutes incorporeal Universes, which I have equally characterized as Universes of reference or Universes of enunciation. Paraphrasing Spinoza, I will say that it is in their essence to exist. Singularly self-affirming (*essentia particularis affirmativa*), they are established on this side of distinctive oppositions of the type $d^{+\infty}$, $d^{-\infty}$. (That is what led to the notation $d^{\pm\infty}$.) A singularization that is synonymous with the internal neccesitation that will give a new existential weight to Assemblages, which will energize them – energy being nothing other than a possible become necessary.

If one takes up Spinoza's modal distinctions, it may be said that at a molar level one remains in the regime of a finite mode, where essence remains distinct from existence. A module exists on condition that the other modules surrounding it 'authorize' it. On the other hand, it ceases to exist from the moment that they exclude it from their field of possibility. Putting to one side the pure and empty consistency of existential grasping, intrinsic determinability (D^i) here is entirely tributary to the extrinsic determinability (D^e) that passes through the cycle of Assemblages. It is the reign of real exo-referred coordinates (in the domain F), and of possibilistic legal constraints of all sorts (in the domain Φ). But this extraneousness of determinability must itself have an 'interior' base, a striation that is proper to it. The function of synapses, constituted from certain sections of Phyla diverted from their original purposes, is to produce this 'interiority' that places it under the regime of the infinite modal essence, which henceforth becomes indistinguishable from existence, or, rather, is such that essence becomes the motor of existence, existential energy (*infinita essendi fruitio*).

In truth, incorporeal Universes are less the effective source of an energetic irrigation of Assemblages than the place from which the energetic requalification of their different domains is brought about. But here we have to reconsider the status of the requalifications, which, from one step to the next, take us back as far as P^c, the Point of Contingencing of the domain of Flows. Effectively, it appears to us that these recursions do not have an occasional character but arise from a general procedure constitutive of Assemblages. Also, we will now call the movement of deterritorialization that has just led us from P^c to U (and which will later bring us back to F passing via T), *procession*, and the successive requalifications that, starting from U, concern the domains of Φ, F and T respectively, *recession* (Figure 7.6).

It will be noted that the movement of procession is diachronic-processual, whereas the recessive requalifications are synchronic-structural. The cycle of procession may be considered as one of reference and the cycle of recession as one of enunciation, or of the existential taking on of consistency.

This passage of the modalities of essentiation from finite to infinite is not sufficient to account for the striation of Universes. The latter is inseparable from the operations that lead to an ontological sliding, that is, the passage from a paradigm of reference to objects to a paradigm of aesthetic consistency – in any case, I can't see how to characterize it otherwise! Universes are not abstract universals.

What gives Universes consistency, what striates them, is the crystallization within them of a singular-singularizing Constellation, ΣU, the best illustrations of which are provided by Art more so than by cult practices. It is no small paradox that the obligatory route for energetic requalification is revealed to be homothetic to the promotion of the eternal return of aesthetic singularities.[3] But there is nothing surprising about this, really. Doesn't the spawning of smooth energies itself pass via the irreducibly singular incarnation that experimentation always constitutes? Cannot

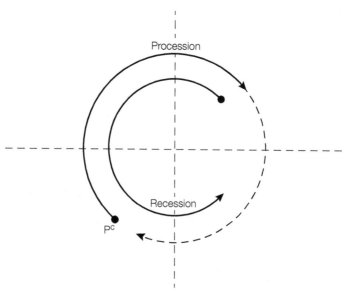

FIGURE 7.6 Procession and recession

technical and scientific setups be assimilated, on many points, to aesthetic performances, and, symmetrically, aren't works of art constructed in the same way as experiments? At the heart of these two registers, existential passages to the act are perhaps not as distant from each other as they seem to the positivist consciousness. Existential action – with a completely different impact to the communicational action of Habermas – operates in the aesthetic field according to a legality without law, the Universe of the beautiful, as Kant emphasized, becoming immanent to form itself. There is nothing of the sort in scientific discursivity, but from this point of view, what of the register of the production of scientific *enunciation*? Is it not under the aegis of singular Constellations of Universes of reference that Thomas Kuhn's famous paradigms[4] set themselves out in their epoch, in a way that is entirely comparable to aesthetic schools and currents?[5] But let us examine in more detail the nature of synapses, the mutational filters that, starting from Phyla, bring about the singularizing striation of Universes.

Synaptic dis-position

In Figure 7.7, we will find the same graph structure as in Figures 6.3 and 6.9, relating to the modular striation of Flows. This is only natural, as synapses integrate, at a deterritorialized level, the operations of existentializing break proper to refrains. But this integration brings with it several differences. The synaptic interval Φ_1'' and Φ_2 is no longer differential and indiscernible, as was the gap between F^{ts} and Se at the Point of Contingencing. On the contrary, it marks an explicit break/cut that is rich in content, albeit a mutilated, 'arbitrarialized' content, rendered a-signifying, that is to say, cut off from its syntagmatic bases and its paradigmatic ties. The whole question is one of knowing how such a content will manage to escape from its status of 'residue' to put itself in a new position of Expression and re-orient the anterior modes of apprehension of states of things. How it will be transmuted into the scene of a double cut/break and double articulation: on the side of the Phyla, with the fractal foldings to which it is latched, and, on the side of the Territories, with a new problematization of enunciation, that is to say, its hypercomplexification, correlative to the entry of components of self-reference. A synapse-scene, a scene-shifter, a dis-positional scene on which is played [out] not the quest, illuminated by divination or hermeneutics, for a lost meaning, but the crystallization of a singularizing Constellation of a Universe of reference (ΣU). It is on the basis of

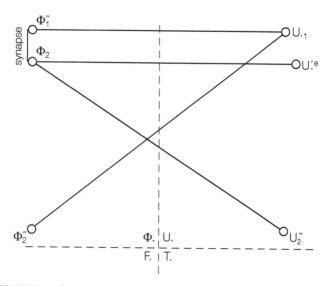

FIGURE 7.7 Synaptic disposition

this double break-bifurcation that we will have to rethink the ruptures of meaning carried off in oneiric discursivity, in symptoms, slips, jokes, etc., which Freud and his successors made undergo their well-known reductionist treatment, taking them for the effects of hidden complexal causes or of a structural play of signifiers, instead of recognizing their essential role in the mutations and metamorphoses of Assemblages of enunciation.

It is true that the Dadaists and, to a lesser extent, the Surrealists (lesser in so far as they were influenced by Freudianism) were in a better position to treat in a creative and open manner the 'optional matters' that these synapses constitute, dice throws whose outcome one is never prevented from influencing, by bending the surface they land on. Phenomenological psychiatry had tried hard to distinguish the symptom from the phenomenon: the symptom channelling the facticity of somatic and behavioural levels, and the phenomenon adorning itself with all the presumed virtues of lived structures.[6] Lacanian psychoanalysis, for its part, also really tried to detach the signifying function of the symptom from its role as 'bearer' of subjectivity ('a signifier represents the subject for another signifier'). But one was still left with the promotion of an abstract subject, working here as matheme of a structurally homogeneous unconscious (constructed in a 'Symbolic' order), constantly recentred there on individuated lived experience. Both remained perfectly incapable of accounting for concrete productions of subjectivity – essentially heterogeneous, multicentred processes, tributary to Assemblages of enunciation meshing with disparate, aleatory and/or historical realities, escaping as much from structural harmonics as from the hermeneutic music of the spheres.

Now, the question is neither to abstract out from signified content, nor to confer on it a separate and autonomous ontological status, but to determine its conversions, these latter no longer being hysteriform, as is the case for refrains, but paranoid, if one holds to this kind of metaphor. How does a problem come to play the game of a refrain in the register of incorporeals? The double, triple, nth game of a 'partialized' content which, whilst remaining attached to its original contingencing, opens up to new fields of virtuality, to new procedures of self-existentialization. How does a corpus of machinic Propositions Mp – this is the way that the phase spaces φ^c of the old expressive function henceforth find themselves requalified (through the recessive inversion of the cycle of the Assemblage, from U towards Φ and T) – represent the new, non-discursive and virtual instances of enunciation ΣU, without for all that denoting or signifying them? These machinic Propositions, as an integral of refrains, are bearers of the symmetric-fractal and deterritorialized representation of the ruptures of contingency, P^c. But they are not only a representation, they are also the effectuation of a pragmatic bifurcation, letting quanta of energy pass that, through concrete machinic operators, will lead to a fourth requalification of the Point of Contingencing,[7] P^c, as signs-particles (S^p).

Synaptic breaking thus diverts the 'natural' movement that, from fold to fold, led the Assemblage of enunciation towards its implosion at the heart of the Plane of Consistency, PoC (the Plane of absolute determinability). Requalified as a machinic Proposition by the mediation of a Constellation of Universes, a synapse blocks the relatively reversible fractalization of the expressive function E.C. so as to processualize the Assemblage of enunciation in the direction of the dissymmetries of Universes. This new abstract machinic Process f(Ma), which installs itself between the domains Φ and U, will be described on the basis of four dimensions, those of singularization, heterogenesis, necessitation and irreversibilization, represented in Figure 7.9, respectively, by the four 'recessive' angles that can be established – going in an anti-clockwise dimension – on the basis of the two diagonals of the square, FΦUT. The figure that is thus composed can also be visualized as a tetrahedron, which will serve us as a graph that is representative of the Abstract machines (Ma) populating the incorporeal Universes, in so far as the latter find themselves caught in a final recessive movement of requalification, this time starting from T.

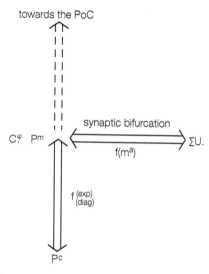

towards the PoC

synaptic bifurcation

$C_?^\varphi$ P^m

$\Sigma U.$

$f(m^a)$

$f\,^{(exp)}_{(diag)}$

Pc

FIGURE 7.8 Synaptic breaking

Singularization here is the deterritorialized equivalent of contingencing operating within sensible modules. It 'fastens' onto the surface of attraction Pm at a Point of Contingencing S^p. But a surplus value of possibility, which will irrigate the diagrammatic function (that is to say the 'other side' of the expressive function), corresponds to this fastening. This surplus value doesn't reside in a growth of positive determinability ($d^{+\infty}$), the fractal process of which is henceforth blocked (although not stratified), it doesn't correspond to a supplement of information, but to a sort of ontological stamp, a decreeing of existential *necessitation*, which constitutes its counterpart of determinability ($d^{-\infty}$) on the side of the axis ΣUT. The virtual enunciation singularized by a Constellation of a Universe (ΣU) thus confers an ontological necessity on the Phyla of possible which are [its responsibility] and which become regular by rights, cause, constant, invariant, imperative, unavoidable…This necessary possibility, I repeat – but will come back to it – also constitutes an energization of the Assemblage that is manifested by the conversion, at the Point of Contingencing, of signaletic Flows into Flows of Sign-particles.

Another implication of synaptic singularization is the establishing of an *irreversibility* of Assemblage processes. One finds again here the internal dissymmetry, announced earlier, concerning the very texture

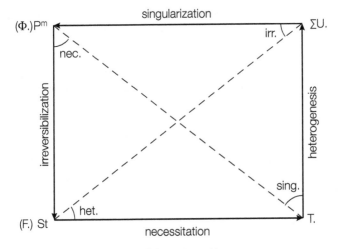

FIGURE 7.9 The tetrahedron of abstract machines

of deterritorialized enunciation. The latter, in effect, finds itself situated, ordered, dated by the singularizing figure that the machinic Proposition constitutes, without it ever being possible to come back to the same point. Hence the fact that the Constellations of Universes could be generically indexed by the signature of a proper name (e.g. Debussyism, Marxism…). It would nevertheless be wrong, on the basis of this state of affairs, to found a correlation between synaptic partialization and the partial character of the objects of the Freudian drive, the material consequence of a symbolic castration that is always lying in wait. It is true that synapses too, do indeed have the double function of delimiting fields of the possible whilst reinforcing their virtual scope, but they have nothing to do with a genetic engendering, nor with a 'corporeified' prop.

There remains the question of *heterogenesis*. In setting itself out to the exclusion of all other Constellations, a Constellation of Universes does not situate itself in relation to them in terms of a figure/ground relationship. It doesn't affirm its difference *against* the others but from its own interior, in an intensive mode of existential autonomization. It is from this taking on of ontological autonomy, this pure affirmation of a being-for-itself – the importation of which results from a requalification coming from the domain T – that the enunciative matrix of a heterogeneity, which one will find at work again in the four corners of the cycle of Assemblages, is born. So, it does not result from a comparative evaluation of distinct entitarian configurations, but from the taking on of consistency of a disparity, a dissymmetry without discursivity, without any pinpointing of alterity. By themselves, incorporeal Universes have no means at their disposal for recentring themselves, to belong to or position themselves in relation to one another. Heterogeneity and alterity are thus for them essentially generated on the basis of crystals of ontological self-affirmation (or hyper-complexity) that existential Territories constitute.

It was necessary to sketch out the viewpoint of the looping of the cycle of Assemblages in the domain T of non-discursive finitude in this way, before returning in a more detailed fashion to the diverse modalities of requalification. This was also in order to indicate the place, at the heart of the condition of the living, of, for example, procedures of individuation and speciation given their rhythm by birth, death, alterity, possibly sex and personal consciousness. Equally it was to indicate in what way these breaks, which, when all is said and done, are aberrant or, at the very least, disturbing, constitute relays of contingency, singularity and finitude that are indispensible to the capture of new fields of possibility.

8 ENUNCIATIVE RECURSION

Like a roundabout at a fairground, at each one of its pulsations, the procession of the cycle of Assemblages induces movements of recession that start up new domains and modify those previously concerned. Thus the Point of Contingencing turns out to be the object of four metamorphoses:

1 in the domain Φ, where it is deployed in a fractal fold E, the initiator of the diagrammatic function, f(diag);

2 in the domain U, where it works as an abstract refrain Ra, synapses functioning as a contingent relay for Constellations of Universes, f(syn);

3 in the domain T, where, echoing its ontic function on the F axis, it releases a pathic (or pathematic) function of self-reference on the axis TU;

4 in its own domain F, where, following a complete turn of the four quadrants after starting at its original position f^{ts} (the point for the application of the tensor mf of the modular function f(mod)), it is transformed into Sp, an energized Sign-particle that leads to the constitution of concrete existential machines, which arise from f(exi).

The point P thus finds itself at the crossroads of the set of functions mentioned previously: f(diag), f(syn), f(path), f(exi), and f(mod).

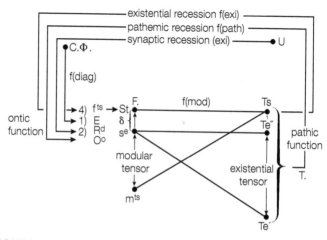

FIGURE 8.1 The four requalifications of the Point of Contingencing

Energetic requalifications

By inverting itself, by becoming a diagrammatic function f(diag), the expressive function f(exp) meshes directly with material flows, and becomes capable of catalysing machinic 'choices', such as feedback, and of bringing about changes of state correlative to energetic conversions. Already that is what is produced when the diagrammatic formula inscribed on my parking permit sets off the mechanism of the entrance barrier: it allows me to transit from a state 'outside' to a state 'inside'. Everything seems to happen as if one crossed two radically distinct thresholds: an an-energetic phase, of a semiotic character (for as long as the permit remains in my pocket), and another, energized phase, once the technical and organic machines (nervous system, muscle system, etc.) get going. At the beginning of Chapter 2, we announced that we would have to confront the aporia of a change of state without a transfer of energy. Here we are! But our first formulation must not be understood as implying the non-existence of charges of energy at the heart of the systems considered. It is simply a matter of a non-transferable energy, which finds itself in a paradoxical state of simultaneous hyper-deceleration and hyper-acceleration $d^{\pm\infty}$, precluding any distinctiveness and, as a consequence, any transfer from one point to another. I don't see any other means than to start from such a postulate. Whoever says change of state, or, more simply, any modification of anything at all (if only through the passive observation of the heterogeneity of one state of things in relation to another), necessarily says energy charge. I don't suppose that any physicist, supposing that she happens to ask herself this kind of question, could accept a departure from such a principle! Consciousness of the most contemplative alterity – that of Satori in Zen experience, for example – stirs up energies, even if they are infinitesimal! It is therefore difficult to object to the idea that signaletic matters and indexes of encoding, afferent to an evaluative enunciation, are energetically charged in such a way as to permit the recordings and memories that are the condition for any passage to the act. On the other hand, it will perhaps be objected that the energy in question lies in the matter of Expression and not in its form. However, it seems to me that such an objection would do nothing but push back the question of the 'gap'[1] existing between observable states of things, pragmatic states of things and the bridges that are established between them. It is better then to accept the position that form is also energy, although in a different way to that circulating in the Carnot cycle. If, in the course of the process one has to accept that complex Assemblages of semiotization come to have effects of great amplitude, then it is necessary to admit the existence, at the most elementary levels of encoding and signaletic expression, of energetically minimal quantum thresholds marking the passage to a register of machinic-pragmatic Effects.

The basic idea is that before any categorization of representation in terms of objectivity and subjectivity a point of view is an act and, at the very least, the prefiguring of an energized interaction. The radically deterritorialized and virtual act of enunciation that is constituted in U is no exception here. It is even this synaptic act (ΣU) that should furnish us with the pillars of the bridge that we are counting on setting up between energy and information. The possible Φ given by a synapse can be said, at one and the same time, to be:

- circumscribed, due to the fact that it results from a choice of traits of determinability, from a 'partialization' of the fields of possibility, which are no longer free to abolish themselves in the Plane of Consistency of determinability;
- fuzzy/vague, because it doesn't stop oscillating between two extreme speeds, either $d^{+\infty}$ when the phase components of the Phylum are in a continuous transition (or in a Rhizome), or $d^{-\infty}$, when these phase components are, on the contrary, disjunct (Figure 7.3).

Thus the cluster of possibilities given in ΣU turns out to be necessary everywhere without being actual anywhere. Here we are then, searching for an infinitesimal unlocalizable, non-separable energy, that is to say an energy that cannot be effectuated in an exclusive fashion in a particularized operation.

The four recursive causalities

Seen from [the point of view of] real chaos, the existence of a virtual chaosmosis could appear to be a fragile extrapolation. But henceforth, the taking into account of enunciative recursion imposes on us a consolidation of its cartographic status. One will even start from the idea that realized chaos is only an aleatory projection of infinitely differentiated and structured chaosmotic processes. Unlike the representation that one ordinarily has of chaos, chaosmosis escapes from the theory of discursive sets and arises instead from meta-modellings of what we will call aggregates or entitarian populations. The laws of internal composition of these populations cease to depend on rational principles of identity, contradiction, the excluded middle and sufficient reason.

In effect, for the fractal processuality that presides over their Assemblage, what is here and now can at the same time perfectly well not be, thus making the reality and virtuality of the same entitarian configuration overlap, implying a radical calling back into question of the concept of simultaneity. Two contradictory propositions can no longer be opposed to one another in as much as they can imply a veritable enunciative decentring and the contingent crossing of a threshold of veracity. In the last place, to suppose that one might persist in accepting that a well-defined play of causes has to correspond to every state of things, [explaining why] it is thus and not otherwise, henceforth, in the framework of this new logic of non-discursive spaces, one will have to admit some singular complications by virtue of the unavoidable heterogeneity of the causalities in question. In this regard, perhaps it is not too rash to try to make the four canonical forms of causality coincide with the four previously described operations of requalification which, beginning from the domains ΦUTF, converge on the Point of Contingencing P:

- *formal* causes correspond to the recession of diagrammatic irreversibilization resulting from the machinic Propositions Pm of the domain Φ;

- *final* causes, or abstract puttings into refrain, correspond to the synaptic recession of singularization, resulting from the Constellations of Universes ΣU of the domain U;

- *efficient,* or energizing, causes correspond to the pathemic recursion of heterogenesis resulting from the existential Territories Te of the domain T;

- *material,* or concrete machinic, causes correspond to the existential recursion and necessitation resulting from the sign particles S^p.

In view of these four modalities of recursive causality, how are matters with regard to our previous problem of the speed of determinability? Let us try, in a single overview, to take up again the definitions previously sketched out.

In the domain of sensible and signaletic Flows we have seen the coexistence of discursive formations striated into two types, associating, in modules of territorialization, bundles of reference series at a hyper-accelerated speed $d^{+\infty}$ between which phase spaces, or spaces where determinability at hyper-slow speeds $d^{-\infty}$ is suspended, are constituted. (cf. § 'The striation of the in-stantiation of Flows'). It is evident that such a striation is synonymous with the separation of two kinds of speeds of determinability. But what is less obvious is to consider that that is the only

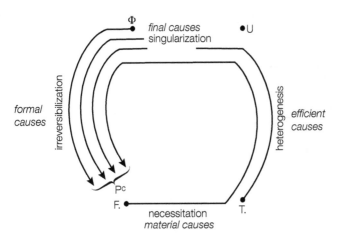

FIGURE 8.2 The four modalities of discursive causality (reprising of Figure 7.8 and Figure 7.9)

ontological case where it will be so, which implies, it has to be said, a radical calling into question of the notions of the instant and of simultaneity.

Let us now come back to our first approach to chaos. From now on we will be led to distinguish two sorts of state at the heart of the Plane of immanence, or the primordial soup of redundancies:

- one is of a discursive chaos implying an infernal disordering at an infinite speed $d^{+\infty}$ of determinability, which seems infinitely accelerated;

- the other is of a non-discursive chaosmosis (that is to say, without any extrinsically circumscribed reference, without any part-part or part-whole relation), which brings about a hyper-ordering at a seemingly infinitely decelerated speed of determinability $d^{-\infty}$.

Why this deceleration of chaosmosis, which confirms immutability? Because even infinite time would not suffice for it to attain its ideal of absolute determinability or, in other words, of unlimited complexification. Finding itself in this way at a perpetual tangent to itself, it is constituted, here and everywhere else, in virtual tension. Always the smile of Alice's Cheshire Cat, in the four corners of the cosmos and nowhere in particular! And it is precisely in this nexus of paradox that the chaotic state joins up with the chaosmotic state, its extreme inverse, the latter only being established at the end of an infinite processual duration, the former dissolving at the first instant. Everything has already dissolved, without there being time to catch a breath! Lapses of time – however short one imagines them to be – like the night of horizonless time, are victims of the same deterritorializing crack that projects them all outside of some attestable real into pure Universes of virtuality. Consequently, it is the very idea that an instant might diachronically run the length of a duration or institute a relation of simultaneity astride two processes that tends to lose its relevance outside purely speculative pathways. It is this irreducible ambivalence $d^{\pm\infty}$ that we are seeking to determine in the cartographic canton called the Constellation of Universes (ΣU).

From the point of view of the speed of determinability, it still remains for us to specify what happens to the entities located in the domains Φ and T. It is appropriate to examine these questions conjointly so as to draw out a symmetrical characteristic in their mode of response, in so far as they pull the modular economy in contrary directions:

- that of a discontinuous fractalization, marked by phase spaces φ working at a speed $d^{+\infty}$ (the domain Φ);

- that of another fractalization, but a continuist one at a speed $d^{-\infty}$ towards pathic operators (the domain T).

Let us first take the latter domain. It is at a speed $d^{-\infty}$ that the striation of the instantiation of flows sorted and separated the reference series or traits of determinability $d^{+\infty}$ within modules, introducing a discontinuity that will be proper to sensible and signaletic registers. One can say that here negative determinability integrates positive determinability ($d^{-\infty} \int d^{+\infty}$). At this stage of the ontology of modules, there is a territorialized circumscription of positive determinations without any explicit recapturing of this circumscription as such. There is simply a negative power of freezing and of the selection of positive traits.

On the other hand, on the side of Φ we have a phase surface φ functioning at a speed $d^{+\infty}$ that recaptures $d^{-\infty}$ negativity, or rather negativities (Figure 6.7). There is a taking on of consistency, a deterritorialized circumscribing of traits that were and that remain diffuse, powdery and unlocalizable...Such a taking on of fractal-molecular consistency defines the Phyla as the integration of negative determinability ($d^{+\infty} \int d^{-\infty}$).

The question of speeds of determinability can presently be summarized by Figure 8.3. That being so, it is clear that we still have too static a description, which still doesn't allow us to confront the difficult question of intermediate temporalizations, which we can longer put off tackling!

Intermediate temporalities

Temporalities that are intermediate between what? Between behaviours of pure discursivity, which are knotted together around those machinic Propositions that are 'chronic' and those that are set out/arranged in a single non-discursive block as an existential Territory (durations). On the one hand, a pseudo-temporality, a pencil-and-paper, or computer-assisted, time; on the other, a unary, Parmenidian time. Between the two, temporalities of subjectification flying past indefinitely in the cursor-ring of a fixed instantaneity. This will be lived, on the one hand, as a trans-processual simultaneity as allowed by myths and meta-modellings objectifying a 'world', and on the other, fecund 'synaptic' moments that singularize a presence in the present, through the finalizing tensions at the horizon of Constellations of Universes.

But what use is a temporality with four dimensions? Immediately it might be said that one cannot confer enough heterogeneity on it, that is

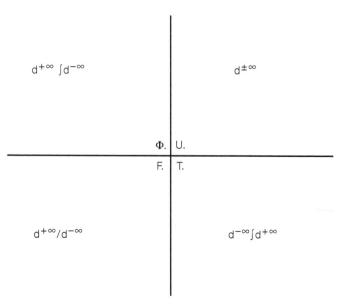

FIGURE 8.3 Speed of determinability

	Singularization Synaptic function Final cause (fecund moments)	
Φ.		U.
Irreversibilization Diagrammatic function Formal cause (objective time)		Heterogenesis Pathemic function Efficient cause (subjective temporalization)
F.	Necessitation Existential function Material causes (durations)	T.

FIGURE 8.4 Temporality in four dimensions

to say, occasions for singularizing its enunciation. Anything but the unidimensionality of a temporalisation reduced to the informational linearity of capitalistic Chronos, a devouring power of translatabilization and of bringing into a generalized equivalence of modes of discursivity, regimes of temporalization and existential durations! It will thus pertain to mythic, aesthetic, schizophrenic and other meta-modellings to map the montages of temporal components, with a base of modules and refrains, etc. that contribute to the speciation of concrete Assemblages of enunciation. However, let us note that when I propose here a description with four dimensions, I am in no way pretending that it is necessary to go through them to explore the chemistry of enunciation! I only intend to indicate that one cannot tackle this domain in the style of naïve or philosophically 'armed' phenomenologists. Times are composite and call incessantly for recompositions on the basis of the most diverse instrumentations and experiments. How is one to spot that it is such and such a type of component that, in such and such an economic context, will get the upper hand? How is one to put to work the procedures of ethico-ethical subjectification that will orient them differently? What conjunction of components can result in the ephemeral or durable metamorphosis, implosion or destabilization that we call birth, death, desire, madness...? Being and time are thus obliged to give precedence to enunciation. Is that not already how Parmenides can be understood when he writes:

> the act of thinking and the object thought are the same thing. Without Being, in which it is uttered, the act of thinking cannot be found; because outside Being nothing is and nothing will be, Destiny trammels it so it is one and immobile.[2]

Is it licit to consider that what is in question is nothing other than the being of enunciation, unary Aïon that Parmenides – unlike Heidegger – has no reason to relate to an ontology anchored in an archaeology of the language of his ancestors (which in all likelihood he didn't care about, any more than he did the gods that his ancestors had the habit of venerating). One could equally locate four causal powers down this same path, the 'goddesses of goods': Diké for the formal causes incarnated in the abstract Machinic propositions of our domain Φ; Moïra, for final causes, this 'accursed share that the initiated can transform into a fecund moment of creative freedom', in the domain U; Ananké, for the causes materializing the circumscription of existential finitude; and faced with all three, the chaosmic hubris of the efficient causes of auto-enunciation. The intersecting of discursive temporalities with existential durations does not go without saying. It is not mechanical, it must be brought about, assembled. An example: at the wheel of my car, I drive drowsily, on 'auto-pilot'. Diverse organic and perceptual temporalities are then at work in a relatively autonomous fashion, in a direct relation of cybernetic enslavement to the machine and the landscape that speeds past. On the one hand, the decelerated duration of diurnal reverie, on the other, an extreme vigilance for the slightest indicator of an incident. Besides, such an incident can connect machinic durations and temporalizations back together again – I mean, really wake me up! Another example: a teacher or even a high-level researcher, who is perfectly at ease in his 'niche' but is literally 'disconnected' in others: dealing with a sudden passion or simply just getting through an airport! What does this kind of intersection consist of? Essentially, it consists in the Assemblage (through the mediation of two operations which have already been defined as fractal-processual-discursive and fractal-recessual-non-discursive) of two distinct chaosmic and modular regimes at the heart of the chaotic soup of the Plane of Consistency.

The chaosmic-synaptic state occurs when an Aïonic temporal tension is constituted, that is to say, when a field of virtuality invades a state of things in a hegemonic fashion, without any concern for the three stratas of before, during and after. The fecund moment of delirium, according to François Tosquelles, the instant of seeing, according to Jacques Lacan, a

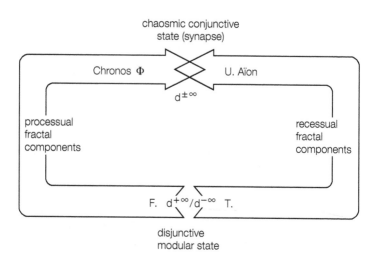

FIGURE 8.5 Chronos and Aïon (repetition of Figure 8.3)

minute of eternity for the Surrealists, Zen Satori, or, more simply, in the field of perception, a gestalt switch...One will note here a new definition of the virtual as the possibility of the possible, as that which existentially authorizes the deployment of a field of possibility, the trigger of a line of discursivity that is itself non-discursive, instituting itself prior to the opposition discursivity/non-discursivity.

The disjunctive modular state, by contrast, secretes its temporalities in a dependence on Aïonic times. A paradoxical dependence as properly speaking, there isn't any effect, counter-effect or interaction between the two types of temporality. All that can be said is that one is the existential condition of the other. When, however, a Chronic time seems to free itself from all Aïonic protection, when it seems to belong only to itself, it is because it has passed into the care of a Constellation of Universes reduced to its simplest expression. A uni-dimensionalized Constellation, a capitalistic Constellation, that, moreover, does not necessarily rise up at the end of a dialectically troubled history, but is outlined at the dawn of the 'Urstaat' of Neolithic times.

Enunciative fractalization

To clarify this enigmatic intersection between intermediate temporalities, we must return to the fractal nature of their texture. The relations between the discursivity of Flows (F) and its capitalization as possibilistic Phyla (Φ) have been described previously in terms of fractal sweeping/scanning. It will be recalled that this sweeping didn't only concern the field of the possible but led equally to the postulation of a passage between molar structures and the molecular operators that work them indirectly by means of the establishment of an infinitesimal deterritorialized continuum (which was then assimilated to a diminishing 'magic skin' baker transformation).

But this provisional description was only called on to take consistency from the moment that another, non-discursive, fractal procedure was introduced, corresponding to the existential positionality of Aïonic Universes operating in the register of enunciations. Let us patiently take up the analysis of these procedures of temporalization again.

Chronic fractalization concerns the systemic articulations and lines of possibility relative to the discursivity of Flows on the basis of attractors that in some way constitute pseudo-territories or deterritorialized Phyla. With Aïonic fractalization, it is no longer a question of territorialized or deterritorialized circumscription at all. It is as if, going against the grain, Aïonic fractalization pushed back down the splinters of time, preventing it from being marked in any way. One crosses a tangent, that of 'infinitesimalizing' reduction, with it. Beyond this limit, a-signifying synapses, which are simultaneously irreversibilizing, singularizing, heterogenesizing and necessitating, push us from the world of memories of redundancies embedded in extrinsic coordinates, into Universes of pure intensive iteration, which have no discursive memory since their very existence acts as such. Synapses can thus be considered operators of 'active forgetting', of existentializing eternal return. Redundancy doesn't stop calling for an extrinsic – syntagmatic and/or paradigmatic – circumscription, even if the latter is engaged in a process of deterritorializing 'shrinkage'. On the other hand, existential iteration remains pure Parmenidian immanence[3] – it has neither inside nor outside, neither figure nor ground, it is a pure body without organs, a pure self-referential affirmation. Existential synapses work as operators for the crossing over of Chronic and Aïonic temporal drives functioning in contrary directions (Figure 8.5). They also constitute a bridge, generating components of passage between the molar registers of discursive sets and molecular registers of non-discursive intensity.

In the Chronic direction, discursivity articulates molar sets or statistical collections according to the principles (Figure 8.6) of:

- envelopment conferring the preeminence of one subset over another;
- the differential solidarity of subsets with regard to sets not participating in the same referent;
- the threshold of rupture and passage between the elements of a subset participating both in the referent of reference and heterogeneous other referents;
- reference transcending each set; the different referents themselves being referred to broader systems of coordinates.

Whilst capitalistic coordinates – of generalized equivalency – are translatable in general energetico-spatio-temporal terms, there are other meta-modelling coordinates that can coexist with their predecessors and which can be more...mythical, or ideological, if one prefers.

In the Aïonic direction, one is dealing more with a discursivity referred to an external context, as there are enunciative instances agglomerated to it. Instead of a fractalization by the encompassing of distinct sets maintaining relations of contiguity, prolonging one another, one is dealing with a non-proximal fractalization, a sort of frozen existential grasping of heterogeneous enunciative nuclei. Enunciative fragments, part or partialized enunciations whose monads are not just separated in time, space and by energetic basin (in so far as they are not directly concerned with these categories of reference), but additionally find themselves heterogenized by the intensive qualities that they happen to be affected by.

Energetico-spatio-temporal coordinates established a referential continuum between separated sets; their operations were deployed at the scale of these sets; it is no longer the same with the operators of intensity or intensification, which work in a dimension of molecular non-separability, the intervention of which is situated at the heart of the enunciative processual genesis of the forms and contents deployed.

In parallel, one must consider, on the one hand, the expansion (or universion) of intensive ordinates, with neither limit, nor time, nor space, nor energy – a sort of hegemonic megalomania proper to each enunciative monad. And, on the other hand, one must consider the fact that there can be no endpoint in the molecular quest for their operator, which recedes towards an infinitesimal tangent seized from their machinic essence. This is to say that unlike the EST operators, intensities and the abstract Machines that pilot them are not on the same level. No ultimate quantum of form, no universal morphogenesis will give us their key. It is a matter of existential qualities that self-organize at the root of being, however far

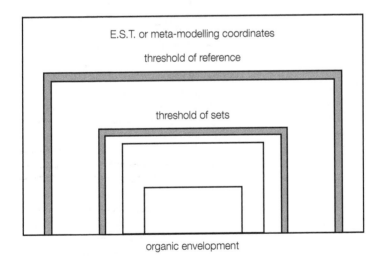

FIGURE 8.6 Chronic discursivity

one considers their genericness to extend. If we attempt to determine a possible foundation for the mode of non-discursive distinctiveness of enunciative monads, the condition of an infinite molecular fractal regression is imposed on us here. By virtue of the fact that they escape from the categories of relation and interaction, it will have to be admitted at the same time that:

1 they have nothing to do with one another, and are thus absolutely distinct;

2 they are nevertheless absolutely indistinct, in such a way that one gains access to them by immediate transferential apprehension, or knowing by affect.

Thus: a hegemony of Affect and an endless flight backwards. If it is licit to characterize domains of complexity succinctly as domains inhabited by principles of incompleteness and uncertainty, those domains whose systemic determination takes flight in a fractal molecular mode, opening up as an abstract machinic chasm, can be characterized as hyper-complex. That this flight 'backwards', this molecular implosion, may find a sort of accomplishment with pragmatic sensori-motor and cognitive memories, in no way implies its non-existence in the 'primitive' regions of machinic Phyla. The place that thus finds itself opened up to chaos, to the aleatory at the heart of the enunciative constitution of the ensemble of the objects of the world, requires that on this side of the structures of determination and predictability (structural territorialization) another virtual level of systemic resumption (systemic deterritorialization) is always outlined.

This active flight demands the assistance of catalytic operators, that is to say operators that remain external to the essence of the process set off. Elsewhere, apropos of the photographs of Keiichi Tahara, I have examined the way that the frame, the framing, the cutting out of forms and of light and Barthes's punctum can function as a machinic index to set off the fractal deterritorialization of a portrait. But this function can operate in a bloc, on the basis of a single relay. In a more general fashion, it is faciali-tarian deterritorialization that functions as a substantial relay for all taking on of signification. The apprehension of meaning is essentially correlative to the facification of a state of things and its horizon. The face of sense and its non-discursive dimension of human comprehensibility is given in a single block. A world hollows itself out infinitely so as to engender transverse relations between heterogeneous Universes of reference in a single moment of impact. The production of subjectivity is nothing other than this fractal machinics of faciality inexorably caught up in a becoming-abstract. A machine of self-exo-reference that knows neither ground nor endpoint to its implosiveness, the better to encompass the totality of the world. The possibility of a 'this side of' must always be preserved. Every element on which it relies is only a trivial intermediary susceptible of substitution, of transposition. Such is the definition of a machinic montage. One will never encounter a basic building block, the ultimate quantum. Today, the element of the living machine is the organ, the cell, the chains of organic chemistry, the building blocks of atoms. Tomorrow it will be particles, quarks… without it being possible to fix an endpoint to this recursion. Essence, act, Aristotelian energeia presuppose the tangential passage of logics of discursivity towards abstract machines of enunciation. It is only by taking into account an irreducible becoming traversing every established ordering that one can return to the apprehension of the differential qualities on the basis of which algorithmic analyses of science are founded.

In relation to the supposedly objectivist descriptions of the human and social sciences, the interest of the operators of schizoanalytic meta-modelling consists in the possibility that they offer of spotting the impact of enunciative processes on…through…in the opposite direction to, the signaletic and sensory weft that paradigmatico-syntagmatic coordinates 'normally' circumscribe. Our speculative cartography of Assemblages of enunciation has led us to four categories of 'enunciative breakthrough', which reach the Flows, Phyla, Universes and Territories from the chaosmos (Figure 8.7). To finish, it remains for us to group together their characteristics.

As a final anticipation, Figure 8.8 represents the stakes of the grasping of these four fundamental dimensions of enunciative hyper-complexity.

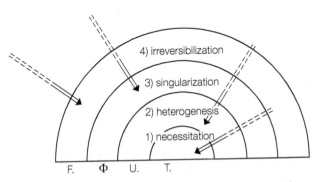

FIGURE 8.7 The four meta-modelling operators

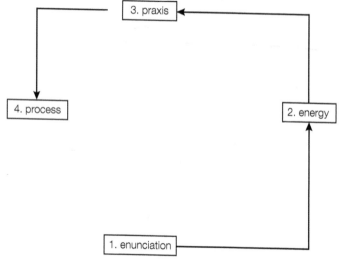

FIGURE 8.8 Enunciative hyper-complexity

Necessitation

At the heart of enunciation a choice for finitude is found, an attachment, without any support, to everything and to nothing with a view to constituting a world. When we examined it previously, we saw modular striation apprehended Flows in a Chronic sense, entirely polarized towards their com-position as deterritorialized Phyla. But here, in the opposite, Aïonic direction, these same Flows no longer have recourse to phase spaces (φ) as extrinsic guarantors of a modular endo-consistency. Dispositional enunciation has no other basis than itself, that is to say, it rests on nothing tangible. By grasping, by pure existential self-affirmation, it certainly relates to other Universes of reference but in a mode that is now non-causal, non-interactive. That is why I define it as pure, sui generis, necessitation. Ignoring every division between inside and outside, modules cannot delimit themselves from one another either. However, that does not prevent them from being affirmed through one another – hence the quality of their intensive becoming established here, which in the subsequent stage will generate an enunciation by generalized transference. The fact that sensible ex-modules now find themselves monadized, if we can put it like that, on the basis of a fractal umbilicus, with no support of any kind, with neither internal nor background world, without either organ or external context, so as to affirm themselves existentially as an empty repetition, to make refrains [ritournellise] in an a-signifying mode, leads them moreover to an irrevocable molecularization (their holographic facet, a metaphor dear to Edgar Morin when he deals with complexity). However they are divided up, however small they are, they still harbour the ensemble of determinations of the whole (determinations that are, for all that, essentially extrinsic D^e) . It is the material texture of Assemblages, in its most intimate grain, that is called on to speak. To say what? Essentially, its own existence, prior to any discursive attribute, an existence that is no less fundamentally 'qualitative'. Whilst in a fractal mode, the determinability $d^{-\infty}$ was free to flee into deterritorialized Phyla, it now finds itself prisoner of an eternitarian duration. What is repeated is no longer a constant of signification but a scheme for the necessity of existence at every instant.[4] Necessitation is thus a resumption of modular contingency when it has been deterritorialized and emptied of its discursivity. It is the persistence of the break at the heart of the discursive fabric, a persistence haunted by the birth-death finitude proper to every non-trivial machine.

But now is the time to offer some illustrations of this register of necessitation, no doubt.

To start with the simplest illustration, let us consider the discrepancy between the form constituted between the inside and outside of a house and the existential Assemblage able to take note of it. For me personally, I have to walk at least 800 metres before I really perceive, through visual adjustments and, above all, by the pattern of air coming into my lungs, that I have effectively left my compartment. Starting from this limit zone, the matter of the outside starts properly to be expressed through my affects, reveries and thoughts.

An equally modular and prototypical passage to the act, if ever there was one, is that of Gottfried Galle, the astronomer of the Berlin Observatory, who graciously agreed to verify the calculations of Le Verrier relative to the presumed trajectory of Neptune, even though some months previously John Couch Adams, a young English astronomer, who had arrived at the same result, found that the astronomer royal, George Biddell Airy, would refuse to take into account his hypotheses.

I am also thinking of the hold of pubescent hormonal speech (correlative to the maturing of the gonads) over the ensemble of temporalization refrains of an adolescent. Or the comparable impact of a 'machinic matter' linked to typing, learning to drive a car, playing an instrument or simply just watching a football match on the telly…And finally, the opening up of virtualities without shores for a subjectivity invested in a poetic matter of expression…

Heterogenesis

Between T and U, along with their crystals of self-organization, pathic operators of heterogenesis bring the entropic dimension. They confer a pseudo-identity on energy sites, with neither contour nor constitutive parts, with no possible 'identificatory' relation, but whose ontological grasping is no less imperative and hegemonic when encountering the slightest alterity. In other words, they are much more the intensive affirmation of a for-itself than the positionality of a difference. We will examine heterogenesis as: the scenic apparatus of the intensities it puts to work; a specific fractal process; existential dating; knowledge by transference; a partial nucleus of self-reference; and a proto-energetic basin.

Through heterogenesis, hegemonically existentializing singular positions find themselves in some way 'negotiated'. We must accept here the paradox of an intensive differentiation as a part of self-ordered systems. Reference is secreted by the system and yet it is not without relation to that of other systems. Everything happens not through composition or the play of elements *partes extra partes*, but through a setting out [disposition] in which each point is the centre of reference for the whole. The gaze constituted by the stage or by video (such as it is at work in family therapy) is prototypical of this dis-position. Here, the elements captured in the scene do not interact (as systems theorists imprudently declare) but enter into existential agglomeration. They are not simply apprehended from the outside, because the enunciative Assemblage is constituted in whole or in part by this fact of being looked at. The flight of the gaze doesn't necessarily have a voyeuristic-persecutionary function here, as the scene apprehends both territorially endogenous and extra-territorially heterogeneous elements of dehiscence. The scene functions like a sponge, if you like, which soaks up a certain type of scattered, deterritorialized being-there.

With heterogenesis, two types of relations are thus differentiated:

- modular, serial and finite relations (FT);
- fractal, non-proximal and infinite relations (TU).

In both cases one is dealing with modes of self-existentialization, but the first are intrinsically territorializing and the second intrinsically deterritorialized (or deterritorialized-deterritorrializing). This second figure of existentialization is no longer territorially enslaved to extrinsic coordinates but has become tributary to processual ordinates. In so doing, its forms have become infinitely transposable and translatable, separated from the status of structure to become a matter for abstract machines. It is no longer just the topological dimensions that are fractalized here but also the dimensions of time and substance. By this new fractal procedure, sensible and abstract qualities invent original relations of transversality. The pathic operators of the Proustian 'Search' clearly indicate to us the recursive paths of temporal passage between 'times' that are distant from one another and between heterogenesized substances (the flavour of the madeleine, the movement between the bells of Martinville, the play between the wasp and the orchid, Vinteuil's little phrase, etc.). We not dealing here with the simple observation of heterogeneity but with a labour of heterogenesis; each dimension demands to be discernibilized, deployed in all its virtualities. Whilst the energetico-temporo-topographical coordinates implied legal transcendent constraints, the scopic dis-position, on the contrary, accommodates aleatory factors in the immanence of the Assemblage. The link that it institutes is an existential glue steeped in molecular bifurcations and degrees of freedom, which it owes to the fact that its fractal folding is no longer formal but operates as an aporetic junction between heterogeneous qualities each one bearing a destiny.

Like an existential stamp, heterogenesis marks the fractal dating of the regime of de- and re-territorialization of an Assemblage of enunciation. This dating, that I will characterize as hyper-fractal, is not relative to the numbering of a fold, like a figure for morphogenetic complexity, but to an abstract formula, the crystal of an event, regulating transversal passageways between different registers. In this regard, the date of the 'Search' is the instant that the narrator's foot steps onto the wobbly paving stone in the courtyard at Guermantes, allowing passageways between the different expressive components, harmony, polyphony and melody together, that inhabit Proust. Qualitative hyper-fractalization thus agglomerates the heterogeneous qualifications in counterpoint to the topographical synaptic fractalization producing new, artificial procedures of subjectification. A matter of expression will find itself invaded by a whole worldliness [mondanéité], as if haunted by an enunciating subjectivity. (The image that comes to mind is that of the toys and utensils that start vibrating as the extra-terrestrials pass by in the Spielberg film *ET*. Except that this invasion is not as sudden. It is the occasion for a deceleration of the regimes of determinability properly constitutive of intermediate temporalities.) One should recall that from T to U one passes from a regime of determinability (or fractality, which amounts to the same thing) separating $d^{+\infty}$ and $d^{-\infty}$ (a modular regime) to a regime where the determinabilities $d^{\pm\infty}$ do not hang together, slide over one another (a synaptic regime). As fractal deterritorialization precedes, or rather, regulates time, it is this stopping and starting of determinability that sets the tempo of this music. The abstract refrains of the component of singularization (which we will come back to further on) are the baton that conducts the starting and stopping of determination, the passage of qualities that have to speak. For example, life can just as easily be considered a decelerated oxidization at the junction of physico-chemical strata as an acceleration of complex chemical eco-system at 37 degrees Centigrade. Depending on the angle one takes, it is an acceleration or a deceleration of determinability which for itself is infinitely slow or infinitely fast – the notion of speed only being relevant at the scale of existential Territories.

This heterogenesis of intensities may seem aberrant, to the point that it will be objected that they escape from the 'normal' modalities of knowledge. And it is true that it is a matter of a knowledge through non-discursive affects. It must, for example, be admitted that the encounter with schizophrenia never results from a cognitive deduction, but is established immediately as an entering into psychotic ordinates. It is the same with aesthetic illumination. A whole background is doubtless necessary for approaching the threshold of enunciation concerned, but crossing this threshold always occurs in one go. Knowledge of the other and knowledge through the other are a continuation of each other. It is at the same time that a musical work informs me and forms me in my capacity and competence for being informed. Affect should stop being thought of as a raw energetic matter. In fact, it is a hyper-complex object, rich with all the fields of potentiality it can open up. The Affect of love, for example, is not resolved at the end of the expectation of a libidinal 'discharge'. By definition it is loaded with the unknown worlds at the crossroads of which it places us. It is a matter here of a generalized transference, which doesn't just concern 'identifiable' persons, but also things, animal and cosmic becomings, whose partial affects see me and whose pathic indices watch me, like a Sphinx at a bend in the path. This gaze is not a simple accident or an avatar of the Superego, it is essentially faciality, as the substance of all humanly significant sense. Every affect is an ambiguous part-man, part-woman, part-animal facilitarian becoming…It looks at me in a strange way, it's after me, it's doing me in [ça me perd], it finds me again at all the crossroads of sense… Like children, psychotics and the 'archaic', the concrete elucidation of heterogenesis should teach us how to decipher the atmospheric alterities that haunt the affective horizons of the living world and its cosmic becomings again.

Heterogenesis brings Affect out of its passivity by conferring on it a power of self-genesis and self-reference. Topographical fractalization was always fixed somewhere on a frozen crest that constituted the delineation of a world. It is no longer the same with the enunciative fractalization that engenders Universes without limits, which ignores all ultimate atomic elements in such a way that it turns round on itself at a molecular tangent to make itself an infinite operative power of subjectification. It takes up the reins: everything seems to stem from it in the rewriting of states of things, but everything of the aleatory, bifurcation, freedom, which then finds itself effectively imported into the Assemblage, really does come from it.

The last point relating to heterogenesis is the equation that it establishes:

$$\text{Enunciation} = \text{Proto-Energy}$$

Our quadrature of enunciation on the basis of the functors FΦTU is not intended to lead back to the classic Kantian opposition of sensibility and understanding, even if it is mediated by a schema. Synaptic refrains, like modular refrains, effectuate abstract machinic Propositions and sign systems directly, by incarnating them in material and existential operations. The fact of sketching out new arrangements for them, whether or not they are accompanied transfers of energetic basins, implies they are loaded with a molecular proto-energy, whose existence I have already conjured up apropos of semiotic energies. Simply to utter a semiotic repetition implies a proto-energetic tension. Let's give an example. After having twice thrown a six, every new dice throw will tend, with growing probabilitarian tension, to 'avoid' the 'excessive' repetition of the same number, a relationship of equiprobability haunting the previous set of dice throws like an entropic horizon. One is in the presence of a deterritorialized virtual energy whose impact on territorialized 'real' energy is perfectly apprehendable. If, by contrast, I happened to throw an 'abnormal' series of sixes, this might signify that the dice was loaded – let us say that it would be playing a singular game in relation to its functional definition. Through trickery, singularization would result in unforeseen potentialities – winnings, for example. By crossing a singular proto-energetic level, a new Constellation of a Universe of reference opens up before me (unjustified winnings – transgression – lies – betrayal – guilt – punishment, etc.). If one can put it like this, the series of sixes takes power in a whole complex Assemblage. Such a proto-energetic investment could be described in modalities as different as:

- the drive;
- the indices constituted by slips of the tongue, etc.;

- displacement, condensation, overdetermination in the primary process of the dream;
- narrative tension;
- contemplative, objectless effusion in the experience of Satori.

Singularization and irreversibilization

Determinability is information before it is assigned a referent. In effect information is always information about something for someone or for a receiver. However, even if determinability remains infinitesimally scattered and powdery (as the ontological status of incorporeal Universes requires), it is nonetheless affected with a pseudo-organization, a virtual dis-position, by virtue of the synaptic Propositions that place it in a Constellation. Assuming that it comes to be stratified within sensible modules – and this supposition is always latent, on the surface of the possible – then the virtual Constellation of traits of determinability loses its fuzziness ($d^{\pm\infty}$) and one passes from incorporeal dis-position to territorialized relations between an instantiation $d^{-\infty}$ and a dis-tantiation $d^{+\infty}$. Virtuality thus 'conserves' the phantom of the stratified state of entities but it is a baroque phantom, subject to infinite substantial and topological metamorphoses that are open to the most exotic of marriages – of the 'sexual relations' between the wasp and orchid type – that can be concocted for it by the Rhizome of machinic Propositions. Whatever the case may be, caught in a Constellation, determinability ($d^{\pm\infty}$) does not have the same freedom as that which errs at the heart of the chaosmos. It is on deterritorialized tracks. It is obliged to respect the principles of irreversibilized ordering, contingentialized constants such as π or Avogadro's number. The changes of register – from physics to chemistry, for example – which I call transfers of basin, are not prohibited but will open up a completely different problem, precisely that of the conversion-conservation-degradation of energies. How does virtual molecular proto-energy ($d^{\pm\infty}$) manage to 'disentangle' itself into $d^{+\infty}$ and $d^{-\infty}$, to pass back through the wall of fractal deconstruction (f(diag)), to invest its capital base of proto-heterogeneity in processes of amplification and multiplication, in order to catalyse and pilot the molar movements of great energy? It should pertain to the concrete machinic requalification to answer this question. A new conversion, which is no longer hysterical nor paranoid but could instead be linked to the schizo process, in so far as it includes a position of reality that is predisposed to all mutations, even the catastrophic.

Synapses result, then, from a rupture in the (relative) reversibility existing between the expressive and the diagrammatic functions. Instead of a simple round trip between the fractal 'descent' of expression and diagrammatic 'ascent' towards the Point of Contingencing (P^c), there is a remainder, an enunciative surplus-value constituting the synaptic effect and through which the irreversibility of energetic entropy rushes. Something will never return; the process is dated, by a proper name, for example. Synapses are thus deterritorialized releases of enunciation and, as such, constitute the incorporeal integrals of sensible refrains.

Through the phantasm, the complex, the archetype...it is already something of this nature that psychoanalysts aimed at. But their aim was not abstract enough, not deterritorialized enough; their feet remained stuck in libidinal clay and materialized determinations. They did not see that matter is also able to speak in the name of hyper-complexity. In fact, it is a matter of certain machinic Propositions breaking their mooring in signifying and diagrammatic functions so as to set to work on the count of two pathemic and existential enunciative functions. This gear change of enunciation may seem a very simple, primary thing, like starting a countdown by pressing a button. But the schematic character of elementary decisionality masks its real dimensions. What happens in fact is the crossing of a threshold of consistency: that of the dis-position of the enunciative scene on the basis of which a Constellation of a Universe of reference can operate. The synapse stamps its 'seal' of the taking on of consistency on it. It initiates a self-enunciative procedure through its character as a caesura, as a-signifying catalysis.

But one can also view things from another angle. Everything derives from the fact that the ultimate reference point is cracked, that absolutely consistent Alterity (the big Other) does not exist. It is from this relativity of alterity that a differential enunciation through enunciative fragments, scattered to the four corners of the cosmos, originates. It speaks in the margin; a self-organizing process can be set off where nothing precise could be expected. In this regard, the Russian Formalists had clearly detected the importance of the uncoupling of form and content ('formalism considers so-called content as one of the aspects of form'[5]). Moreover, it is not a question of making this a simple observation but of putting in gear analytic praxes on that basis. What may be in question is, for example, perhaps a labour of form consisting in 'slowing' it down, in darkening it, in 'making it visible by increasing the difficulty and duration of perception', in short, all the procedures of 'defamiliarization'[6] that will give so many meta-modelling materials that can permit an initiatory enunciation to take off.

	Necessitation	Heterogenesis	Singularization	Irreversibilization
Domain of origin	F	T	U	Φ
Recession	existential f(exi)	pathemic f(path)	synaptic f(syn)	diagrammatic f(diag)
Causality	material	efficient	final	formal
Mythographic reference	Ananke	Hubris	Moira	Dike $_\cdot$
Determinability	$d^{+\infty} / d^{-\infty}$	$d^{-\infty} \int d^{+\infty}$	$d^{\pm\infty}$,	$d^{+\infty} \int d^{-\infty}$
Temporalization	durations	dates	fecund moments	objective times

FIGURE 8.9 Enunciative dimensions

THE REFRAINS OF BEING AND SENSE
(Analysis Of The Dream About A.D.)

That the nonsense of the dream has a possible use goes back to the oldest forms of subjectification. Syntagmatic ruptures, semantic proliferations, pragmatic inductions: there is no domain of the dream that cannot play a bifurcating role with regard to the dominant significations and norms of the waking state. My aim here is to show that, from the moment that one opts for a model of the unconscious that is open to the future and is broadened out to the heterogeneous semiotic components that can interfere in it, there is no reason to oppose two logics, one of the primary process relating to latent content and one of repression as the condition for access to consciousness. The signifying distortions of the dream no longer arise from an interpretation of its deep contents but participate in a machinics on the surface of its text. The part objects that work it are not mutilated by a symbolic castration but are at work as autonomized operators of subjectification. The cutting, the breaking of sense is only a manifestation of a subjectification in the nascent state. It is the fractalization that is necessary and sufficient for something to occur where everything was closed. It is a deterritorializing opening.

To illustrate this problematic, I have chosen one of my own dreams, which, like a hologram, comprises numerous long-standing over-determinations that I have found at all the important junctions of my existence.

The dream text

In the company of Yasha David and his wife, I leave house A, which looks onto a large square that seems to belong more to a big market town in the provinces than to a major city. Bordering the two longest sides of

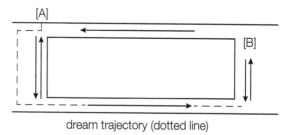

dream trajectory (dotted line)

The dream trajectory

this square are two streets that go one way in opposite directions. Those bordering the two shortest sides of the square are two-way. The ensemble constitutes a circuit that I traverse three sides of during the dream.

We are on the point of going our separate ways when I notice that I don't really know where I parked my car. First I decide to look around the square. Yasha believes he can remember where it is. He and his wife accompany me whilst I look. We arrive at point B, situated on the right-hand side of the square and I am seized by the wish to thank Yasha for the success of our search together. But I hold back the phrase that I was on the point of saying, because I notice that I was going to call him Gilles. I talk of the risks that we have run together: we were on the edge of an abyss. 'I start again', it was as if we had clung to the side of an abyss, but in the end we managed to get out…In an outburst of sympathy, I ready myself to embrace them both. Once again, I withhold my first movement: remembering that I had been told that Yasha is supposedly jealous for his wife, I make do with clasping them both with my arms.

Associative commentary and narrative developments

Yasha David

A Czech intellectual who is a refugee in France, with whom I worked for more than a year on developing some significant events for Kafka's centenary. It led to us having so many difficulties with the management of the Centre Georges Pompidou that on numerous occasions we thought we would have to abandon the project.

Yasha David's wife

I don't know her very well, having only met her two or three times. When noting down this dream I noticed that it wasn't really her in the dream, but Héléna Gallard – whose first name is really written Aléna – the wife of another friend. She is also of Czechoslovakian origin and also worked on a project for a Kafka exhibition, but only in its preparatory phase. I had already confused Aléna with Yasha David's wife on several occasions. I met Aléna and her husband Jean Gallard on several occasions, in Mexico then in Paris and Amsterdam. I experience a warm sympathy for this couple, perhaps even a sort of fascination. But I sense that they are having certain difficulties, which I don't manage to discern the nature of very clearly.

The rectangular square

Straightaway it evokes the principal square of an old Mexican city in an Eastern province the name of which I know very well but which eludes me when I write the dream down. By cross-checking I finally recover the name: Michoacan. The name of the city has to be Pascuaro. I have stopped over in a hotel located on this square. I have retained a powerful impression of it, because of its provincial charm and because it seems destined to remain the same through the passing centuries. I remember having thought 'that is where I would like to end my days'. In the background of this Mexican evocation, there resonates a very old memory of Normandy, of a large, dark square in the town of Louviers, to which the 'rue au Coq', where I stayed with my maternal grandmother, led. It was only several days after having noted down this dream that I was to discover, with surprise, that in fact it had to be the main square in Mer, a little town on the banks of the Loire, close to where I currently live for half the week. However, it is not the Mer of today that it is a question of in the dream but the Mer of more than 40 years ago, during what was called the 'exodus', when millions of French people set about fleeing the German invasion of 1940. I don't know how, but my parents managed to rent a little house there, situated at precisely point A of the place in the dream. We were counting on staying there for the rest of the war, ready to go south of the Loire if necessary. This prospect literally enchanted me. (I have to say that I experienced this upheaval of my life as an extraordinary adventure!) But right at the start of the next day we had to leave in a hurry, following the announcement that the bridges over the Loire were going to be blown up in the face of the German advance.

The direction of traffic around the square

The existence of a vectorial problematic superimposed on the figurative representation of the dream is related to two formative components:

1   A dream, a year earlier, that I called 'the dream of the ball with the parquet flooring' in which my second son, as a very young child, was separated from me in a tense atmosphere. We were at a ball. I had cause to leave through a door on the right of a large quadrilateral, then to return through a door on the left, and then to make a difficult crossing through the dancers from left to right.

2   A graph, which was also quadrangular, setting out a redefinition of the unconscious on the basis of four basic entities: Flows, machinic Phyla, existential Territories and incorporeal Universes.[1] But there was a question left hanging for me about this graph, which had also already animated the formal composition of the 'the dream of the ball with the parquet flooring'. It concerned the symmetry, which was too obvious for my liking, of the inter-entitarian transformations, along the abscissae and ordinates of my schema. In the dream presented here, one can also apprehend a zone, in the upper part of the circuit that is, if not uncrossable, at least implies a detour, and consequently, a breaking of symmetry. The hesitations, uncertainties, inhibitions, forgetting and slips that constitute the texture of this dream all seem to gravitate around this same zone, which I once characterized as 'vacuolic'.[2]

The forgetting of the car

I forgot my car twice: once in the dream-space and once with the name of its maker, because whilst transcribing the dream it is the letters 'BMW' that appear, instead of 'Renault'. This substitution, of one make of car, which I owned 20 years ago, for the one I currently own, also refers to another dream, in such a way that one can consider that we are dealing here with a junction between dreams, rather than with an enclosed signifying corpus. Let's note that this constitutes a modality of oneiric activity that is much more frequent than is generally believed.[3] In this other dream, I had also lost my car, which this time was the BMW of the past, but the scene took place in the context of the years of upheaval when I actually owned it. I came down the Rue Gay-Lussac – a name that I frequently censor so as to try to find it, and then I continue my journey by bicycle. On the other side of the Boulevard Saint-Michel,[4] I find myself in a meeting of the Socialist Party whose platform the Green Party was chased from by strong-armed stewards headed by Lionel Jospin in person. But I will return to the dream of the Place in Mer. We can pick out four a-signifying indices with regard to my losing the Renault:

1. Being lost, it constitutes a hole in space, and this spatial cutting out of a familiar object – which in a way forms a part of my Ego – echoes the opening of the door of house A. This putting into parentheses of an Ego object doesn't damage its referential character, by which I mean that the dream car doesn't stop being a Renault.

2. I feel that the passage from a fully spelled out name 'Renault' to a name in initials 'BMW' is affected with a certain quality of sense.

3. I note a hesitation concerning the order of connection between this sequence of forgetting where I left the car and that of the slip relating to Yasha David. This hesitation echoes my perplexity with regard to Yasha David's declaration that he can perhaps remember where I left my car.

4. Finally, I can't ignore the most stupid, mechanical association, which consists in extending the question of forgetting in the form of a question 'where is the self…analysis?'[5] It is true that I recently re-read the correspondence between Freud and Fliess and that I have asked myself about this curious, disguised homosexual relation on the basis of which Freud assembled the enunciation of his self-analysis.

The slip of the tongue in the dream

It is Gilles Deleuze's name that comes to mind, instead of that of Yasha David, in this intense interior that I constitute for myself in this dream. This substitution will function as a matrix of enunciation on the basis of which will be generated:

- polyphonic dialogical sequences (in Mikhail Bakhtin's sense)[6] essentially linking female persons: Adelaide, Arlette Donati, Alena Gallard, Micheline Kao, my mother, my grandmother…;

- harmonic Constellations of heterogeneous levels of enunciation, which will be examined later on.

The abyss

Three directions of association present themselves:

- a speleological reference that I haven't managed to elucidate;
- a text by Samuel Beckett entitled *The Lost Ones* in which a whole population survives by hanging onto a circular wall;
- a test that I invented in my youth and pompously baptized the 'Test of socio-existential integration', for which the initial instructions tended to be nullified as the procedure progressed.

Inhibition faced with jealousy

Having had 20 years of diaries stolen from me during a recent burglary, a friend undertook to reconstitute a 'memory' for me, by interviewing me about my past and also by questioning my friends about me. When she told me that she was going to interview Arlette Donati, with whom I had lived for seven years during this period in the 1960s, I thought that she would probably talk to her about some of my jealous behaviour over her, and about which I would have preferred that she skip over. But here, the by now classic Freudian logic of denial is playing out in full: 'I'm not jealous, because it is Yasha David who is jealous'.

A polyphonic analysis of the manifest lines of subjectification

It is a matter of picking out parallel and intersecting lines of sense, from a point of view similar to that of Bakhtin's dialogism. Only then will we seek to characterize the synapses of sense that catalyse a function (ΣU) of Constellations of Universes of reference, starting from a deterritorializing and fractalizing rupture. In the first place, we will distinguish the manifest Phyla of discursive sense, such as they are given on the surface of the written text of the dream, from the latent Phyla, such as they develop in the course of an oral explication, from an 'associative' point of view. We can distinguish five principal manifest Phyla:

1. around the town, the square and the closed circuit of the surrounding streets;
2. the lost car;

3 Yasha David and the lapsus that he brings about in the dream with regard to Gilles Deleuze;

4 a cave;

5 inhibition with regard to jealousy.

It will be noticed that the only component that foregrounds proper names is the third, which will occupy a particular place with regard to the other four, as a synaptic operator. The heterogeneity of these components will also be noticed.

The first is given as an iconic visual relation, which we will classify under the category of existential Territories (Te);

The second puts into play an absent machine, a potentiality that may or may not be there, which will be classified under discursive Phylas (Φ);

The third is a mental process of everyday psychopathology, which will be classified under the category of synapses;

The fourth is a signified utterance that will be transformed into an iconic utterance in this course of its associative developments. In this sense it is a chaotic black hole, the reverse of an existential Territory;

The fifth is a coarté affect (in the sense that Rorschach uses this term) that will be attached to non-discursive Universes of reference.

Analysis of the latent lines of subjectification

Development of the first component. The referent of the square in the dream was immediately identified from an iconic point of view, but the proper name of the town concerned required several days to appear. It is the town of Mer. The other references, to Mexico and Normandy (Pascuaro and Louviers) will remain in the background of the primary reference, even if first of all they are given before it. (It is as if the primary reference had to cross several thresholds of resistance.) One should be careful not to pass too quickly from the lexeme 'Mer' to the phonematic structure 'mère' [mother]. 'Mer' is a proper name that is connected with my father by association, as he took the decision, during the exodus, to get us lodgings in this town and on precisely this Place. It is significant for me that the final 'e' of Mer and the grave accent have fallen into the sea [mer]. It is the mother minus something, the mother relinquished of everything she has in her arms and on her back, and it is the father who is much freer in his movements and also much more distant.

The maternal background, by contrast, is found, undivided, with the square at Louviers, which is more or less adjacent to a park where, I believe, I can recall my mother pushed me in a pram.

As for the third dimension of the constellation, that of the square in Pascuaro, Mexico, with its connotation of a peaceful death, we will only be able to come back to it after an examination of the labour of the dream's central synapse.

What one can retain from this is that the door of the house at A leads onto an Existential Territory composed of mother and father.

Development of the second component. In fact, at the end of the cultural event at the Centre Georges Pompidou, which Gilles Deleuze had participated in, I had suggested to Yasha David that I take him back home. We left together for the car park under the Centre. I realized that I had forgotten where I had left my car. We walked round the different levels of the car park for a long time until, to my great shame, I realized that I had come on foot. That was in reality, but I have dreamed very frequently about forgetting where I had left my car.

Likewise, I will only be able to tackle the connection with Rue Gay-Lussac, the Green, the Socialist Party, etc. after the labour of the synapse. In the meantime, it must be underlined that for me the theme of the car corresponds to that of the desiring machine. My life was turned upside down when I – very belatedly, because I was 35 – gained my driving licence. The indirect consequence of this was the acquiring of an independence that was to result in a divorce, amongst other things. It was my father who, on his deathbed, had insisted, in a very particular way, that I pass my driving test. He felt isolated, too reliant on my mother and wanted me to come and see him more often. I recall also that he had given me a 50-franc note so that I would register for the test. That moved me a great deal because he didn't really realize that, at that time, 50 francs was no longer a great deal of money.

Having to deal with the third synaptic component separately, the fourth and fifth components do not, for the moment, call for any particular developing.

Analysis of the synaptic component

The deterritorializing and fractalizing dream operator is an abstract apparatus that is manifest from two elements:

- a forgetting, that of the car;
- a slip, bearing on Yasha David's name.

These two elements can be grasped within the same, triply articulated phrase:

I'm looking for my $\dfrac{\text{Renault}}{\text{BMW}}$ in $\dfrac{\text{Mer}}{\text{Rue Gay Lussac}}$ with $\dfrac{\text{Yasha David}}{\text{Gilles Deleuze}}$

      (forgetting)   (lapsus)

It should be noted that the first articulation is itself organized in a complex fashion. I dream that I have forgotten where my car is, but at the same time, I forget the name of the car, for which I substitute that of another manufacturer, BMW. I remember having driven through violent demonstrations in this car. At the time, I was living with Arlette Donati and my collaboration with Gilles Deleuze was to begin shortly after. There is, then, a present period, Renault-Yasha David, and a more glamorous period BMW-1968-Arlette Donati-Gilles Deleuze. But the ancient period does not repress the present period by a simple dialectical opposition. It includes a dialectical dimension from which a machinic surplus value results, which will work in the other domains of subjectification. It is essentially a matter of a movement of deterritorialization manifesting itself by the passage from the fully spelled out name 'Renault' to the initials 'BMW'. We will see in what follows that this initialling will swarm over neighbouring proper names and thus permit the development of the first abstract machinic nucleus.

Let us note that contemporaneous to this dream, I had a very problematic relationship with an Italian woman called Adelaide, who I had a habit of calling A.D.

We thus have a transformation that can be summarized in the following table:

1984	Renault	A.D.	Yasha David
1968	BMW	Arlette Donati	Gilles Deleuze

Everything is as if the initialling of the period 1968 climbed back up to 1984, passing from Arlette Donati to A.D. (Adelaide).

Analysis of the harmonic Constellations of levels of enunciation

The polyphonic lines developed according to their own spaces of sense as a function of their respective machinic Propositions, themselves embedded in extrinsic rhizomatic coordinates. Thus, the town square developed into the town of Mer, into Louviers, in Pascuaro, then into father-mother, etc.

Now it is a matter of better outlining the deterritorialized enunciative nuclei that speak in the dream as much as in reality, since from the point of view of the production of subjectivity that I am placing myself in here, there is no longer any way to keep the latent unconscious contents and the consciously explicit utterances separate. These affectants, or interpretants, in Charles Sanders Peirce's sense, are non-discursive in as much as they constitute deterritorialized Universes on the basis of which heterogeneous modes of semiotization are organized.

An example of the heterogeneity of such a component engendering discontinuous enunciative fragments: the passage from Renault to BMW or the slippage from Arlette Donati to A.D., with, in the latter case, the addition that the deterritorialization of the abbreviation here is correlative to a phonological reterritorialization, as it is on this plane that A.D. functions in the name Adelaide.

Let us note equally that these partial enunciative nuclei cannot be designated as such through syntagmatic chains or paradigmatic axes. Here they are only indexed by proper names, convoked on the basis of three successive lovers: Micheline Kao, Arlette Donati and A.D. One might imagine that code names or inchoate verbs have as their mission to bring about this same a-signifying rupture, which authorizes the putting to work of an enunciative existential function. Instead of being prisoner of a signifying quadrature, the synaptic semiotic chain here finds itself in a position to generate a fractal proliferation that will explore the diverse resources of the imaginary and enable an advance with an unresolved problem, that of the relationship between birth and death in so far as it can generate inhibition, in this instance.

A first partial harmonic nucleus is organized around components 1 and 4 of the dream, that is, those of the father-mother Territory and the cave, which, as a function of its intrinsic coordinates, attracts the components of an enunciative field. It will be recalled here that the dominant form of expression of component 1 is essentially of a visual order. Coming out of A, I enter into the superposed background worlds of mother-Louviers-Pascuaro. This iconic component is, however, doubled and – one might say – troubled, by a certain phonological syncretism, which will be manifested on two points:

1 the transformation of Mer into mother (mère);
2 the transformation of Michoacan into Micheline Kao, who was in a way my first wife, although I wasn't formally married to her.

These superposed background worlds constitute as if an ice palace on the basis of which I apprehend a zone-cave manifesting itself as point B, through the uncertainty, lack and caesura relative to the forgetting of the car.

The existential Territory of Mer remains enclosed on itself like a cycle track. However, it is cracked, a cave vibrates in it in a tangential way. And I can only apprehend this cave from the outside, metaphorically or metonymically, through the proper names that are pinned onto it by association.

It is the second harmonic nucleus that will allow me to outline it a little more closely. It results from the application of the synapse constituted by component 3 to the second machinic component and the fifth affective component. The Renault-BMW shift makes me move from a regressive-deathly world towards a sort of trajectory of initiation. I come down Rue Gay-Lussac, first on foot then by bicycle. Evidently there is 'gay' homosexuality in this street, but above all the memory of the most violent demonstrations of May 1968. On the morning of 10 May I arrived there too late, at ten o'clock, after the battle with the police, just in time to go and look for injured friends. In any case, I was uneasy during street fighting; I was inhibited with regard to physical confrontation with the police. One thus finds here a double matrix for coarté affect: inhibition in the face of fighting and in the face of homosexuality.

But it is an inhibition that changes because the background worlds cease to stage themselves as in a mirror, so as to link together processually in the meeting with the Greens, the altercation with Lionel Jospin and in an endless continuity, the evocation of the ethnologist friends: Cartry, Clastres, Adler, etc., and of the first psychotic patient in therapy who I took to them, on a motorbike, on the other side of the Rue Gay-Lussac, precisely, that is, Rue Monsieur-le-Prince...And one should also add Lucien Sebag and another dream, situated opposite the room of the Mutualité, where this time the themes of death and music find themselves knotted together. In short, a whole world of diverse activities of creative machinic linkage!

It is the semiotic diversification with the play of the grapheme and the phoneme around A.D., like in a crossword puzzle, that allows me to articulate and differentiate the imaginary blockage conveyed by the component territorialized on Mer. Nevertheless, one will find a residual reterritorialization with the coarté affect of jealousy. Although during these different periods, with Arlette Donati and with A.D., I was a convinced believer in sexual liberation, that didn't stop me being jealous when one of my partners effectively seized on this freedom. This nucleus of inhibition, which for a long time played out around Arlette Donati and led me to go and look for her in my BMW several times, is found with the ambivalence around Yasha and Gilles, but as a nucleus of neutrality where, by convention, it is established that the problematic of jealousy will not come into it.

In the last analysis, what does the dream propose to us? Beyond the fixation on native lands, a problematic of desiring machines can restart processual existential lines. However, something doesn't stop skidding out of control, a forgetting, an inhibition, a loss of consistency…Under these conditions, it is better not to rush anything and above all never to forget the *self-analysis* of the slip of the tongue and forgetting within the dream, the only way of warding off an anxiety about death, characterized as both essential and derisory by the gesture of the dying father offering me a 50-franc note.

REFRAINS AND
EXISTENTIAL AFFECTS

'If I am afraid of robbers in my dreams, the robbers, to be sure, are imaginary, but the fear of them is real' noted Freud in *The Interpretation of Dreams*.[1] The content of an oneiric message can be transformed, faked, mutilated, but not its affective dimension, its thymic component. Affect sticks to subjectivity, it is glischroid in character, to borrow Minkowski's qualification for describing epilepsy. Except that it sticks as much to the subjectivity of its enunciator as to that of its addressee and, in so doing, it disqualifies the enunciative dichotomy: locutor-auditor. Spinoza had discerned this transitive character of affect perfectly 'from the fact that we imagine someone like us to be affected with an affect, we are affected with a like affect', from which resulted what he called 'an emulation of desire' and the unfolding of multipolar affective compositions. Thus the sadness that we feel through that of the other becomes commiseration, whilst it is 'impossible that we represent hatred towards us by those similar to us, without hating them in return; and this hatred cannot happen without a desire for destruction that is manifest in anger and cruelty'. Affect is thus essentially a pre-personal category, establishing itself 'before' the circumscription of identities, and manifesting itself by transfers that are as unlocalizable from the point of view of their origin as from that of their destination. Somewhere, there is hatred in the same way that, in animist societies, beneficent or harmful influences circulate through the spirits of ancestors, and, concurrently, totemic animals, or through the 'mana' of a sacred place, the power of a ritual tattoo, a ceremonial dance, the story of a myth, etc. A polyvocity, then, of components of semiotization which are nevertheless still in search of their existential consummation.

As much the colour of the human soul as of animal becomings and cosmic magics, affect remains fuzzy, atmospheric,[2] and yet is perfectly apprehendable, in so far as it is characterized by the existence of thresholds of passage and of reversals of polarity. The difficulty here resides in the delimitation not being discursive, that is to say, not being founded in systems of distinctive oppositions that are set out in linear sequences of intelligibility or capitalized in informatic memories that are compatible with one another. Assimilable in this respect to Bergsonian duration, affect does not arise from categories that are extensional, susceptible of being numbered, but from intensive and intentional categories, corresponding to an existential auto-positioning. As soon as one seeks to quantify an affect, one immediately loses its qualitative dimensions and its potential for singularization, for heterogenesis, in other words the evental compositions, the 'haecceities' that it promotes. That is what happened to Freud when he wanted to make affect the qualitative expression of the quantity of drive energy (libido) and its variations. Affect is the process of existential appropriation by the continuous creation of heterogeneous durations of being. For this reason, we would certainly be well advised to give up treating it under the aegis of scientific paradigms so as to turn deliberately towards ethico-aesthetic paradigms.

That, it seems to me, is what Mikhail Bakhtin invites us to do, when, in order to specify aesthetic enunciation in relation to ethical evaluation and objective knowledge, he places the accent on its character of 'encompassing by the outside of content', the 'feeling of value' and on the fact that it leads to experiencing oneself as creator of form.[3] By drawing affect towards the aesthetic object, what I would like to underline is that it is in no way the passive correlate of enunciation, but its motor. It is true that this is somewhat paradoxical, because affect is non-discursive, entailing no energetic expenditure, and this is what has led us to qualify it as deterritorialized machinism.

The finitude, the consummation, the existential singularization of the person in her relation to herself, as much as in the circumscription of her domain of alterity, do not go without saying, are not given either by rights or in fact, but result from complex processes of the production of subjectivity. And in very particular historical conditions, artistic creation represented an outgrowth and an extraordinary exacerbation of this production. Also, rather than reducing subjectivity to only being the result of signifying operations, as the structuralists wished (in this regard, one is still under the influence of the celebrated Lacanian formula according to which a signifier was supposed to represent the subject for another signifier) it will be preferable to map the diverse components of subjectivity in their fundamental heterogeneity. Even in the case of the composition of a literary form, which nevertheless seems entirely tributary to language, Bakhtin underlines how reductive it would be to restrict oneself to the raw material of the signifier to account for it. Opposing the creative personality, organized from the interior (to which he assimilates the contemplator of the work of art), to the passive personality of the character, the object of literary vision, organized from the exterior,[4] he is led to distinguish five 'aspects' of linguistic material, so as to draw out an ultimate level of verbal affect assuming the feeling of engendering at the same time: sound, meaning, syntagmatic links, the phatic valorization of an emotional and volitional order.[5] The verbal activity of engendering a signifying sound thus correlates with an appropriation of rhythm, of intonation, of the motor elements of mimicry, the articulatory tension, the internal gesticulations of the narration (creative of movement), the figurative activity of metaphor and the whole internal élan of the person 'actively assumes through utterances a certain value-and-meaning position'.[6] But Bakhtin is keen to make it very clear that this feeling cannot be reduced to that of a brute organic movement, engendering the physical reality of the word, but that it is also the engendering of the sense of appreciation:

> a feeling of generating both meaning and evaluation, that is, a feeling of moving and assuming a position as a whole human being – of a movement into which both the organism and the meaning-directed acitivity are drawn, because both the flesh and the spirit of the word are generated together in their concrete unity.[7]

Whilst being non-discursive, this active power of affect is nonetheless complex and I would even characterize it as hyper-complex, wanting to indicate thereby that it is an instance of the engendering of complex, processuality in the nascent state, the locus of the proliferation of mutating becomings. With affect, the question is henceforth posed of a dis-position of enunciation on the basis of the modular components of proto-enunciation. The affect speaks to me, or at least it speaks through me. The dark red of my curtain enters into an existential Constellation with the dusk, when darkness is falling, to engender an uncanny Affect which devalues the clarities and urgencies which imposed themselves on me several instants earlier and it makes the world sink into a void which seems irremediable. On the other hand, other scenes, other Existential Territories, can become the support for highly differentiated Affects. For example, the leitmotifs of *Das Rheingold* will induce innumerable sentimental, mythical, historical, social references in me. Or the evocation of a humanitarian problem will set off a complex feeling of repulsion, of revolt and compassion. Whilst continuing to have a confined existence for themselves, from the moment that such scenic dis-positions, or dis-positions of territorialization, start to overflow my immediate environment and engage procedures of memory and cognition, I find myself tributary to an Assemblage of enunciation with multiple heads. The individuated subjectification in me that is authorized to speak in the first person is no longer anything more than the fluctuating intersection, the conscious 'terminal' of these diverse components of temporalization. With the curtain and the late hour, the affect – which could be called sensible – was given as immediately there, whilst with problematic objects, its spatio-temporal congruence dissolves and its procedures of elucidation threaten to flee in all directions.

However, my idea is that problematic affects are the basis of sensible affects and not the other way round. Here the complex ceases to be based on the simple (as in those conceptions prevailing in scientific paradigms), so as to organize synchronic distributions and diachronic becomings as its own economy allows.

Let's take up these two aspects one at a time.

As the precarious result of a composition of heterogenous modules of semiotization, its identity permanently compromised by the proliferation of Phyla of problematization that work it, in its 'rich' version, Affect is constantly questing to re-capture itself. Besides, it is essentially from this ontological flight 'backwards', consecutive to an infinite movement of fractal virtualization[8] that its power of existential self-affirmation results. On a phenomenological plane, this question of the crossing of a threshold by Affect, with a view to attaining sufficient consistency, is posed by most psychopathological syndromes. On this side of such a threshold, it is the sphere of 'pathic time' – according to the felicitous expression of von Gebsattel[9] – that finds itself threatened. Equally, one may recall Binswanger's incisive chiasm regarding autism, which is characterized less by an empty time – boredom, typically – than by a void of time.[10] Psychopathological syndromes reveal, without doubt better than any other Assemblage, what I would call the inchoate dimensions inherent to Affect, some of which literally set to work on their own count. This doesn't in the least signify that normality ought to be characterized by a harmonious equilibrium between the modular components of temporalization. Normality can be just as 'disordered' as other [mental] tableaux. Some phenomenologists have even reported a syndrome of hyper-normality in melancholy.[11] The discordance between the different ways of beating time – what I will call its setting into refrains [ritornellisations] – is not specific to abnormal subjectivity. Instead, what characterizes the latter is that one mode of temporalization gets the upper hand over all the others, temporarily or definitively. The normal psyche, on the other hand, is more or less in a position to pass from one mode to another, as Robert Musil has Ulrich say magnificently: 'the sane person is full of countless insanities and the insane person is possessed only by one'.[12] The exploration of the expressive levels of pathic temporalization has not yet been seriously undertaken. It seems to me that the repercussions that might be expected from it would largely exceed the strict field of psychopathology and would be particularly significant in the linguistic domain. I imagine that the analysis of the modal and aspectual consequences of the obsessive or melancholic holding back of time could lead to the formulation of a more general function of the inhibition of enunciation, and, symmetrically, that of its mad, manic acceleration (*Ideenfluss*) to a function of liquefaction. ('The maniac is continually seized by an infinite range of references, always actual, fleeting and interchangeable. His temporalization is "reduced to an absolute momentalization" (that) ignores all duration and disappears like melancholic temporalization.')[13] I can also imagine the use that semioticians could make of a study, that would, without a doubt, be much more arduous, of the gap between the mute expression of the catatonic and the fantastic 'interior gesticulation' – to borrow an expression from Bakhtin – for which it is the mask. In a more general fashion, one will have to admit that the disordering of rhythms of enunciation and the semiotic discordances that result from it cannot be grasped in a homogeneous register of meaning production. They always refer to power takeovers by extralinguistic components: somatic, ethological, mythographic, institutional, economic, aesthetic, etc. The affair is less visible with the 'normal' exercise of speech, by virtue of the fact that existential affects are more disciplined in it, subjected to a law of homogenization and generalized equivalence.

Under the generic term 'refrain', I will group reiterated discursive sequences, closed on themselves, having as their function an extrinsic catalysis of existential affects. Refrains can take rhythmic or plastic form, be prosodic segments, faciality traits, emblems of recognition, leitmotifs, signatures, proper names or their invocational equivalents; equally they can be established transversally between different substances – this is the case with Proust's 'refrains of lost time', which constantly enter into correspondence with each other.[14] They can be of a sensible order (the madeleine dipped in tea, the disjointed paving of the courtyard of the Hotel de Guermantes; Vinteuil's little phrase, the plastic compositions around the bell-tower of Martinville…); or a problematic order (the ambience in the Verdurin's salon); just as much as of the order of faciality (Odette's face). To situate their position as the junction between the sensible and problematic dimensions of enunciation, I propose to 'enframe' the relation of signification (f(sign) (that is to say, the relation of reciprocal presupposition or of solidarity between the form of Expression and the form of Content, in Hjelmslev's terms) of four semiotic functions relating to the Referent and to Enunciation. We will thus have:

1. a denotational function, f(den), corresponding to the relations between form of Content and Referent;

2. a diagrammatic function, f(diag), corresponding to the relations between matter of Expression and Referent;

3. a function of sensible affect (refrain), corresponding to the relations between Enunciation and form of Expression;

4. a function of problematic Affects (abstract machine), corresponding to the relations between Enunciation and the form of Content.

Let's note that in so far as one can conceivably keep the significational, denotational and diagrammatic functions within the traditional semantic and syntactic domains, it is not a question here of enclosing the two functions of existential affect in a third drawer that would be labelled 'pragmatic'. As Hjelmslev forcefully underlined, linguistics doesn't arise from an autonomous axiomatization (any more so than any other semiotic system).[15] And it is from the side of the concatenation of these partial enunciative Territories that a generalized flight of systems of expression from the side of the social, the 'pre-personal', the ethical and the aesthetic operates.

What can one expect from our bifaced refrain-abstract machine? Essentially a locating and deciphering of the existential praxial operators that are established at the junction of Expression and Content. A junction where, I insist, nothing is played out in advance in a perfect structuralist synchrony, but where everything is always an affair of contingent Assemblages, of heterogenesis, of irreversibilization, of singularization. With Hjelmslev, we have learned of the fundamental reversibility between form of Expression and form of Content overhanging the heterogeneity of substances and matters that are their support. But, with Bakhtin, we have learned to read the layering of enunciation, its polyphony and its multicentring. How do we reconcile the existence of this intersection formally unifying Expression and Content with that of the multivalence-multifluence of Enunciation? How, for example, do we understand that the heterogeneous voices of delirium or of creation can combine in the Assemblage of productions of sense outside commonsense? Productions that, far from being established in the position of a deficit from a cognitive point of view, sometimes allow access to highly enriching existential truths? Linguists have long refused to consider enunciation head-on, they only wanted to take its incursions into the structural framework of syntactico-semantic processes into account. In fact, enunciation is not at all a distant suburb of language. It constitutes the active core of linguistic and semiotic creativity. And if linguists were really inclined to take on board its function of singularization, it seems to me that they would be well advised, if not to substitute proper names for the categorial symbols that dominate the syntagmatic and semantic trees that they have inherited from the Chomskyans and post-Chomskyans, then at least to propagate the Rhizomes that cling to these proper names. We must learn again the games of the refrains that fix the existential ordering of the sensible environment and support the meta-modelling scenes of the most abstract problematic Affects. Let us get an overview of some examples.

Marcel Duchamp's bottle-rack functions as the trigger for a Constellation of Universes of reference that sets off intimate reminiscences – the cellar of the house, beams of light on the cobwebs, adolescent solitude – as much as it does connotations of a cultural and economic order – the epoch in which bottles were still washed using a brush...The Benjaminian aura[16] or Barthes's punctum[17] also arise from this kind of singular refrain-making. Again, it is this refrain-making which confers a sense of scale on architectural Assemblages;[18] what sometimes miniscule details does the perception of a child walking down the dismal passageways of a social housing estate fasten on to? How, starting from a distressing seriality, does he succeed in consummating his discovery of a world of magical haloes? Without this aura, without this refrain-making of the sensible world – which in any case is established in the deterritorialized prolonging of ethological[19] and archaic[20] refrains, the objects that surround us would lose their 'air' of familiarity and would topple into an anguishing strangeness.

Refrains of Expression are of prime importance in sensible Affects: for example, the intonation of an actor will fix the melodramatic turn of an act, or the 'serious voice' of a father will trigger the wrath of the Superego (American researchers have even managed to demonstrate that the most tight-lipped of smiles entails, in the manner of Pavlovian reflexes, anti-depressive biosomatic effects!). On the other hand, the prevalence of refrains of Content, or abstract machines, is affirmed with problematic Affects, which operate as much in the direction of individualization as of social serialization. (Besides, the two procedures are not antagonistic: existential options are not mutually exclusive in this register but entertain relations of segmentarity, substitution and agglomeration.) For example, an icon from the Orthodox Church does not have as its primary finality the representation of a Saint, but the opening of a territory of enunciation to a believer, making her enter into direct communication with the saint.[21] The facial refrain draws its intensity from the way that it intervenes as a shifter – in the sense of a 'change of decor' – at the heart of a palimpsest superposing the Existential Territories of the body and those of persono-logical, conjugal, domestic, ethnic, etc. identities. In a completely different register, a signature appended to a banking document also functions as a refrain of capitalist normalization: what is behind this scrawl? Not simply the person that it denotes but also the assonances of power that it triggers amongst people in high places.

The human sciences – psychoanalysis in particular – have long accus-tomed us to thinking affect in terms of an elementary entity. But there also exist complex affects, inaugurating irreversible diachronic ruptures that should be called: Christ-affect, Debussy-affect, Lenin-affect. It is in this way that for decades a Constellation of existential refrains has given access to a 'Leninist-language' engaging specific procedures as much of the rhetorical and lexical order as of the phonological, prosodic or facial orders, etc. The crossing of a threshold – or initiation – that legitimates a relation of full existential belonging to a group subject depends on a certain concatenation and taking on of consistency of these components, thus put into refrain. Some time ago I tried to show, for example, that Leon Trotsky never really succeeded in crossing the threshold of consistency of the collective Assemblage of the Bolshevik Party.[22]

Enunciation is like the conductor who sometimes accepts his loss of control of the members of the orchestra: at certain moments, it is the pleasure of articulation or rhythm, if not an inflated style, which sets out to play a solo and to impose it on others. Let's emphasize that if an Assemblage of enunciation can include multiple social voices, it equally takes on pre-personal voices, capable of bringing about an aesthetic ecstasis, a mystic effusion or an ethological panic – an agoraphobic syndrome, for example – as much as an ethical imperative. One can see that all forms of concerted emancipation are conceivable. A good conductor will not attempt despotically to overcode all the parts on the score, but will be looking for the collective crossing of the threshold at which the aesthetic object designated by the name at the top of the score is attained. 'That's it! You've got it!' Tempo, accents, phrasing, the balancing of parts, harmonies, rhythms and timbres: everything conspires in the reinvention of the work and its propulsion towards new orbits of deterritorialized sensibility…

Affect is not, then, a state that is passively submitted to, as its ordinary representation amongst the 'psy' disciplines would have it. It is a complex subjective territoriality of proto-enunciation, the locus of a labour, of a potential praxis, bearing on two conjoint dimensions:

1   A process of extrinsic dissymmetrization, which polarizes an intentionality towards fields of non-discursive value (or Universes

of reference). This sort of ethicization of subjectivity is correlative of a historicization and of a singularization of its existential trajectory;

2 A process of intrinsic symmetrization, evoking not only the aesthetic attainment of Bakhtin but also the fractalization of Benoît Mandelbrot,[23] which confers the consistency of a deterritorialized object and a grasping of auto-existentializing enunciative autonomy on affect.

Let's listen once again to Bakhtin:

> through its own strength, the word transposes the consummating form into content. Thus, a request in the lyric – an aesthetically organized request – begins to be sufficient unto itself and does not need satisfaction (it is satisfied, as it were, by the very form of its expression); a prayer ceases to need assistance; repentance ceases to need forgiveness, and so on. Making use of the material alone, form brings any event and ethical tension to the fullness of completion. With the help of the material alone, the author assumes a creative, productive position with regard to content, that is, with regard to cognitive and ethical values. The author enters, as it were, the isolated event and becomes the creator in it, without becoming a participant.[24]

This function of consummation as the disjunction of content – in the sense that an electricity meter can malfunction –, this self-generation of enunciation seems entirely satisfactory to me. But the other traits by which Bakhtin characterizes signifying aesthetic form, to wit: unification, individuation, totalization and isolation,[25] seem to me to call for some development. Isolation: yes but active isolation, moving in the direction of what I have elsewhere called a processual setting into a-signifiance. Unification, individuation and totalization: certainly, but 'multiplicating'. It is here that I would like to introduce this other idea of a fractal taking on of consistency. In reality, the unity of the object is only the movement of subjectification. Nothing is given in itself. Consistency is only gained by a perpetual headlong flight of the for-itself, which conquers an existential Territory at the very same time as it loses it, nevertheless seeking to retain a stroboscopic memory of it. Reference here is no longer anything other than the support for a reiterative refrain. What matters is the break, the gap, which will make it turn around on itself and which will engender not only a sentiment of being – a sensible Affect – but also an active way of being – a problematic Affect.

This deterritorializing reiteration is equally effectuated along two synchronic and diachronic axes, no longer separated this time into autonomized extrinsic coordinates but woven together in intensive ordinates:

1   Intentional ordinates in accordance with which each affective territory is the object of a fractalization. This can be illustrated by the symmetrical internal relations developed in the so-called baker transformation in mathematics.[26] I understand by this that it is by an inchoate tension, a permanent 'work in progress', that the 'taking on of being' of affect is renewed, acquires consistency. None of its partitions [scores], even if they are infinitesimal, escape from procedures of existential homothety deployed – outside the registers of discursive extensity – by sensible and problematic refrains. Not only are all the spatio-temporal angles of approach explored and subsumed but the set (or the integral) of points of view of scale (to come back once again to this fundamental category of architecturology) are so too.

2   A trans-monadic axis, or axis of transversality, which confers a transitive character on enunciation, making it drift constantly from one existential Territory to another, generating singularizing dates and durations from it (once again the privileged example here is that of the Proustian refrains).

Subjectification is an intersecting of actual and virtual enunciative points of view. It wants to be everything without division and is in fact nothing, or nearly nothing, because it is irremediably fragmentary, perpetually shifting, spaced out. Finitude, existential consummation, result from the crossing of a threshold which is in no way a demarcation, a circumscription. Self and other agglomerate at the heart of an ethical intentionality and the aesthetic promotion of an end. What completely falsifies the reading of psychoanalytic authors when they deal with the Ego, is that one literally doesn't know what they are talking about: because they haven't given themselves the means of understanding that the Ego is not a discursive set entertaining Gestalt relations with a referent. Also, one cannot reasonably accept the articulations of it that they propose. Certainly, it is always possible to turn it into a 'displaced' representation, to construct a meta-modelling scene with regard to it and to decree that it is identified with this scene. In a way, we have hardly any other means for speaking about it, for sketching or writing something about it. It nonetheless remains the case that the Ego is the whole world, I am everything! Like the cosmos, I don't recognize any limits to myself. If, perchance, it was different, if I was to fall back on my body, then there would be a difficulty. The Ego arises from a logic of all or nothing. There always exists a part of me that finds it difficult to tolerate that someone can decree that there is no me beyond this territory. No! It is still me beyond, even if another territory endeavours to force itself on me – unless the question of the Ego stops being posed and all possibility of auto-enunciation abolished. A frightful and unnameable perspective that we prefer not to look in the face, and which generally leads us to talk about something else...

It is because Affect is not a massive elementary energy, but the deterritorialized matter of enunciation, a highly differentiated integral of insight and 'outsight' that one can have something to do with it, that it can be worked on. Not in the style of traditional psychoanalysts, that is to say, through modelling identifications and symbolic integrations, but by deploying its ethico-aesthetic dimensions through the mediation of refrains. (On this point I agree with Emmanuel Levinas when he makes an intrinsic link between faciality and ethics.)[27] Consider, for example, the symptomatic refrains populating the psychological automatisms of Pierre Janet, the experiences of primary delirium of Karl Jaspers or the fantasmatic unconscious of Freud. Two attitudes are possible: that which makes of them a fixed state of fact and that which starts from the idea that nothing is played out in advance, that analytico-aesthetic and ethico-social practices are able to open such refrains up to new fields of possibility. Originally, Freudianism created a veritable mutation in an Assemblage of enunciation. Its techniques of interpretation, its interventions into oneiric and psychopathological refrains only had a bearing on semantic contents – the illusory revelation of a 'latent content' – in appearance. In fact its entire art consisted in making its refrains play out on novel scenes of affect: free association, suggestion, the transference...so many new ways of saying and seeing things! But what psychoanalysis missed, in the course of its historical development, is the heterogenesis of the semiotic components of its enunciation. Originally, the Freudian unconscious still took into account two matters of expression, the linguistic and the iconic, but with its structuralization, psychoanalysis pretended to reduce everything to the signifier, even to the 'matheme'. Everything leads me to think that, on the contrary, it would be preferable for psychoanalysis to multiply and to differentiate the expressive components that it puts into play, as much as possible. And for its own Assemblages of enunciation not to be arranged next to the couch, such that the dialectic of the gaze is radically foreclosed. Analysis has everything to gain from enlarging its means of intervention; it can work with speech, but equally with modelling clay (like Gisela Pankow), or with video, cinema, theatre, institutional structures, family interactions, etc. In short, everything that allows the a-signifying facets of the refrains that it encounters to be stimulated, in such a way that it is better able to set off their catalytic functions of crystallizing new Universes of reference (the fractalizing function). In these conditions, analysis no longer rests on the interpretation of fantasms and the displacement of affects but endeavours to render both operative, to score them with a new range (in the musical sense). Its basic work consists in detecting encysted singularities – what turns around on itself, what insists in the void, what obstinately refuses the dominant [self] evidence, what puts itself in a position contrary to the sense of manifest interests...– and to explore their pragmatic virtualities.

What is the reductionist bent of the signifier – on which psychoanalytic affect (with its increasingly empty transference, its more and more stereotypical and aseptic exchanges) hasn't stopped slipping – supported by? To my mind it is inseparable from the much more general curvature of capitalistic Universes in the direction of the entropy of the equivalence of significations. A world where one thing is worth no more than another; where every existential singularity is methodologically devalued; where in particular, the affects of contingency, relative to old age, illness, madness, are emptied of their existential stigmata and become mere abstract parameters, managed by a network of welfare support services – everything bathed in an ineffable but omnipresent atmosphere of anxiety and unconscious guilt.[28] Weberian disenchantment, the correlative, it will be recalled, of a devaluing, of a 'sacramental anti-magic'[29] or of an all-out re-enchantment of productions of subjectivity by the depolarization of collective Universes of reference against the values of generalized equivalence and to the benefit of an infinite multiplication of existential *captures of value*? Although the current inflation of computational and communicational logics hardly seems to lead in this direction, it seems to me that it is indeed on the promotion of social and aesthetic analytic practices preparing the advent of just such a postmedia era that our future, at whatever level it is considered, depends.

GENET REGAINED

Perhaps the massacres at Chatila in September 1982 were not a turning point. They happened. I was affected by them. I talked about them. But while the act of writing came later, after a period of incubation, nevertheless in a moment like that or those when a single cell departs from its usual metabolism and the original link is created of a future, unsuspected cancer, or of a piece of lace, so I decided to write this book. The matter became more pressing when some political prisoners urged me not to travel to France. Anything not to do with the book came to seem so far away as to be invisible. [1]

Jean Genet was to die four years later, whilst he was correcting the proofs of *Prisoner of Love*, an immense book, beyond the ordinary measures of literature – which might explain, without excusing, why so many critics have missed its real importance.

A book in waves. Ten times, 20 times, the same scenes, the same characters arrive in the backwash to project new flotsam and jetsam of memory. 'Souvenirs', Genet modestly subtitles it, '*souvenirs*, which were meant to be read as reporting';[2] 'images' he specifies in the introduction. A book of images, a book of margins to give space to a singular polyphony in which the most secret dimensions of the poet will be knotted together (evidently I am not talking about his sexuality here, which as everyone knows, is already a national treasure), with the 'metaphysical struggles'[3] conducted by the Fedayeen and the Black Panthers in counterpoint to his perpetual wandering.[4]

'Was the Palestinian revolution really written on the void, an artifice superimposed on a nothingness, and is the white page, and every little blank space between the words, more real than the black characters themselves?'[5] Would this revolution have been nothing but a pretext for him to write literature? What, then, would separate him from all those 'poets of the revolution' that he mocks so cruelly?[6] But evidently this 'passage via writing'[7] of his Palestinian experience is in no way comparable to a vulgar enterprize of literary recuperation. He detested the idea of being treated as a man of letters so much that during the incessant debate that he had with himself throughout the book, on the legitimacy of his attempt, it seems that the idea never even occurred to him that a similar accusation could be made about him.

This visceral refusal of the position of the writer, which would force him to camp on the bourgeois side of the barricade, did not escape Jean-Paul Sartre at all.[8] But he nonetheless apprehended Genet from an exclusively literary angle and considered that his destiny inexorably called on him to 'end up' in literature. It thereby appears that given the test of time, the colossal and sumptuous monument – if not mausoleum – that Sartre built for him, in the form of a 700-page preface, turns out to be rather ill-fitting for the calibre of personality that Genet was subsequently to reveal. It is not that it was too ambitious, but rather that it also missed the processual driving force of his life and his work. According to Sartre, Genet went through three metamorphoses: that of the thief, that of the aesthete and that of the writer, and they made him pass successively from the act to the gesture, from the gesture to the word, then from the word to the work.[9]

> Genet began to write in order to affirm his solitude, to be self-sufficient, and it was the writing itself that, by virtue of its problems, gradually led him to seek readers. As a result of the virtues – and the inadequacies – of words, this onanist transformed himself into a writer.[10]

One would in some way be dealing with the transformation of a psychopathic pervert and delinquent into a 'rhetorician',[11] a prisoner of the duly pacified imaginary and soul. 'Genet, the sole hero of his books, has fallen entirely into the imaginary, he becomes the imaginary *in person*'.[12] Although evidently distinguished from Freudian conceptions, one sees that Sartre's existential psychoanalysis has nevertheless retained a certain schematic quality, certain reductionist tics, I would say. Genet's work is compared to the humanization of religions, which replace human sacrifices by symbolic sacrifices;[13] the writing of each one of his books functions as a 'cathartic attack of possession' or a psychodrama.[14] The novel *Our Lady of the Flowers* is assimilated to a detoxification of narcissism[15] and after ten years of literature which, according to Sartre, are worth a psychoanalytic cure,[16] the recovery of the patient, who has finally resolved to have a little family, is triumphantly announced to us 'Somewhere between Saint-Raphaël and Nice a house is waiting for him'.[17] A miracle of literature! And above all, classic Sartre! Naïve, compassionate and secretly conformist! All of that is all well and good but it is not in this direction that the future was to turn. Genet would never have settled down, he was never to 'attach' himself to a Territory, to choose a house, if not in the mode of nihilation (to paraphrase Sartre). I'm thinking of the daydream of the house where he was born that he relates to us in *Prisoner of Love*, implanted in a place 'out of space' and which is nevertheless glimpsed for a few moments on the Turkish coast. He looks through an open window at the garden, the sea and, further away, the island of Cyprus, whilst the incantatory phrase 'And from here, out of danger, I'll watch a naval battle in broad daylight' forces itself on him.[18] A bewitching that is threatened immediately by the superimposition of another image, this time much older and Jordanian, of a little house 'with romanesque porches [...], with their semicircular vaults supported on four marble columns'. He was then in the company of a senior Palestinian leader to whom he said: 'See how beautiful it looks on the rock!' 'The PLO will let it to you for six months if you like.' It immediately became grey and dirty'.[19]

Thus Genet did not fall into either aestheticism or literary profes-sionalism. The fact that he was recognized as one of the greatest writers of the twentieth century did not lead him to give up aesthetic wandering and didn't even prompt him into giving up thieving. Figuratively, he continued to assimilate the latter to poetic apperception ('the poetry lies in his full awareness of being a thief');[20] in reality, he carefully maintained his contacts with old or potential convicts,[21] and, when the opportunity arose, he would steal from his publishers or sponsors, certain of whom, it is said, were obligingly complicit. Explanation by means of Freudian psychogenetic stages, whether revised by Sartre or not, is deficient. In particular, it doesn't allow us to understand why – if the condition of the writer suited him so well – he would cease all literary or theatrical production for 20 years. And the reason for this dazzling resurgence a few years before his death? We will only be able to find our way here, in my opinion, if we consider that for this exceptional being, 'before' life and 'before' the work, there was always a subter-ranean process, an essential dynamic, a creative madness that literally subjugated him. It is something of this order that he is aiming at in 1983 when – to someone who asks him if it is still in reference to his literary work that he published an article on the Chatila massacre in the *Revue d'études palestiniennes* – he replies

it is thanks not to the books that I have written but to my disposition, which I get myself into, where life has put me thirty years ago to write books, that a year ago I was able to write the short essay you are talking about...[22] In relation to this primary disposition, his life and work were only ever sort of sub-products, subject to every variation, every eclipse.

It is just the same with the habitual dichotomies between the real and the imaginary. Let us listen to what he says in this same interview when he concedes that in associating with the Black Panthers, then with the Palestinians, he was acting more as a function of the real world than as a function of the world of the dream or the world of grammar – but, he adds straightaway, only to the extent that one opposes the real world to the world of dreams: 'Of course, if one pushes the analysis further, one knows very well that the dreaming also belongs to the real world. Dreams are realities'.[23] It is clear that right to the end of his life, Genet never passed through the famous stages of development and adaptation to the real that it is claimed are linked together around weaning, potty training, the Oedipus and castration complexes, the pre- and post-pubescent patency periods. For him, everything functioned at the same time. He never gave up his dreams and his infantile 'perversions'. Yet that would not prevent him from being engaged, in the most lucid, the most 'adult' fashion, in contemporary historical realities. I will add that it would be vain to try to save the psychogenetic schema by having recourse, not to the Real-Imaginary dyad but to the structuralist triad that adds the Symbolic to it, because evidently his triumphant entrance into the 'symbolic order', with literature and theatre, had no redemptive effect, as far as he was concerned. Decidedly, sublimation did not work for him! Rather than a dialectical exhaustion, his mastery of writing only resulted in an exacerbation of his contradictions and his lacerations. Despite a certain soothing, noticeable on reading *Prisoner of Love*, Genet gave up none of his madness: the madness of desire, the madness of revolt, the madness of beauty.

We must search elsewhere, orient ourselves towards something that would order the real, the imagination and creation differently. Something that would not make of them separate instances but would lead them to engender each other. An imaginary-symbolic producing new realities, a subjective disposition capable of receiving all the charges of the imaginary conveyed by the real…One could legitimately join the phrases where Genet's subjectivity falls back onto the most 'limited' of realities to those where the real irrupts outside of him in an 'objective' process of subjectification. One would thus pass in a continuous fashion from the thesis of mere reportage ('As I'm not an archivist or a historian or anything like it, I'll only have spoken of my life in order to tell the story, a story of the Palestinians,')[24] to the declarations – which are so astonishing coming from an apologist for every kind of betrayal[25] – in which he worries about betraying the information mission that he initially assigned himself (by virtue of the fact that he orders the episodes that he lives through in the Palestinian resistance 'in the same seeming disorder as the images in a dream',)[26] 'more imagination than [his] nightmares and [his] memories',[27] an idea that he incarnates in the matrix-image of moss, lichen, grasses, eglantines, fig trees[28] cracking the most mineral of realities, and which he doubles up on the side of actuality with the image of the Palestinian people hanging on to life through lumps of concrete from the camps destroyed by Israeli bombs, then from an older point of view with that of the tap in the wall.[29]

There is a whole theory to be elaborated on the function of oscillation, eclipse, evanescence, effacing, in Genet's oeuvre.[30] This theme keeps coming back. One of the prototypical images that he offers us of it (equally present in a very similar form in Kafka) is that of the vapour from a boiler, which 'steams up a window, then gradually disappears, leaving the window clear, the landscape suddenly visible and the room extended perhaps to infinity'.[31] Adjacent to this image – because one image always calls up another – there is the hand and sponge moving to and fro over a blackboard, rubbing out the chalk writing.[32] A deterritorialization of space, time and words. The Fedayee is also essentially a being of disappearance, 'he turns into the path, and I'll no longer be able to see his face, only his back and his shadow'.[33] His struggle as such also arises from eclipse, 'some inexpressible feeling warned me that the rebellion was fading, flagging, was about to turn into the path and disappear'.[34] And finally it is Genet in person who is abolished, shrinking infinitely towards the line of the horizon.[35] Except one must be careful not to think that these are simple phenomena of annihilation. All these effacements leave trails behind them like stroboscopic after-images of other universes; their shadow play announces the coming to light of new existential dimensions: 'the fact that they were like ghosts, appearing and disappearing, lent them (the Fedayeen) a life more powerful than that of things that never evaporate and whose image is there all the time. Or rather the Fedayeen's existence was so powerful it could afford those sudden, almost courteous evanescences, relieving me of too insistent and tiring a presence'.[36] At the time of *Screens*, when Genet asked Roger Blin that his mise en scène illuminate the world of the dead, there is no doubt that it was already a subjugation of the living that he had in mind.[37] At death's door he himself sometimes feels his skin become phosphorescent, 'as a parchment shade does when a lamp is lit'.[38] But one should not, for all that, think that these transformations announce any mystical revelations. No, they only participate in an entire life's work on perception, the imagination and their various modes of semiotization.

Sartre abusively projected his own conception of imaging consciousness as a derealizing function onto Genet.[39] In so doing, he condemned him to remain surrounded by an imaginary that was entirely invested with his malevolent phantasmagoria, and denied him any effective escape from accursed solitude. It is true that in Genet the creative process always fully appealed to fabulation[40] – whether masturbatory or not – but his fundamental aim nevertheless remains a poetics with a social bearing. The writing of his first texts is inseparable from his experience of the penal condition. His 'theatre of cruelty' revolved around the themes of prostitution, negritude, colonial wars…Let's not forget that at the outset, *Prisoner of Love* was a militant work, written at the personal request of Yasser Arafat, as Genet likes to recall, doubled with a more general reflection on the deeper meaning of what, starting at the end of the 1960s, were the demonic movements (the Zengakuren, the Red Guards, the Berkely Revolt, the Black Panthers, May 68 in Paris, the Palestinians).[41] Certainly, he was very careful not to give these revolutionary undertakings blanket approval. He rejects their wooden language, their dogmatism; he appreciates their appropriate dose of 'theatricality' for the media (the 'comedians of the revolution'[42]) and his lucidity is formidable when it is a matter of denouncing the bureaucratic and corrupt aspects of the Palestinian movement that he had discovered.[43] But what fascinates him in these 'lively rings' these 'telluric faults', as he calls them,[44] is everything that goes beyond the particularity of their interests, their fundamental precarity as much as their metaphysical commitments. He is particularly attached to one of their essential mechanisms, which is what might be called their image function: the ways of being and dressing of the Black Panthers, which almost overnight change the way that black people as a whole perceive the colour of their skin or the texture of their hair, for example. Here Genet deciphers the dimensions of the body, sex, the dance of intonations of the voice and of gestures, a whole enunciative texture – one might say, a whole eventuation [événementiation] that is infinitely more profound than what they have been reduced to today under the term 'look'. Regarding the eponymous heroes whose names have been affirmed throughout history, he speaks of 'fabulous images', citing Socrates, Christ, Saladin, Saint-Just…They draw their potency from being at once exemplary and singularizing, 'not because [they are] powerful, but because [they] exist'.[45] But I believe that one can legitimately broaden this expression to all the imaginary formations that, from this same perspective, acquire a particular – transversal – capacity to bridge times of life, existential levels as much as social segments, even – why not – cosmic stratifications. Because we have to seek Genet in all these places simultaneously. In this respect he is indeed a man of this century, one who, more than any other perhaps, will have given birth to new ways of seeing the world. I repeat: Genet is a man of the real. I would like to say: a man of the future real. He is not a Saint, as Sartre pretended to believe, and above all not a Saint condemned to metamorphose perpetually into a vermin, who would be called on to convert history into the categories of myth.[46] In fact, myths and their images only matter to him in as much as collective operators succeed in conferring on them a historical consistency. In these conditions, becoming a 'solitary and fabulous hero', who is exemplary and thus singular[47] ceases to be contrary to collective fusion. 'I was all desire for the group as a whole, he writes, with regard to the Black Panthers, but my desire was fulfilled by the fact that they existed'.[48] Becoming the hero of forms of sensibility to come, alongside a handful of others – Kafka, Artaud, Pasolini – is entirely in accord with his will to effacement or even his desire for invisibility.[49] Exit, then, the solitude of the accursed poet! To agree to bring his 'dreamer function' to the Panthers and then the Palestinians is not an element in the derealization of these movements, as he still asks himself, sometimes, seemingly in an imaginary dialogue with Sartre. It is perhaps even a means of conferring on them a more intense subjective consistency. 'So, in their revolt, the Palestinians took on the weight – oh, I'm afraid of being very literary – but they took on the weight of Cézanne's paintings'.[50]

At the same time, it is worth asking oneself what this welcoming of a character like Genet – even to their secret bases – implies for a movement such as Fatah. Here is a movement that does not just raise funds, buy arms, get diplomatic and mass media support but also demands poetry! And not from just anyone, not from a laudator of the 'socialist realist' type, but from the shiftiest, the most deviant of authors, from whom any militant who is normally constituted – and that is the whole question – would rightly have expected the worst cowardice, the most infamous treason. But that would have been to forget that Genet could only betray through fidelity to himself. However the case may be, he did insist on laying his cards on the table: 'The day that the Palestinians are institutionalized, I won't be at their side. I won't be there the day that the Palestinians become a nation like other nations.' Is it not a very interesting revolution that thus accommodates itself to such an attitude on the part of a 'fellow traveller'? Better still, which seems to have encouraged it. Something to keep an eye on! I call this creative instance that is established 'before' the manifestation of life and of the work, and which allows Genet to pass from a derealizing fabulation to these 'fabulous images' that produce the real, 'processual praxis'. It is constituted by three levels – modular, polyphonic, synaptic – that entertain synchronic relations, and not of three stages.

The level of modular crystallizations

A multitude of fragments of sense sweep helter-skelter across the world and the psyche. Everyone who has been well brought up, that is to say, every soul whose reflexes and mind have been duly normalized, knows how to discipline essentially heretical, dissident and perverse voices. But Genet was not well brought up, and he never intended being reborn into the common world ('I will always be haunted by the idea of a murder that will irremediably separate me from your world'). Rather than living this turbulence in the way that it is generally lived, under the gaze of the other, as so many calamities, abysses of anxiety and guilt, he decides to live with it, to tame it, transmute it ('Repudiating the virtues of your world, criminals hopelessly agree to organize a forbidden universe'[51]). By way of rhythms, refrains, passwords, magical-mnemotechnical formulae, he takes partial control of this primary processuality of sense. He learns how to make the worst horrors of punishment, humiliation and prison change sign, change into signs and make of them intensely erotico-aesthetic values. Sartre has this superb formula regarding *Our Lady of Flowers*: it was the collection of his erotic talismans. But what really must be seen is that this entire labour of the primary recrystallization of sense bears indifferently on the perception of the world and on language. I needed to drill into a mass of language, he writes, in *Diary of a Thief*, and like an echo, in *Prisoner of Love* he describes a world that hollows itself out 'in the time it takes to think that prison is hollow, or full of holes and cavities, a man can imagine in each of them a time and a rhythm different from those of the stars'.[52] In one case, it is the signifier that leads the dance, in the other, it is the signified. In fact, it is the traditional opposition between expression and content that proves to be relative and deficient here. What matters to Genet is not the communication of a message but the constitution of an expression that everywhere exceeds its linguistic components.

> Languages may be an easily learned method of communicating ideas, but by 'language' shouldn't we really mean something else? Words, and above all syntax, conveyed to the young almost before vocabulary, together with stones and straw and the names of grasses, streams, tadpoles, minnows, the seasons and their changes, the names of illnesses.[53]

From this point of view, the figures of the signifier and the figures of the signified will have to converge such that a matter of expression will impregnate a context and, reciprocally, so a context will imprint its impulses, its paradigmatic perversions, on discursive chains (whether or not they are of a linguistic order).

Starting with a particularly important module for *Prisoner of Love*, one that crystallizes around the names 'Fatah' and 'Palestinian', let us consider these diverse access routes. Genet begins by scrutinizing the scriptural matter of 'Fatah'. This word was forged artificially on the basis of the initials FTH: Fa for Flasteen= Palestine; Th for Tahrir = Liberation; Ha for Haraka = Movement.[54] Since he gains nothing from this, he turns to possibilities of the 'clandestine' germination of semantic content. Let us note that at this stage he stays with the significations surfacing in Arabic – he doesn't give in to 'free associations'. 'Fatah' begins by being charged with the senses of 'fissure, chink, opening…a victory willed by God' it then entails 'meftah' = key and the fact it contains the three basic letters of 'Fatah', then 'Fatiha', the name of the opening surat of the Koran. It will be noticed that this triple transformation diagonally reconstitutes the original structure of the initials FA.TH.HA:

So, here the signified has moved into the position of the structural key for the signifier! A game for children and philologists, Genet exclaims! However, that is not the essential point. What is essential here is that through this association of ideas, he succeeds in constellating three Universes of reference: sexual, divine and revolutionary 'behind the three words derived from the same root as Fatah lurk the idea of a struggle (for victory), sexual violence (the key in the lock), and battle won through the grace of God'.[55] We are not far from Freud, but the Freud of the good years, the mad years of *The Interpretation of Dreams* and *Jokes and Their Relation to the Unconscious*.

With the word 'Palestinian' one quits the terrain of letters and etymologies (Palestinian = Philistine) for that of phonemes and the timbre of the voice, 'four syllables whose mystery doubtless came from the nocturnal element of their most precious enemies.'[56] Genet explains that a shuddering, an affect of sadness, linked to a key image – that of a grave waiting like a shadow at the feet of every fighter – is triggered in him just on hearing the word 'Palesti'.[57] This rectangular shadow, which doesn't stop following him around, is like the label of his singularity, the guarantee of his complete lucidity in the face of death and is unlike the white world, which 'moves forward without a shadow'.[58] One rediscovers the same type of modular schema, where the light finds itself treated by shadow in numerous variations on the theme of Black and White in their relation to writing: 'In white America, the Blacks are the characters in which history is written.They are the ink that gives the white page a meaning.'[59] Beyond any Manichaeism, the function of the Fatah-Palestian module seems to be to relink contraries at the most extreme points of their antagonism. Even the rivalry between 'Palestine shall conquer' and 'Israel shall live' seems to harbour traces of a hyper-paradoxical complicity between landless peoples of yesterday and today. That being the case, the primary quality of the Palestinians, as has already been said, resides in their resolute acceptance of finitude, whereas the Israelis, on the other hand, persist in their addiction to pernicious dreams of eternal life.[60]

Let us also signal other fantastic manifestations of this module, in which the Palestinian revolution appears to him in a hypnagogic image as the tail of a caged tiger sketching out a 'hyperbolic flourish and brushing its tired curve onto its flank', to find an inimitable taste of the familiarity of slang.[61]

I've tried to illustrate this first modular level of processual praxis on the basis of an example that is relatively circumscribed from a textual point of view, and always with a minimum of semantic safeguards. But I could just as easily have started from more deterritorialized modules: I've already mentioned the problematic of the drilling of holes in the real and in language; I'm also thinking of the technique of 'flattening' Hamza's mother ('like a flat cardboard dummy'[62]) who could only have played the key role at the heart of the 'family romance' forged by Genet to the extent that she previously underwent this modular treatment. Or the extraordinary game of cards without cards which is pursued throughout the book, like a red thread, an abstract machine for flaking, layering the real and predisposing it to being charged with new possibilities. Certainly, many other writers have built up their creation on similar modular concatenations to these. In the first place, of course, one should cite Proust, with his cortège of leitmotifs, of fecund moments, of refrains.[63] But beyond the relatively anecdotal fact that in Genet the loose paving stones – on the basis of which memories start to proliferate – are no longer situated in the courtyard at Guermantes or in St Mark's cathedral but in the devasted camps of Shabra and Chatila,[64] I believe that there is also another type of use of intensive traits in his work which he frees on this occasion. He is not imprisoned in the universe of memory. On the contrary, the process was ceaselessly exposed to the encounter of heterogeneous realities that could inflect it, make it fluctuate far from pre-existing equilibria, or even derail it. I'm not saying that Proust went round in circles! A whole world finds its expression in his work too. But it is a world mastered like a well-tempered clavier, a definitively closed world. There is a plus (and perhaps, in a different sense, a minus) in Genet: the opening up of the expanses of the ocean, the insistent presence of death, finitude, the risk of total and definitive incomprehension.

The polyphonic level of fabulous images

At this level it is no longer a matter of drawing out from each primary module the voices that can be expressed through it, but of enlarging fields of virtuality, allowing new Universes of reference and singular modalities of expression to emerge by conjugating heterogeneous voices. In two words, it is a matter of producing another real, correlative to another subjectivity.

It may happen that a module engenders distended significations that are so contrary to one another that it ends up losing control of them (for example, when, in *Funeral Rites,* Genet wrote the word 'Hitlerian' and saw the Church of the Trinity advance towards him like the eagle of the Third Reich).[65] It is completely different when several modules entertain what Mikhail Bakhtin calls dialogic relations. Not only can the most unheard of exchanges be supported, but additionally they can engender a surplus value of sense, a supplement of singularity, an existential taking consistency. Proust had superimposed the amorous dance of a wasp and an orchid onto the voyeuristic revelation of the guilty relations between Charlus and Jupien.[66] In Genet, the flower is linked to the convict:

> The convict's outfit is pink and white striped. Though it was at my heart's bidding that I chose the universe wherein I delight, I have at least the power of finding in it the many meanings I wish to find: there is a close relationship between flowers and convicts.[67]

So, two or three universes crystallize together: jail, flowers, poetry… Anything else? The agitation that results from the oscillation between flowers and jailbirds, Genet specifies in a note.

With the example of the game of cards without cards, we have already signalled that an intermediary module could supplant the terms that it joins together and set to work on its own count. The game of cards is the feast of Obon in Japan, during which the dead are supposed to come back to visit the living[68], it is a 'dry masturbation'[69], it is a way of characterizing the Palestinians [70], it is the imaginary guitar of Lieutenant Mubarak [71], it is the trickery of the brother of the knight of Grieux, who allow Nabila, a Lebanese nurse, to be associated with Manon Lescaut, it is a world of silhouettes, it is writing, which is only 'eyewash' [72], and, ultimately, it is nothing in particular, it is a style, a principle of deterritorialization…But the 'fabulous images' will go further in acquiring autonomy. Let us now try to define more specifically their modalities of expression. The best example that we can offer of them is Mubarak, the Sudanese lieutenant, a senior officer in the PLO. He is a composite character of whom it is impossible to assess how much of Genet's portrait of him is imaginary:[73] a negro with tribal markings, a lover of cheap junk, a 'fabulous animal', a skilled soldier from Sandhurst military college, a reader of Spinoza, a dancer to African rock, a pervert, voyeur, pimp, whore, this graceful black man is one of the rare protagonists in *Prisoner of Love* who succeeded in bringing Genet out of what was his sexual reservednesss, at least psychically, during his Palestinian wanderings. 'He wallowed in my discomfiture'. [74] But what is it, exactly, that touches him in this abundant character? It seems that it is certain traits that pass across several avatars: the timbre of his voice ('his sperm seemed to be transmitted through the guttural tones of his voice' [75]) and his way of speaking French like Maurice Chevalier…his limping, a trait they shared, and also his silhouette, which is very important! In this regard, we should note a curious transferring of an existential cutout between the narrator and the Sudanese man, one day when the latter was amusing himself by imitating his [walk], in response to an imitation that Genet had himself just tried out:

> He imitated me going up and down some mud steps. Thanks to him I saw myself as a huge figure outlined against an almost black sky, descending in the distance, though nearby, a bit stooped with the weariness of age and from marching up and down hills as high to me as the clouds over Nablus, and limping at the end of the day. The limp was simplified and exaggerated, but just like the way I walked. I realised I was looking at myself for the first time, not in a so-called Psyche-mirror or cheval glass but through eyes that had found me out…[76]

Let's be clear that the fabulous image here has nothing do with the image one [comes up against] in the mirror of the psyche or in that of pure alterity. There is no longer any reflecting-reflected mirage, any imaginary supercharged with identifications, phantasms or anything else of this kind. It is to Mubarak that Genet owes his power to apprehend himself from an angle that is all the more true, all the more real for having been reworked, rewritten, repainted, mise en scène again. As a counterpart, he has a polychromatic memory of Mubarak, dominated by violet and Prussian Blue [77]. A multi-colour negro[78] who makes the Constellation of Universes of sex, violence and theological virtue – around which he had been turning for so long – more intelligible. A negro chameleon at the crossroads of his dreams of Africa, his prison loves, black America, and the shadowy part of the Palestinian struggles. It appears here that the time of Archibald's imprecations in *The Blacks* really is over: 'Let Negroes negrify themselves. Let them persist to the point of madness in what they're condemned to, in their ebony, in their odor, in their yellow eyes, in their cannibal tastes'.[79] Black is no longer the other side of White, nor its limit. It has become the probe-head – 'the laughing Panthers wore a dense furry sex on their heads'[80] able to explore the repressed values of the West and its logics, where 'discontinuity and number, those two names of death' as Sartre writes,[81] are suspended. However, we will have to make space for another enunciative procedure, because the fabulous image in turn shows its limitations! Mubarak wavers, cracks, breaks up in a fragmenting of the body and the world; a continuity solution for the process threatens:

I was surprised to see the world bisected. The image took the form of a person there at the moment when it happened. It's a moment that seems short when the knife is sharp, but which seemed long as Lieutenant Mubarak walked in front of me in the setting sun. He was the knife, or rather the handle of the knife that was slicing the world in two … The lieutenant, walking before me and separating the light from darkness.[82]

The synaptic level of existential operators

Both the modular concatenation of cosmic and signaletic fluctuations and the 'fabulous' harmonizing of voices that were not generically destined to meet each other, left the subject without any hold on the creative process: neither from a position of passive contemplation nor from a position of active orchestration. Now it is enunciation as such which he aims at. In a certain fashion it is a return to the idea of primitive swallowing. Is it a crazed attempt at self-mastery (of ipseity, in Sartre's terminology) or rather – as we will see – a methodical enterprize of the production of a mutant subjectivity? Everything will depend here on the capacity of the aforementioned process to avoid being imprisoned by the phantasm.

One day in October 1971, Genet makes the acquaintance of a couple of Palestinians – Hamza and his mother – in a refugee camp in Jordan. This encounter, which he was profoundly affected by without ever managing to understand why, will lead him to re-evaluate his relation to the Palestinian revolution and will give a direction to the book project that was to end up as *Prisoner of Love*. What I call an existential operator or synapse is constituted from it, that is to say, an Assemblage that is at once psychic, material and social, able to put in place a new type of enunciation and, as a consequence, a new subjective production. His reflection, the journeys, but above all, a long search for dreams and lost revolutions, were to converge on the setting up of this instance.

Hamza is a 17-year-old combatant to whom Genet was entrusted by his Palestinian friends. They will only spend a few hours together, before and after the young man leaves on a mission against the Jordanian army, which had just begun to attack the PLO's bases. Subsequently, Genet won't have any news of him for 14 years: certain rumours will make him believe that he died during torture, until he finally manages to find a trace of him in Germany. On that night, Hamza's mother had put Genet up in her son's room. He remembers with emotion the moment when she came into the darkened room to bring him a Turkish coffee and a glass of water on a tray. He stayed silent, with his eyes closed. He realized that this woman was, quite naturally, bringing him coffee as if he were her son. Genet experiences genuine love at first sight for this unknown couple who, in his own words, became a 'fixed mark' which guided him. 'My fixed mark might be called love, but what sort of love was it that had germinated, grown and spread in me for fourteen years for a boy and an old woman I'd only ever seen for twenty-four hours?'[83].

All the elements of fabulous conversion previously described can be found here, the same semiotic distortions, with Hamza's silhouette cut out against a thick shadow, in particular. When he evokes the mother opening the door of the bedroom, for example, he always sees the son next to her, immense,

> in the end I never imagined just one image on its own: there was always a couple, one of them seen in ordinary attitudes and realistic dimensions while the other was a gigantic presence of mythological substance and proportions. It might be summed up as an apparition of a colossal couple, one human and the other fabulous.[84]

But another labour, which I will call one of sanctification, is added to this labour of 'fabulous image creation' if I may call it that. The mother-Hamza couple literally finds itself bound to the pieta-Christ couple, in a sort of family romance, like those in which some children attribute themselves a noble heredity, in which, not content with being an orphan, Genet voluptuously occupies all the places – of husband, wife, crucified victim and so on.[85] He had already a conducted a similar religious transformation a long time before, by magnifying the penal colony: "I call the Virgin Mother and Guiana the Comforters of the Afflicted."[86] But evidently the Holy Land lends itself much better to this kind of operation! We will note in passing that in both cases one finds oneself in the presence of a deterritorialized earth, but one notes that Genet is all the more nostalgic for prison given that the latter has been abolished, is a dream prison and that he is all the more compassionate with regard to the Palestinian desire to recover their lands given that he reckons achieving this is problematic. However, the essential point lies in the supplement of processual power that is brought to the fabulous image by this narrative graft of a religious origin. The image is not just a crossroads for heterogeneous voices/pathways; it works for itself; in a certain way it becomes self-sufficient, self-referent, self-processual. This doesn't prevent it from enlarging its field of action over memory and the occurrences of events. Like the fabulous image, its function is to produce a singular temporality, a specific way of discursivizing subjectivity. But it proceeds to do so in an even more open manner, ceasing to turn round and round the contours of an icon but constantly deploying new lines of possibility. Genet experimented with his self-divination procedure in his prison time:

it was within me that I established this divinity – origin and disposition of myself. I swallowed it. I dedicated to it songs of my own invention. At night I would whistle. The melody was a religious one. It was slow. Its rhythm was somewhat heavy. I thought I was thereby entering into communication with God: which is what happened, God being only the hope and fervor contained in my song.[87]

However, it will be admitted that this is a God in need of a bit of air! In fact, the Virgin Mary-prison coupling represented a veritable tour de force for trying to overcome a crack in the universe that could seem irrevocable, uncurable. Sartre's equation imaginary – derealization – evil – solitude was never far away.[88] With Lieutenant Mubarak, good and evil, black and white begin to entertain relations that are complex in a different way. Reality not only opens up, it is charged with infinite virtualities. However, the character still remains too massively mythological, barely fit to enter into fine-grained subjectification procedures and finally, as we have seen, he himself becomes the agent for a new splitting of the world. Everything changes with the synaptic double articulation:

$$
\text{Genet} \begin{cases} \text{Hamza–Mother} \\ \\ \text{Christ–Virgin Mary} \end{cases}
$$

The term 'synaptic' aims to underline that one is right to expect something very different to simple rearrangements or harmonics of sense from this operator: a pragmatic effect, an existential surplus value, the release of new Constellations of Universes of reference. Relations are now less identitarian, less personological – however tempting it may be to reduce them to Oedipus and incest.[89] Henceforth, numen no longer affixes itself to the marrow of images, but finds itself distilled in much more molecular praxes, if you will, appropriate for transforming the everyday perception of the world and its eschatological horizons.[90] Besides, Hamza is not even a believer, he is neither Muslim nor Christian. That wouldn't change anything. And when, after 14 years of eclipse, he will 'rise from the dead' for Genet, married to a German, probably the father of a whole rabble, that will not desacralize him, it will not take apart our existential operator. This is for the good reason that its efficacity doesn't reside in its visible cogs but in a machine of abstract intensities, conjugating Universes of jouissance, poetry, freedom, death to come, in a new way…Through it, something comes undone for Genet. Through it, another Genet is born. An end to the faultline, the laceration. He explains that he has 'cut this couple out to suit [him]self, cut it out from a contininuum that included space and time and all the connections with country, family and kin.'[91] Even the past, present and future seem to want to be superposed, in one of those retroactive smoothings of time dear to Réné Thom, in such a way that it seems to him that the Palestinian revolution is an integral part of his oldest memories.[92] And what if death too was, in truth, nothing more than a resurrection of the instant: a wellspring of absence, of potential. 'To have been dangerous for a thousandth of a second, to have been handsome for a thousandth of a thousandth of a second, to have been that, or happy or something, and then to rest – what more can one want?'[93]

ARCHITECTURAL ENUNCIATION

For millennia and perhaps in imitation of crustaceans or termites, human beings have had the habit of surrounding themselves with shells of all kinds. The buildings, clothes, cars, images and messages that they endlessly secrete, stick to their skin, adhere to the flesh of their existence just as much as their bones do. There nevertheless exists a notable difference between humans, crustaceans and termites, which is that so far no one has detected corporations of architects, tailors or media 'professionals' in the last two species. Whatever the case may be, one observes that for a very long period of history it is to an ecolithical expression of the sort that builds ziggurats, demolishes the Bastille, takes the Winter Palace that we owe the delineation of social Assemblages. Except that recently, besides stone being hidden behind steel, concrete and glass, it is above all in terms of speeds of communication and the mastery of information that the division of powers is played out. Under these conditions, architects no longer really know which saint to pray to! What use today would it be to invoke Le Corbusier in a city like Mexico, for example, which is careering deliriously towards its 40 millionth inhabitant! Even Baron Hausmann wouldn't be able to do anything about it! Politicians, technocrats, engineers deal with this sort of thing by having as little recourse as possible to the men of an art that Hegel nonetheless put in first place. Certainly architects retain control of a minimal niche in the domain of sumptuary constructions. But we know that positions are expensive in this domain, and, short of accepting – like a postmodern dandy – the politico-financial wheeler-dealering that they imply at every step, their rare occupiers are generally doomed to an under-handed degrading of their creative talents. The paths of pure theory,[1] of utopia,[2] of a nostalgic return to the past,[3] remain. Or even that of critical contestation, although the times scarcely seem to lend themselves to it!

The object of architecture has been smashed to pieces. It is useless to hold on to what it was or what it ought to be! Situated at the inter-section of political stakes of the first importance, of democratic and ethnic tensions, of economic, social and regional antagonisms that are nowhere near resolved, spurred on by constant technological and industrial mutations, it is irreversibly condemned to being dragged and pulled in every direction. However, nothing implies that one must take the eclectic side in this state of affairs, which on the contrary perhaps calls for an exacerbation of the ethico-political choices that have always been subjacent to the exercise of this profession. It is henceforth impossible to take refuge behind art for art's sake or pure science in good faith.[4] Reinventing architecture can no longer signify the relaunching of a style, a school, a theory with a hegemonic vocation, but the recomposition of *architectural enunciation*, and, in a sense, the trade of the architect, under today's conditions.

Once it is no longer the goal of the architect to be the artist of built forms but to offer his services in revealing the virtual desires of spaces, places, trajectories and territories, he will have to undertake the analysis of the relations of individual and collective corporeality by constantly singularizing his approach. Moreover, he will have to become an intercessor between these desires, brought to light, and the interests that they thwart. In other words, he will have to become an artist and an artisan of sensible and relational lived experience. Understand that I do not particularly intend to make him recline on the psychoanalytic couch, so as to make him accept such a decentring of his role. On the contrary, I consider that it is the architect who finds he is in the position of having to analyse certain specific functions of subjectification himself.[5] In this way and in the company of numerous other social and cultural operators, he could constitute an essential relay at the heart of multiple-headed Assemblages of enunciation, able to take analytic and pragmatic responsibility for contemporary productions of subjectivity. As a consequence, one really is a long way here from only seeing the architect in the simple position of critical observer!

With the accent thus displaced from the object to the project – whatever the characteristics of its semiotic expression and semantic content may be – an architectural work henceforth calls for a specific elaboration of its enunciative 'matter': how is one to be an architect today? Which part of oneself is to be mobilized? In what way must one engage and with what operators? What relative importance will developers, engineers, urbanists, actual and potential users have for him? To what point will it be licit to compromise with the diverse parties present? It is a matter here of a highly elaborated transferential economy that I propose to examine from the angle of the two modalities of consistency of the enunciation of an architectural *concept*:

- one is polyphonic, of the order of the *percept*, inherent to the deployment of components contributing to its discursive setting into existence;
- the other is ethico-aesthetic, of the order of the *affect*, inherent to its non-discursive 'taking on of being'.

The polyphonic components

Under the category of scale, Philippe Boudon has inventoried 20 angles from which to attack the architectural object, which essentially turn out to be centred on the category of space. He has proposed regrouping them in four categories:

- those that refer to real space itself (geographical optical scales of visibility, proximity and surveyed lots of land);
- those that refer architectural space to an external referent (symbolic, formal, technical, functional scales, scales of extension, dimensional, socio-cultural and economic symbolics, the symbolics of the model);
- those that refer architectural space to its representation (geometrical, cartographic and representation scales);
- finally, those of the architectural approach in so far as it comes and goes constantly between these different spaces ('put to scale', 'give the scale of', etc.).[6]

One could doubtless list further components of this nature. But by taking the point of view of enunciation and no longer that of a simple taxonomic enumeration of modes of spatialization, it is evident that their potential number becomes properly infinite. Every virtual enunciation roams in the vicinity of the architectural object. As Henri Lier writes 'every signifying architectural work grasps itself as able to be different to what it is. An abode is never the abode but it refers to the abode; it is one of its possibilities, appearing as such.'[7] Nevertheless, on this continuous spectrum of virtual enunciations, I have retained eight types of Assemblages corresponding to the 'voices' that seem to me to be effectively enacted in contemporary architecture.

1 *A geopolitical enunciation* taking into account the points of the compass, the unevenness of the terrain, demographic climatic

givens, as well as changes in the long duration such as the trend to secularization, dear to Fernand Braudel,[8] which affect the drifting centre of gravity of the 'city archipelagos'[9] as a function of the fluctuations of the world economy.[10]

2   *An urbanistic enunciation* relative to laws, regulations, habits and customs concerning the size of terrains, the disposition and size of buildings as much as the contamination mechanisms of model and image (relating to what Philippe Boudon calls the 'scale of proximity'). Interlocutors here can be incarnated in the 'hard' form of bureaucrats, State bodies or in the vague form of collective states of mind or opinion, more or less relayed through the media.

3   *An economic enunciation*, the capitalistic expression of relations of force between different individual and collective systems of valorization. Starting from an evaluation relative to costs and demands in terms of expected profit, prestige, political impact and social utility, it leads to the fixing of a market value for real estate and to 'piloting' the choices and amounts of investment in the domain of construction.

4   *A functional enunciation* or infrastructure function [fonction d'équipement] that considers built spaces in terms of their specific utilization. Collective apparatuses, as much as apparatuses meant for private use, are integrated at the heart of a double network of:

   i   'horizontal' complementary relations positioning each constructed segment in the ensemble of urban structures that today are interconnected at the heart of worldwide capitalism;[11]

   ii 'vertical' relations of integration ranging from micro-facilities (light, air, communication, etc.) to the macro-facilities of infrastructure.

   As Paul Virilio writes

   today…the essence of what we insist on calling urbanism is composed/decomposed by these transfer, transit and transmission systems, these transport and transmigration networks whose immaterial configuration reiterates the cadastral organisation and building of ornaments. If there are monuments today, they are certainly not of the visible order, despite the twists and turns of architectural excess. No longer part of perceptible appearances nor of the aesthetic of the apparition of volumes assembled under the sun, this monumental disproportion now resides within the obscure luminescence of terminals, consoles and other electronic night-stands.'[12]

Consequently the collective enunciators here are:

- Social stratifications according to resources, age groups, regional particularities, ethnic segregation, etc.;

- Social bodies sectorized as a function either of their specialist activities of an economic order or their welfare situation (hospitalization, imprisonment, etc.);

- Planners, experts, technicians of all kind who are in a position to state the constraints and norms of architectural writing.

5 *A technical enunciation* that implies a capturing of the speech of the equipment and more generally the materials of construction involved in, for example,

> fixing the slope of a roof as a function of the relative permeability of the material employed, the thickness of a wall as a function of its load, the dimensions of a material as a function of its handleability or transportability or its putting to work.[13]

The interlocutory relays here are not only with construction engineers but also chemists, who invent new materials every month, electrical and communication engineers and, little by little, the entirety of scientific and technical disciplines.

6 *A signifying enunciation* the aim of which is, independently of functional semantemes, to assign a significant content to a built form shared by a human community that is more or less extended but always delimited by the ensemble of other communities not sharing this same type of content. One finds several of Philippe Boudon's scales again here. The scale that results in a building incarnating a symbolic form independently of its size (for example, the cruciform plan of Christian churches). The scale that traces the disposition of a construction on the basis of an explicit ideological model (the ideal city of Vitruvius, the 'rural', 'industrial' or 'exchange' cities of Le Corbusier...). The scale at which, on the contrary, a more or less unconscious socio-cultural scheme intervenes (like the central patio that Arabic builders have in all likelihood inherited from Ancient Rome), or the even vaguer scale that confers a global style on the laying out of a city (such as the atmosphere of being closed in on itself of small Tuscan towns, which is light years away from the opening onto a transfinite spatium of North-American agglomerations, clinging to the flow of a freeway as they do).

7 *An enunciation of existential territorialization* of a perspectival as much as of an ethological order, which I will link to the three types of space that Vittorio Ugo has distinguished for us:[14]

- Euclidean spaces, under the aegis of Apollo, which position an object-identity in a univocal fashion in the framework of an axiomatico-deductive logic, and at the heart of which is inscribed an 'architecture that is primary and elementary in all the clarity of its crystalline perfection, always identical to itself and devoid of any ambiguity or internal contradiction';

- projective spaces, under the aegis of Morpheus, which position forms with a modulated identity, metamorphic perspectives, which affirm the primacy of 'the imaginary over reality, of the gaze over speech, extension over use, the project over perception';

- labyrinthine topological spaces functioning as existential places,[15] under the aegis of Dionysus, according to a geometry of the envelopment of the tactile body which already refers us to the register of affects.

Architectural space is one concrete operator among many of the metabolism between the objects of the outside and the intensities of the inside. But if, from Vitruvius to Le Corbusier – passing via Leonardo da Vinci – the play of correspondences between the human body and habitat have been explored ceaselessly, perhaps it is now a matter less of considering the latter from a formal angle but from a point of view that can be characterized as organic. As Massimo Cacciari writes 'every authentic organism is labyrinthine.'[16] We will refer to the multiple fractal dimension of the labyrinthine (or rhizomatic) characteristic of existential territorialization later on.

8 *A scriptural enunciation* that articulates the ensemble of other enunciative components. Because of the diagrammatic distance that it introduces between expression and content, and through the coefficients of creativity that it generates, architectural design promotes new potentialities, new Constellations of Universes of reference, beginning with those that preside over the deployment of the ethico-aesthetic aspects of the built object.

Ethico-aesthetic ordinates

Architectural enunciation doesn't only involve diachronic discursive components. It equally implies a taking consistency of synchronic existential dimensions or levels of ordinates. Following Bakhtin, I will distinguish three types:[17]

- Cognitive ordinates, that is, the energetico-spatio-temporal coordinates that arise from the logics of discursive sets. It is in this register that the scriptural enunciation of architecture concatenates the first five types of Assemblage of enunciation previously listed;

- Axiological ordinates encompassing the ensemble of systems of anthropocentric valorization, as much of an ethical as of an economic and political order;

- Aesthetic ordinates determining the thresholds of consummation of an entity, an object or a structural ensemble, in so far as these start to emit sense and form on their own count. It pertains to these ethico-aesthetic ordinates to make the components of signifying enunciation and existential deterritorialization interface with other components. Thus the built, the lived and the incorporeal find themselves rearticulated with one another, although capitalist societies haven't stopped eliminating every trace of subjective singularization from their architecture and town planning, to the profit of rigourous functional, informational and communicational transparency.

Don't misunderstand me: the singularization of which it is a question here is not a simple affair of 'spiritual compensation', a 'personalization' dispensed as a kind of 'after-sales service'. It arises from instances that operate at the heart of the architectural object and confer its most intrinsic consistency on it. Under its external discursive face, this object is established at the intersection of a thousand tensions that pull it in every direction; but under its ethico-aesthetic enunciative faces it holds itself together in a non-discursive mode, the phenomenological access to which is given to us through the particular experience of spatialized Affects. On this side of a threshold of cognitive consistency, the architectural object topples over into the imaginary, the dream, delirium, whereas on this side of a threshold of axiological consistency, the dimensions of it that are the bearers of alterity and desire crumble – like the cinematic images that

Australian Aboriginals turned away from long ago because they found nothing of interest in them. On this side of an aesthetic threshold of consistency, it ceases to catch the existence of the forms and intensities called on to inhabit it.

As a consequence, in the last analysis, the specificity of the architect's art would be his capacity to apprehend these Affects of spatialized enunciation. Except one has to admit that it is a matter of paradoxical objects, which cannot be located in the coordinates of ordinary rationality and which one can only approach indirectly, through meta-modelling, aesthetic detour, mythical or ideological narrative. Like Melanie Klein's part objects[18] or the transitional objects of Winnicott,[19] this kind of affect is established transversally across the most heterogeneous of levels. Not in order to homogenize them but, on the contrary, to engage them more deeply in fractal processes of heterogenesis. The architectural form is not called on to function as a gestalt closed in on itself, but as a catalytic operator triggering chain reactions at the heart of modes of semiotization that make us escape from ourselves and open us up to original fields of possibility. The feeling of intimacy and existential singularity connected to the aura exuded by familiar surroundings, an old residence or a landscape inhabited by our memories, establishes itself in a rupture with substanceless redundancies and it can generate proliferation and lines of flight in every register of the desire to live, the refusal to give in to the dominant inertia. For example, it is the same movement of existential territorialization and synchronic taking consistency that will make things as different as: a box for shoes and treasures under the bed of a child hospitalized in a medico-psychological boarding school; the password-refrain that he perhaps shares with some mates; the place at the heart of the particular Constellation he occupies in the refectory; a totem-tree in the playground and an outline [découpe] of the sky known only by him all 'work' together. It is up to the architect, if not to compose all these fragmentary components of subjectification harmoniously, at least not to mutilate the essentials of their virtualities in advance!

To work in this way for the recomposition of existential Territories, in the context of our societies devastated by capitalistic Flows, the architect would thus have to be capable of detecting and exploiting processually the catalytic points of singularities that can be incarnated in the sensible dimensions of the architectural apparatus as well as in the most complex of formal compositions and institutional problematics. Every cartographic method for achieving this is licit, once the architect's *commitment* – let us not step back from this old Sartrean concept, which has long been taboo – finds its own regime of ethico-aesthetic autonomization. The only criterion for truth that will be imposed on him will then be an effect of existential consummation and superabundance of being, which he will not fail to encounter once he has the good fortune to find himself carried off by a process of eventization, that is to say, of the historical enrichment and re-singularization of desire and of values.

ETHICO-AESTHETIC REFRAINS IN THE THEATRE OF WITKIEWICZ

Enunciation rests on a constantly modified subjectification. That is to say, one cannot connect it and disconnect it as one would a computer. One never stops arranging it and decomposing it so as to recompose it on different bases. From this point of view, theatre work may constitute one of its most significant paradigms.

Certain operators, which I call sensible refrains, mark the phase transitions from one Assemblage of enunciation to another. Example: the ceremony relating to a fetish object capable of setting off a perverse enunciation. Or, in the opposite direction, an inhibition, a slip of the tongue, a lapsus that throws a register of enunciation to which subjectification thought itself well secured out of gear. But there are also more complex operators that are not directly apprehendable in terms of concrete expression, which I call problematic refrains, or abstract machines. Certain of the narrative montages of Witkiewicz's theatre will serve to illustrate this second modality, particularly those that are centred on the theme of the loved woman who is killed at her own request.

Allow me two more brief remarks before examining *The Pragmatists,*[1] which is one of the two pretexts for our meeting today, from this point of view.

Concrete and sensible or abstract, phantasmatic and problematic: what purpose do these refrains really serve? Let us make it clear straightaway that we will not make a hermeneutic use of them here, nor seek to extract 'latent contents', even eschatological messages, from them! This is because for us they are essentially existential shifters having as their mission the putting into place, the circumscription, singularization and support – from the point of view of their consistency – of Universes of reference, Universes which, moreover, remain fundamentally unlocalizable, incorporeal, with neither organ nor spatio-temporal limit. Thus symptom-refrains make us cross the threshold of a hysterical, obsessional or paranoid apprehension of the world (in a direct relation of existential appropriation as much as by way of external witnessing). A minimal faciality refrain will allow a baby, shortly after being born, to cling to a maternal Umwelt. A modal pentatonic refrain, deployed on the basis of a handful of notes, will project us into the Debussyist universe. A play of gestural, vestimentary, intonational refrains will freeze us in the judicial libido – a somewhat morbid world of offences and punishment. Nothing here happens naturally, of its own accord. Triggers, operators, specifically assembled catalysers are needed.

And what characterizes such refrains, what allows them to be recognized? As a general rule it is a matter of expressive concatenations whose syntagmatic weft or discourse of content find themselves brutally interrupted, the effect of which is to prohibit a particular chain from deploying its relational antennae, leading it, on the contrary, to coil up on itself and go round and round to infinity. When things go badly, this repetition triggers an implosion of the expressive system, which can find itself carried off in a generalized rout, whilst it can equally happen that a positive setting into refrain activates this same segment of expression or content and starts to generate a process that will play a role of self-referenced enunciative nucleus.

Now let us come to the 'pragmatists'. The polyphony developed by its five principal characters is established on the basis of a sort of original bass or 'tenor' full-song that will remain subjacent throughout the whole of the development of the play. The degree zero of expression, this inexhaustible flow of speech, this uninterrupted internal chattering, is assimilated to a conversation with the loved woman – Mammalia, as it happens – who paradoxically is completely mute and only expresses herself through more or less hysterical mimicking and gesticulation. 'This ghastly torture is the essence of my life. Talking with a woman! My God! Was I created only to be something through which the stream of existence could flow, without ever stopping for even a second.'[2] But later, this chattering will be the object of a less pejorative appreciation, when – relayed to Masculette (an asexual young girl who is nonetheless full of grace) – the author will characterize it as an indispensible chord in the symphony that constitutes his existence 'isn't conversation the most significant way of experiencing life? Let's talk about anything at all... Actually, just the fact of talking itself...With words the wealth of possibilities is far greater than with events.'[3]

We will not remain with this associative flow and a seizing of enunciation will be granted in this play to the double character Plasfodor

Mimecker and Graf Franz von Telek (called von Trottek in the version presented by Philippe Adrien). There is a great deal to say about the strategy of the double in Witkiewicz, beginning with the doubling of his own public identity as Witkacy. (On this point I refer to Daniel Gérold's study *Les doubles dans l'oeuvre de Witkacy.*)[4] At the time Witkiewicz wrote this play it was still a well-known theme, on which he performed a sort of détournement. Let us remember above all that it is less the Hoffmanesque mystery or the psychoanalytic investigation that matters here than the mise en scène of an ethico-political wrenching that is incessant in the same collection.

> Witkacy was constantly torn by a 'double system of values', as he himself wrote, by a double constraint that translates the conflict between aesthetics and morality, a tension that pulled him towards two absolutely contradictory poles simultaneously, Pure Form in Art and, in life, the socialisation that would bring equality and justice to the human herd – two diametrically opposed solutions to the metaphysical problem.

Plasfodor Mimecker is charged with incarnating a demand for aesthetic authenticity that borders on a desire for abolition. 'To live means to create the unknown!' but as the conditions hardly lend themselves to this, it would be better to disappear! 'I've had enough of that! I've blocked off all the exits forever. Only death, hers and mine, will be my sole work!'[5] Quite the opposite of this, his brother-in-law, von Telek, illustrates a ferocious, quasi-bestial life drive. Half a dozen times in the course of the play, a refrain will come to his mouth 'I'm healthy as a bull!' Avid to dine out, with orgies, spiritualism and diverse stimulants added, he is characterized as a 'director of the Ministry of Poisons' but also, and in a somewhat contradictory fashion, as the boss of the union of teetotallers. Sometimes it is a matter of 'teetotaling tramps' and sometimes of 'mechanized teetotalers'. To clarify this point, it would be worth resituating this denunciation of teetotalling, which occurs on several occasions throughout the play, in the context of what were, in pre-World War 1 Germany, campaigns in favour of abstinence, at the heart of numerous youth movements (which in a way prefigure National Socialism). Let us note equally that Thomas Mann criticized this abstinent scum using the voice of one of the characters of *Magic Mountain*. That being so, von Telek is first defined as a pragmatist for whom every move is valid and who, in the domain of art in particular, is ready to exploit no matter what special effect of the day. His last discovery of this sort is something between a non-spatial sculpture and a music that is immobilized in space…But his big idea is to open up a fantastic and macabre cabaret, a sort of club that would produce a 'certain reality' on the basis of all kinds of bizarre things. And he banks on Plasfodor ending up resolving to become its director, despite his obstinate refusal to give up his isolation, so that he might devote himself to who knows what enterprize of socialization and adaptation!

In appearance the dice are cast for the two brothers-in-law, whose rivalry is fuelled by an old incestuous relationship between von Telek and his sister Mamalia, and by a current amorous relationship with Masculette, who is in Plasfodor's service. In every domain the pragmatists appear to be called on to triumph over passionate idealists, all the more so given that at the end of the last act, von Telek, with the health of a bull, is the sole survivor of the intrigue (having in fact eliminated all the other protagonists either through violent death or by disappearing in the gulf of nonsense that borders one side of the scenery). And yet the play is much less Manichean than it appears. Because I haven't yet mentioned the existence of the principal character, I mean the Chinese Mummy, this infernal mummy-machine, this abstract machinic refrain who in truth alone calls the tune. At the start she is introduced by von Telek, being in a way part of his moving circus, but she quickly turns against her manager, who she ends up terrorizing. In fact, an old complicity links her to von Telek's rival Plasfodor, having been seduced by him five years earlier, in a bamboo hut in Saigon. This led him to drink her blood, down to the last drop, something that had the additional benefit of plunging Mammalia into a definitive silence and, as a result, bound her to him forever. Why these veins emptied of their blood? In my opinion it is because it is only through such an ordeal that the Chinese princess that the Mummy was could become a deterritorialized being capable of casting off all the moorings of time and space and confront the problematic that the Janus Bifrons called Witkiewicz-Witkacy runs up against. It pertains to the operator of enunciation henceforth constituted by this magical mummy to convert the old desire for abolition into a desire for pure creation, *ex nihilo*: 'nothing dominates anything, she declares, everything comes into being by itself as part of the whole world, which is only the eye of Nothingness turned in on itself'. She defines herself as the 'Great Connection of Everything with Everything' and as such she can call into question no matter what segment of reality, leading Plasphodorus to cry 'That damned Mummy is the most real Character of us all. It is because of her that reality's crept in among us.'[6]

One of the instruments used by this new operator of enunciation to convert the things of the ordinary world into an incorporeal hyper- or sur-reality and to embrace a much desired 'strangeness of existence' is a machine reminiscent of those of Kafka or Raymond Roussel. A hideous convex plastron that sometimes draws near to and sometimes moves away from Plasfodor. Through its intermediary, virtual threads join together the dream and real life, whilst Plasfodor sinks deep into bottomless abysses: 'soft as down and black as the starless night.' However, this descent is nonetheless torture because the 'sleep without dreams in the Infinity of all that is and ceases to be' that it leads to is identified with Mammalia, who is considered 'punishment personified, which is self-embodied without anyone directing it.'[7] Thus the passion for abolition will not stop arising from a paradigm associating woman, mother and death and it will pertain to the Assemblage of enunciation to put to work a procedure of an entirely different nature so as finally to succeed in warding off the omnipresence of a guilt without object. This task will fall to a threnody, constructed on the phonological basis of the name Mammalia, and which this time is reminiscent of certain of Antonin Artaud's sound poems.

> Ma a a a la ra ga a a a ta
> Ka ma ra ta ka a a la.
> Ma ga ra ta ma ga ha a
> Ma ge ere ka la wa ta pa a a.

It will be recalled that the first intervention of the Mummy in relation to Mammalia had rendered her mute. Her new 'treatment' is more radical still as it consists in making her undergo a double deterritorialization:

1   of her name, transformed into an a-signifying refrain arising from a purely poetic rhythm;

2   of her incarnation as a character, to the extent that, at the end of the play, as I have already signalled, she and Plasfodor will find themselves projected by the Mummy into a black abyss where, before disappearing definitively, she will rediscover her voice one last time, just long enough to emit a frightful cry.

Must one thereby understand that guilt will have been liquidated at the very same time as its Oedipal object, that is, the woman-mother, finds itself sublimated in an aesthetic production? Be careful! The least one can say is that in Witkiewicz, the concept of sublimation is hardly in favour! 'What I am talking about isn't any lousy teetotaling spirituality.'[8] It is rather a matter of a direct transmutation bearing on heterogeneous orders of reality. It is already in this way that the savagery of white desire was formerly converted by the princess of the blue lotus into a play of the colours yellow and black on a palette set up in the pictorial and racial registers at the same time.

Let us signal that this immediate hold over the narrative thread by the distinctive oppositions of colours constitutes a sort of leitmotif in the theatrical oeuvre of Witkiewicz: an example is the ensemble of costumes and scenery of *Gyubal Wahazar* which are composed of yellow, red and black. In *The Water Hen* Witkiewicz speaks of 'little pictures that God makes with his magic pastels'.[9]

Verbal refrains – 'the health of a bull', a-signifying refrains, coloured and plastic refrains, the tics of the characters contribute to the promotion of a problematic refrain articulated on the following nexus: the apparatuses for the conversion of the passion for abolition into aesthetic creation constantly find themselves threatened by the intrusion of the woman-mother as object of desire. How is such a desire to be silenced? One can tear out the tongues of women, one can also neutralize their femininity – that is what will be done on a small scale with Masculette in *The Pragmatists*. It is also what will be done on a large scale in *Gyubal Wahazar*, in which the proto-fascist leader decrees a division of women into two categories: real women, who will be mechanized pitilessly and the 'masculettes, that I turn into men by means of the appropriate transplant of certain glands'.[10] Another solution will consist in killing the loved woman, if possible at her request, as is the case in *The Pragmatists*. For its part, the water hen is killed two times over, once fantasmatically, and the other, in the end, for good. But one senses clearly that in fact it is killed infinitely, in a repetitive, compulsive fashion. The narrative tension of eternal return. An obsessive eroticism, always with the threat that the Ego will close up on itself, like an atrocious trap of solitude. 'My system is unshakeable, cries Gyubal Wahazar. It transposes my own torments into universal values. I am the first martyr of my six-dimensional continuum. No-one has the right to suffer less than I do.'[11] Hence one sees that torture machines, which are so frequent in Witkiewicz's oeuvre, constitute a sort of final expedient, an ultimate hook for alterity. To ward off death by processualizing creation without for all that prostituting it seems to me to be the problematic refrain that inhabits the theatre of Witkiewicz. It might be characterized as cathartic – on condition that one acknowledges that it struggles as much against an endogenous threat of implosion as against the prefabricated myths of psychoanalysis or initiatives in psychological readaptation or re-socialization. Its proclaimed objective, which seems to echo Antonin Artaud's theatre of cruelty, is 'Dadaism in life' and not just in the work of art. An open, prospective, re-singularing analysis, let's say…but it is time for me to stop, otherwise I will start talking to you about schizoanalysis!

KEIICHI TAHARA'S FACIALITY MACHINE[1]

What is a photographic portrait? The impression of a face taken so as to produce a representation, but also the borrowing of certain traits of this face for completely different ends, such as the denotation of a proper name, the evocation of a memory, the triggering of an Affect…It is on this second aspect of the portrait that Keiichi Tahara primarily works. In fact, he only retains from his 'subjects' those traits that he can use to prepare the landscapes that obsess him and, above all, so as to obtain a certain effect of subjectification, towards which his oeuvre as a whole tends. What is it a matter of? Of a transfer of enunciation: instead of it being you, the spectator, who contemplates the photograph, it is suddenly the photograph that surprises you, which starts to scrutinize you, which interpellates you, penetrates you right to the soul.

By means of the hundred or so photographs of personalities collected in the present album, it is possible to take apart the Taharian machine that brings about this effect. It essentially comprises three components that we will examine in succession:

- a deterritorializing cutting out of the face;
- a fractal rupture of the gaze;
- the attaching of an original proliferation of significations – which thus find themselves attached to the proper name – to this apparatus.

Considered without any particular aesthetic qualification, the human face already originates in the detaching of a gestalt figure from an animal muzzle as ground. A face, which is culturally acceptable, is thus obliged to bend to the typical intervals of authorized significant movements. (For example, a smile that exceeds a certain threshold of size would refer to the grimacing of an autistic person or a moron.) However, Keiichi Tahara endeavours to work the traits of faciality in registers of framing and lighting effects that would bring them out of these pre-established montages of signification and would reveal original potentialities. Thus, the faces to which he is attached will find themselves carried off towards non-human, animal, vegetable, mineral, cosmic becomings of abstract composition... that are constitutive of what one might call prospective unconscious dimensions.

This play of framing can proceed at a general level. In contrast to the general frame of the photo, which finds its angles systematically rounded off in an effect of fuzzification, this type of internal reframing can be carried out by way of a window (e.g. Christian Boltanski)[2] or even a mirror.[3] It can equally be done by the implanting of frames that are lateral to the face or to the person and it then consists in a tableau,[4] in quadrangular objects[5] or even in a rectangle of light hanging over the scene.[6] The combinations of the two procedures are frequent. For example, the window at which Boltanski appears itself encompasses other windows and these three stages of fractalization by the nesting of frames then find themselves prolonged by the multitude of layers and branches that seem to envelop the person represented in American shot.[7] This fractalization of framing can sometimes result in a generalized disruption.[8] On other occasions, as is the case with Bram van Velde, it leads, inversely, to a static putting into perspective, conferring on the person a sort of stamp of petrification and eternity. In more than half the portraits, the play of light operates by a vertical cut that bars the face with a fractal line of shadow. The most typical case in this regard is doubtless the portrait of Ricardo Bofill, which opens the collection. In effect, all that subsists of his face is a narrow vertical strip that represents barely a quarter of the photograph's surface, whilst the left eyebrow, the eye, a transverse wrinkle and the corner of his mouth comprise the luminous mass that remains. When the vertical cut is external to the face,[9] and equally when it stays at a tangent to it,[10] the cut stays in the form of a straight line. In the case of Buren, it finds itself multiplied like a series of...columns! It is much rarer for the luminous cut to be horizontal. However, that is the case with Iannis Xenakis, when it brings to mind a musical score cut vertically by a stave. Let us note, with Maurice Rheims a different form of horizontal and vertical crossover and a similar cross-cutting with François Truffaut, to which a detachment of the head, pure and simple, is added.

Another rather frequent method of deterritorialization of the face by the play of light consists in making a small part of it emerge from a large dark mass.[11] It is also worth signalling the use of blurring by the decentring of focal distance,[12] by local shifting[13] or by the use of cigarette smoke,[14] and distinguishing the blurred face in the foreground from general blurring.[15]

Considered for themselves, in their serial effect, or in association, the ensemble of these procedures of deterritorializing cutting out prepare the ground for the putting to work of the second component, that for its part will no longer be content just with fractalizing the spatial frame but the Assemblage of enunciation too.

From the first, decidedly prototypical, portrait of Ricardo Bofill, what seems to me to be the heart of Keiichi Tahara's aesthetic goal finds itself laid bare. To apprehend it, it is worth pinpointing the play of complementarity that is established between the visible eye of the left of his face and the invisible eye of the right of his face, which is ready to reappear in a fugitive but fulgurant, quasi-hallucinatory fashion, on the basis of the miniscule trace of white that remains of it. It is from this metonymic coming and going that the existential effect of being-seen-by-the-portrait originates, a theme that was dear to the Surrealists and which I have already evoked. We are now in a situation in which the ensemble of faciality traits has been destabilized by the deterritorializing treatment of lighting and framing. Henceforth, the structural key to the image no longer adheres to the 'photographic referent' such as Roland Barthes defines it ('I call "photographic referent" not the *optionally* real thing to which an image or a sign refers but the *necessarily* real thing which has been placed before the lens, without which there would be no photograph')[16]. It finds itself transferred to the imaging intentionality of the spectator. My gaze finds itself 'dragged into' the bringing into existence of Bofill; without it, his soul would be scattered to the four winds. But this appropriation turns back on me, sticks to me like a sucker. In its precariousness, this being-there sticks to my skin. It doesn't stop gazing at me from my interior. In short, I am bewitched, the evil eye is put on me, I am expropriated of my interiority.

The vis-à-vis of the photographs equally works at extracting an autonomous, abyssally fractalized gaze. A face-profile movement can be sketched out, a contrast of light, of posture…all things that animate and hollow out representation. In this regard, two of the most significant portraits concern Arman, in which relations of complementarity are established between his beard in the left foreground and a sculpture made of metallic pincers in the right background, the half-lit face on the left and the black profile on the right, the eyes in shadow corresponding to the full opening of the eye-window protected by bars.

One ought in addition to take stock of other modes of enactment of this same existential effect:

- The obscuring of the eyes of Maurice Rheims by means of a horizontal bar of shadow or his being completely back-lit;

- The half-closed eyes of Mario Merz, on whose eyelids a glimmer of light appears, constituting a sort of second vision;
- The reflection of the frames of the spectacles of Degottex, which are substituted for the brightness of his gaze;
- The total vitrification of the blind gaze of Juliette Man Ray, the emission of a luminous cross from the lenses of Levi-Strauss's spectacles or the luminous effervescence of Maurice Rheims's eye;
- The white of the eye which stands out on the face;[17]
- Or, in a more frequent fashion, the iris,[18] or perhaps cornea,[19] that becomes the seat of the emission of a light-gaze.

It is thus on the basis of a fracture of sense that this existential transfer of enunciation is set off, the portrait's capturing of the gaze. Roland Barthes had apprehended this phenomenon through the opposition he makes between the 'stadium', in which the signification of the photo is coded, and the 'punctum' 'sting, speck, cut, little hole – and also a cast of the dice… that accident which pricks me'.[20] He described the force of metonymic expansion of this point of rupture and established a difference between the punctum, founded on a 'detail' that interferes in the register of forms and what he calls a stigmata punctum, which for its part intervenes in a harrowing domain of Time, its lacerating emphasis. But, for me, this stubbornness of facticity – 'that-has-been' – with which the intentionality of the image collides is no more than a case (his meditation on the photograph of his dead mother, for example) that perpetuates a memory folded in on itself. Keiichi Tahara's portraits indicate another path for us, because his principal concern evidently resides neither in denoting the identity of his 'subjects' nor in circumscribing the charges of signification of which they are the bearers. Certainly one sometimes finds references to the domain that confers their fame on them here, but always in the mode of indirect allusions. Here their attested faciality no longer totalizes faciality traits. On the contrary, these start to interfere with contextual traits. They bring deterritorialized Universes of existential reference into existence. But, thinking about it, are we not in the presence of a general faciality function? The face of Christ, like the traces on the Turin Shroud, hasn't stopped haunting Western capitalistic subjectivity, like those of Presidents Washington, Lincoln and Jackson on the American dollar! All signification is inhabited by a deterritorialized faciality that confers on it less its formal sense than its existential substance. What talks to me as a sensible quality, as a gestalt, as an abstract problematic, always does so as an enunciative nucleus incarnated in a face (facialitarian reterritorialization). The voice itself finds itself pre-disposed by this kind of non-discursive faciality, which imposes itself as the presence to itself of an absolutely different present. It is not a matter here of the presence of a 'big Other' in the structuralist lineage of Lacan, but of an alterity modulated by the big and the small turns of history and by the mutation of technological Phyla.

In this regard, to consider photography as a more or less surpassed step in a line that would progressively lead us to cinema, video, computer-assisted digital imaging, etc. would be an unfortunate misunderstanding. As Roland Barthes forcefully underlined, it is in the photograph, more than any other art form, that the existential temporality of the machines of representation lies. Most other media are too talkative, their narrative programmes dominating enunciation too brutally, substituting for it, expropriating the free processes of subjectification of which photography alone can allow the powers of partial temporalization to be deployed (with the exception of the comic strip perhaps, which is capable of equalling it on this terrain).

The very particular interest of Keiichi Tahara's work, in the lineage of his greatest predecessors, consists in diversifying and making the maximum play of what I will call the machinic components of the 'armed' gaze. One meets again here, in new modalities, this sort of subjective effacing of the photographer that Moholy-Nagy sought and which led him, more than half a century ago, to distinguish the production of eight types of gaze: abstract, exact, rapid, slow, intensified, penetrative, simultaneous and distorted.[21] This sort of deterritorializing and de-subjectifying treatment of the portrait consists in staging, in 'landscapifying' a processual faciality on the basis of traits that are offered passively to the enunciator. Let us consider once again some examples.

In the portrait of Kounelis, two discs of raw light break away from the eyes, literally tearing the gaze towards us. They echo an equally rounded glimmer of light that doubles the right-hand side of the face like a collapsed halo. Consequently it is the whole photograph that becomes an eye, the head itself being nothing more than a bulging pupil. The molecular mystery of Arman, where it is a white globule that is parasitic on his nostril and resonates with other circles and white traces behind his head, in counterpoint to the absent eye, on the one hand, and on the other, with the photo facing him, the sculpture of metallic pincers. In the case of Buren, the two white globules have become two conspicuously overexposed white shirt buttons, vibrating with a population of large-headed pins that become thorns on a map of Europe folded into a Chinese screen. Two large lampshades have taken the place of eyes in the portrait of Philippe Sollers and this time the punctum has been displaced to the edge of the tableau, in a way that makes one think of a painting by Jasper Johns, with its stencilled numerals and letters. And finally Robbe-Grillet, where, this time it is two cuneiform signs of light that mark the bottom of the photo, like two capsule satellites starting out on their umpteenth trajectory. (The previous works of Keiichi Tahara already frequently had recourse to this type of 'parasiting', including through the use of reflections in glass frames.)

Keiichi said to me one day 'I first have to understand through the gaze, even when I don't take a photo. Then the impression stays in my head and there's no longer any difficulty...' To understand here is to free oneself from the superimposed significations that are imposed on the facialitarian landscape as if by themselves, it is to allow oneself to be dominated by the other gazes that organize themselves before your eyes. The importance of the multiple fractal cracks engendered by the photographic apparatus as conceived by Keiichi Tahara resides in the fact that, leaving certain interpretative sequences yawning, it leads these latter to reiterate themselves emptily, indefinitely, and to secrete new existential stases, accompanied by new lines of sense and new Universes of reference. The partial nuclei of enunciation and existential taking body that thus find themselves established enter into transverse correspondence with part objects (in the sense that Freudians gave to this term) and connect the scopic drive to a Constellation of other spheres of interest and desire. The proper names that Keiichi Tahara brings us to apprehend from an unforeseen angle then become the notes of a musicality that everywhere exceeds them. It is no longer a question, I repeat, of denoting an identity or of connoting a message. We are no longer in the register of identifications and mediatized communications. It is by immediate transference without any hesitation that these deterritorialized bodies are given to us, without limit and without organs, constituting so many effects indexed simply through their proper names.

'CRACKS IN THE STREET'

In response to the invitation to your conference, I had suggested calling my paper 'The Existentialising Functions of Discourse'.[1] But after having crossed the Atlantic this proposition became 'Cracks in the Text of the State'. Already that gives us quite a lot to think about! Subsequently, it was explained to me that for a meeting placing itself under the auspices of an organization devoted to literature, it would be a good idea to stick to the idea of the text. OK! But it nonetheless remains that when I speak of discourse, it is only incidentally a question of text or even of language. Discourse, discursivity is for me first of all a trajectory, the wandering of Lenz, for example, reconstituted by Büchner in the profound life of forms, the encounter with the soul of rocks, metals, water, plants…[2] Or the immobile peregrination that grasping a Zen garden consists of, to the point that, achieving the total presence of Satori, it is closed to any communication.[3] Or, indeed, even an autistic child's fascination with the slow formation of a drop of water, the endlessly reiterated falling of which he greets with the same explosion of joy and jouissance (in *Ce gamin-là*, the film Renaud Victor devoted to the experiments of Fernand Deligny).

But some will wonder what this discursivity outside the text might be were it not taken up in the literary treatment of a Büchner, supported by Buddhist texts or overdetermined by the poetico-philosophical reading that a Fernand Deligny can give of it? Certainly minimizing the role of the text and of the writing machine in the putting to work of these mute redundancies and in the deployment of the Universes of virtuality of which they are the bearers is not part of my aim. Besides, nowadays modes of non-verbal semiotization are evidently called on to lead a life that is symbiotic not only to speech and writing but is also computer-assisted. Let's say all that works together, without any precedence or folding back of one domain onto another. So, I'm OK with the title 'Cracks in the Text' that was suggested to me and with the diverse modalities of textual discontinuity that your letter of invitation enumerated: gaps, ruptures, interstices,

slippages, margins, crises, liminal periods, peripheries, frames, silences…
OK to all that, on condition, though, that it is not taken as a pretext to
definitively silence the other forms of discursivity that persist in inhabiting
our world!

'Cracks in the street.' For the statement proposed, a composite memory
of three paintings by Balthus on the theme of the street, is substituted. The
context is in Old Paris, between the Place Saint-Germain des Prés and the
Place Saint-Michel.

In the 1929 painting one finds a dozen characters, peacefully going
about their day-to-day business, and a horse in harness in the background
facing to the left. In the foreground, a moon-faced young man, his right
hand on his heart, stares at the spectator of the painting. It would be better
to say: seems to stare, because in truth his bewildered gaze remains folded
in on itself. Let us say that he is turned towards us, gazing at him.

The horse has disappeared from the second version, from 1933, in
which the urban décor has been stylized and the perspective thrown out
of joint. The canvas is bigger, the characters more solid, at least those
who find themselves in the foreground. The moon-faced boy, still with
his hand on his heart, has moved into a secondary plane in the image.
His left shoulder is hidden by the dark silhouette of a woman seen from
behind, whose hair is inscribed in the frame of a shop in the background,
composing a sort of Chinese ideogram of a red colour. This woman holds
out her right arm towards the pavement, her open palm facing forwards,
as if to catch the wind or, equally, to grab the thigh of another woman,
also seen from behind but situated much further away (who seems to
carry a 20-year-old toddler in a sailor's uniform in her arms). Despite
the discrepancies owing to perspective, the gestures of the man and the
woman in each of these couples respond to each other head on, binding
them to one another like the front and the reverse of a new race of
androgynous beings.

Let us note that these curious pairings only constitute two cases amongst
the dozens of others that one could pick out on this same canvas. In effect,
like pieces on a chess board that has been knocked slightly, the gestures,
postures, profiles, facial traits, folds of clothing of all the characters have
been diverted from their 'natural' position so as to be re-orientated in such
a way that they answer to an enigmatic play of correspondences, one of
the principal keys to which resides in the strategy of gazes. Commentators
have not failed to note the empty, 'disconnected' character of these latter.
However, the essential point does not lie in this empty character but in
the imperious occupation of space that results from their redistribution
in a radar-like system of surveillance, through which the hegemony of a

seeing without a subject, without any object, with no purpose, predominates. A sort of panoptic superego that is all the more disconcerting for its being established in an atmosphere that has been compared to that of the 'commedia dell'arte'.

This coppery sparkle, worthy of Janáček or Stravinsky, have deserted *Le passage du Commerce Saint-André,* the third version of the painting, which saw the light of day 20 years later. A different, much more molecular treatment of plastic elements has been substituted for the rutilant relations of surface and colour and for the dance of gazes that generated a systematic disordering of the coordinates of our ordinary world (to illuminate it anew but so as finally to bring us back to it). It is something that initiates a soft topology, intensive graduations that are subliminal but which nevertheless project us into an irreversible mutation of the universe. It is no longer on the brutally discernibilized entities that the work of rupture and setting adrift bears but on the overall canvas, each fragment of which, as in a holographic image, carries the complexity of the whole. With the painting now being as tall as it is wide, its surface three times bigger than that of the first version, the size of the characters has become relatively smaller. There are no more than eight of them, to which a doll has been added. Like the actors in a Robert Wilson play, they develop around a white dog, which is facing to the right, in the central position (and which might also make one think of a lamb). Yes, perhaps it is a theatre, because the façade of the principal building has descended like a backdrop and the lateral façades have been set up in false perspective like scenery at the sides of the stage. But it could equally be a Zen composition for the city, associating living and inanimate forms. Now the eyes are blurred; the gazes appear to have emigrated into the sightless windows that everywhere encircle the scene. From one of them, the round head of a child seems to rise like a Cartesian diver. In another, up and to the right – the only one with blinds attached – the sleeve of a white jacket, hanging there by the virtue of the Holy Spirit, emerges in a scarcely believable position.

I have lingered a little on these three paintings because they will permit me to illustrate the three ideas I would like to propose to you.

From the first, the irreducible polyvocity of the components of expression that contribute to the production of an aesthetic effect, is reaffirmed: components loaded with sense, conveying 'recognizable' forms, those that are the bearers of history and of cultural messages, and those a-signifying components that rest on the play of lines of the Affects of colour. No hermeneutics, no structural overcoding can compromise the heterogeneity and functional autonomy of these components, the guarantors of the processual opening of the work, no signifying operation can 'resolve' the interlaced paths of aesthetic discursivity. Before coming here, some of my friends had warned me: above all, don't declare war again on structuralism and postmodernism, as you have a habit of doing! You ought to know that in the United States this sort of thing is never really taken seriously, even when it becomes noisily fashionable.

But what can you do?! For the last couple of decades, like myxomatosis for rabbits in the European countryside, the plague of the signifier has so ravaged the human sciences and our literature, disappearing only to reappear in other guises, that I have some difficulty getting rid of my distrust! Staying with the first of Balthus's *streets*, a simple example will show that the signifier has no ontological priority over the signified, but also that the latter can pass into the position of 'trump card'. As we know, one of the expressive procedures of this artist consists of painting in the manner of the early Italians. This painting in particular has been compared to two works by Piero della Francesca *The Legend of the True Cross* and *The Queen of Sheba*, in the chapel of San Francesco d'Arezzo.[4] In whatever manner it comes to light, clearly and distinctly or through a vague intelligibility, this cultural connotation impregnates the whole set of expressive components with an aura of the archaic that is determining for the awakening of a certain kind of Affect. But where, under these conditions, is one to localize a signifying caesura generative of sense? In the things said or in the way of saying them? In the figures of Content or in the discursive chains of Expression? This is a false dilemma! Because the veritable processual splitting resides in the capacity of the enunciation to keep the functors of Expression and the functors of Content separate and working together, without any priority of either one over the other and that for the excellent reason that they all participate in the same deterritorialized formalism, as the Danish linguist Hjelmslev had postulated.

This leads me to my second series of reflections. The aesthetic rupture of discursivity is not undergone passively, the heterogeneity of registers to which it leads must be conceived as a heterogenesis. It is enacted by operators that I characterize as concrete machines and which, at one and the same time, dissociate and gather together matters of expression, 'polyphonize' them, as Bakhtin would have it, and transversalize them, that is to say, make them shift between their diverse levels of deterritorialized forms and processes, which I call abstract machines. Pierre Klossowski, Balthus's brother, has clearly shown the essentially productive character, the existentializing function, of this kind of aesthetic suspension of speech, in a commentary dedicated fully to these canvases:

> a non-discursive mode of expression, the painting doesn't double but suppresses the speech that fights against oblivion. But whilst speech also dispatches many other things to oblivion, so as to actualise certain others, the image has as its content oblivion itself: it ignores the time that devours and distances, in it past existence subsists, omnipresent. That is why perspective in painting gives as much importance to the distant as to the close object, the 'foreground' and the 'background' only being a division of the same surface.[5]

Let's leave to one side Pierre Klossowksi's characterization of pictorial expression as non-discursive. It is merely a matter of terminology: on one side of enunciation, the apprehension of a work of painting is discursive, whilst on the other side, of content, it ceases to be so. The whole problem is one of locating the concrete operators that will allow us to pass from one to the other. For now we will retain from what Klossowski says only the possibility of painting acceding to a memory of being that escapes from spatio-temporal coordinates, that is to say, to an impossible, aporetic memory. Martin Heidegger has written that every attempt to think Being changes it into a being and destroys its essence. And such an absence of solution, according to him, is a sign indicating that 'we must stop dreaming of finding exits but of finally setting foot on this site supposedly without any exit, instead of chasing the usual exits'.[6] Existence is not a given by rights, a gain, it is a contingent production that is constantly called into question, a rupture of equilibrium, a headlong flight establishing itself in a defensive mode, or in a regime of proliferation, in response to all these cracks, these gaps, these ruptures…

Balthus's second version of *La rue* leads us to pick out two other important characteristics of this existential function when it is organized in aesthetic Assemblages. In the first place it sets off what, following Jakobson, I will call a phatic operator. Through it, certain ruptures of form, certain dissolutions of pre-established perceptual schema, certain diversions of sense find themselves converted into new enunciative cutouts. This can be seen clearly here, with the exaggerated gesticulations of certain of the painted figures and with the 'stuck on' aspect that their silhouettes take. These significant plastic elements, torn away from the internal logic of the 'subject' of the painting, start to gesticulate, make signs to, interpellate the spectator. Already, in the canvas of 1929 the character in the foreground, who looked at us without seeing us, attempted to establish a complicity with us and the scene unfolding in the street, as if he wanted to drag us in. In that of 1933, this link is distended because the gaze of this same character, now on a secondary plane, has been totally depersonalized. But the participation of the spectator is nonetheless required and far from finding itself diminished, it is intensified to the point that it is now the scene itself that has become the bearer of a sort of substantified clairvoyance, traversing us throughout, troubling us in our very depths. Our own gaze has ceased to be contemplative; it is captured, fascinated and henceforth functions as a transmission belt between a gaze-machine at work in the painting and the unconscious processes that it triggers in us. A curious trans-human, trans-machinic relation of inter-subjectivity is established. Let us underline that the plastic elements on which this phatic function is based arise indifferently from both the formal register of expression and the register of significant contents, in such a way that the harmonics of lines, form and colour speak to us here as much as the indices and symbols that are the ostensive bearers of a message.

The second characteristic of the existential function that is set into relief in the painting of 1933 in particular is related to the threatening tonality (which I have already signalled by characterizing it as superegoistic) that this panoptic and phatic enunciative cutout finds itself affected by. It derives from the irremediable precariousness of the apparatus thus put in place entering into resonance with our own ancestral fear of fragmentation and dismembering. The effect that the cracking of structures of sense closed in on themselves and the detachment and autonomization of plastic composition interpellating us, pulling us by the sleeve, have is that the painting itself takes on this fear, absorbs it like blotting paper, then relays it back to us in a form that both intimidates and wards off misfortune. What do they want of us, this gaze and this voice that are now unlocalizable? But now fragility, uncertainty, vacuity, aporia turn out to be the guarantors of existential consistency and Kierkergaardian splinters, the ultimate points of singularity, become the catalytic nuclei of the unfolding of new Universes of reference. Tertullian's paradox echoes back to us: 'the Son of God is dead: it is wholly credible, because it is unsound. And, buried, He rose again: it is certain, because impossible.'[7]

At this point it would still be advisable to elucidate the specific position of this function of existential collapse in the domain of literature, how it promotes refrains of complexity that rupture discursivity. But it is now time to pass to my third and last series of considerations.

The painter has set out on his canvas processual operators to enslave our vision (enslave in a sense close to that of cybernetics; in other words controlling at a distance, creating feedback and opening up new lines of possibility. One could even say that he has connected us to a kind of proto-software). In the second version one found oneself in the presence of two principal operators:

1   A technique of cutting-out, of the disarticulation of motifs that led to them being fixed as 'tableaux vivants' (still following Klossowski), to discernibilize them violently, in such a way as make them emit new references of sense.

2   An a-signifying composition of lines and colours taking possession of the whole canvas in multiple fashions. The result was the entry of enunciation into a fundamentally metastable Constellation of existential Universes oscillating between a 'commedia dell'arte' pole of the dance of forms, of the invention of original becomings, and a superegoistic pole of the petrification of the bewitching of gazes.

The operator of *Le passage du Commerce Saint-André* will conjugate the two previous operators, transforming them. The treatment through the exaggerated cutting-out of forms now finds itself inverted in a sort of imperceptible 'shifting' which relaxes and de-contrasts the motif-background relations. The impact of the 'cracking' is displaced from molar ensembles to molecular intensities; the powdery grain of pictorial matter takes primacy over the structurally qualified relations. The breaking down of the dynamic of gazes throws facts and gestures, which to that point had been hooked onto the eyes of the characters like a garland, off centre. It is the painting itself, taken as a whole, which makes itself into a gaze and an originary instance of sense, implanting a 'becoming Balthus' at the heart of our ways of seeing the world.

But what can confer such a power of subjective mutation, taking us far from well-worn paths, on this kind of operator? Doubtless there is no general speculative response to this question, which each aesthetic Assemblage has to take up again from zero! The enigmatic power that the *Passage* by Balthus is loaded with resides in the fact that its real 'subject' is, precisely, nothing other than this operator... of passage, transversality, of the transfer of subjectivity. It appears to me that in this case we are dealing with an operation proceeding through the molecular fracturing of forms that are correlative to an intensification of the modulation of colour, at the heart, moreover, of a restricted palette. This visible, though vague, fracture induces another, this time definitely invisible, fracture operating at the heart of the psyche. Referring to the research of Benoît Mandelbrot on 'fractal objects',[8] I would like to say that a double, objective and subjective, process of 'fractalization' is operating here. It will be recalled that a fractal set is indefinitely extensible through internal homethety and that its representation tends to lose any fixed identitarian contour – at least when it is generated in a stochastic fashion. In my view it would be worth broadening fractal analysis beyond the frames of geometry and physics in which it was born and applying it to the description of certain limit states of the psyche and the socius. Thus the dream could be considered a fractal state of representation, and I don't doubt that going down this route, certain questions like those of the dualism of drives, the 'splitting' of the Ego, the symbolic break and the castration complex might be freed from the impasse in which Freudianism and its structuralist relays left them.

Winnicott's notion of the transitional object would also particularly merit being rethought. What is an operator for the transition of reference? How do the subjectivity converters that make us pass from one Constellation of Universes to another function? With *Le passage du Commerce Saint-André* we can see that in certain circumstances a pictorial representation can trigger a fractal impulse that indicates and vectorizes a transformation that echoes 'in a cascade' (according to Mandelbrot's fine expression) not just from one spatial dimension to another but equally across other temporal and incorporeal dimensions. In the era of artificial intelligence, is it not finally time to rid oneself of the massive oppositions between mind and body once and for all, and to study the interface operators between these two modalities of existence?

The principal characteristics of the fractal impulse convertor put to work by Balthus can be summarized in three points:

1   It permits an escape from systems of representation closed in on themselves; it eats away at their limits in such a way as to make them work as a 'strange attractor' of transversality.

2   Its intrinsic processuality leads to a constant repositioning of its ontological references and to a modification of the existential dimensions of its enunciation, dimensions that are synonymous with permanent resingularization.

3   The fact that it escapes from the pre-established circumscribing of sense leads to its deployment in self-referenced fields of expression that can be considered as so many instances of the self-production of subjectivity.

The stakes of such a fractalization of the psyche are not lacking in ethico-political repercussions. It is a question of the constraining, 'one way', discursivity of capitalist subjectification, which can thereby find itself expropriated by multi-centred, heterogeneous, polyphonic, polyvocal approaches established far from 'pre-coded' equilibria. It calls for the return in force of the Signified, of the 'iconic', of the non-digital, of the symptom, in short a certain 'democratic' liberation of molecular populations.

Allow me, in the guise of a conclusion, to make three remarks relating to linguistics, music and logical positivism.

Linguists and semiologists haven't completely ignored the existence of this existential function inherent in diverse modalities of discursivity – and not, I repeat, just in linguistic discourse.[9] But hitherto they have opted to keep it in the drawer marked 'pragmatics', the third drawer below those of syntax and semantics. Contrary to the linguists and semiologists, I would like to have shown that its dimensions of polyphony, of a-signifying rupture generative of enunciation and of processual fractalization give it a completely different scope. It is true that it has an essential place in semiological fields (for example, in the use of accents, intonation, prosodic traits, etc.), but its role is nonetheless fundamental in the constitution of: existential Territories arising from human ethology (amongst others); rituals and refrains of social demarcation; even the facialitarian compositions, the 'part objects' and transitional objects around which the psyche is organized…Through all these possible procedures of fractalization, of processualization and of existential recomposition, this third function of discursivity (established concurrently with those of signification and denotation) engenders modalities of individual and/or collective subjectification that set to work across/through dominant subjective formations. In other words, subjectivity is in a position to take hold of its own fate, through their mediation.

Music could equally offer us a privileged terrain for the exploration of this processual fractalization of 'objective subjectivities.' It would be necessary for us to retrace the history of the 'smoothing' of voices and noises under the conjoint action of instrumental machines, scriptural machines and the advent of new Assemblages of collective listening. And how on that basis a new sonorous matter was forged, lending itself excellently to the fractal breaches that led music to its modern processuality. It would also be necessary to take up again in detail: the conversion of modal musics into tonal music, correlative to the division of the scale into intervals that are equal and – by virtue of this – slightly out in relation to natural harmonics; the transgression of the old prohibition against the triton, called the 'Devil's' interval,[10] which resulted in the octave being artificially divided into two equal parts and then, in the prolonging of the equalization of 'temperament', the resulting dodecaphonics and atonality. One might then establish that each one of the steps in the deterritorialization of sonorous matter was catalysed by a play of 'little differences' resulting from a molecular fractalization of the basic musical entities. The return of the voice, of rhythms and timbres and transfigured noises in music would then be clarified in parallel and as if in counterpoint.[11]

NOTES

TN refers to Translatory's Notes.

Translator's introduction

1 'Pour Félix' in Gilles Deleuze *Deux régimes de fous. Textes et entretiens 1975–1995* Paris, Minuit, 2003, p.357.

2 Cf. the arguments about 'untranslateables' developed in B. Cassin (ed.) *Vocabulaire européen des philosophies: Dictionnaire des intraduisibles* Paris, Seuil, 2004.

3 Janell Watson *Guattari's Diagrammatic Thought: Writing between Lacan and Deleuze* London, Continuum, 2009.

4 Gilles Deleuze *Negotiations 1972–1990* trans. M. Joughin, New York, Columbia University Press, 1995, p.14 (translation modified).

5 See the comment on Deleuze and the oeuvre in the entry for 10 June 1972 in Félix Guattari *The Anti-Oedipus Papers* trans. K. Gotman, New York, Semiotext(e), 2006, pp.399–400.

6 See for more on this Éric Alliez and Andrew Goffey's 'Introduction' in *The Guattari Effect* London, Continuum, 2011.

7 See François Dosse *Gilles Deleuze Félix Guattari Biographie Croisee* Paris, La Découverte, 2007, p.68 and the discussion of Guattari's relation to Joyce in Peter Pel Palbart 'The Deterritorialized Unconscious' in Alliez and Goffey *The Guattari Effect* op. cit. pp.68–83.

8 Several aspects of argot, for example, are well worth underlining in this respect – its somewhat secret nature, linked to the social and political position of the groups that speak it; its use of often highly artificial procedures for the construction of its vocabulary, for example. The latter has been outlined by Marcel Schwob in his *Étude sur l'argot français* Paris, Émille Bouillon, 1889. See more generally on argot Alice Becker-Ho *Les princes du jargon* Paris, Gallimard, 1993.

9 Félix Guattari *L'Inconscient machinique* Paris, Recherches, 1979, p.75.

10 In this respect, Guattarian pragmatics presents an interesting challenge to the arguments debated by Cassin and Badiou in their discussion of Lacan and metaphysics. See Alain Badiou and Barbara Cassin *Il n'y a pas de rapport sexuel. Deux leçons sur 'L'Étourdit' de Lacan* Paris, Fayard, 2010.

11 See E. P. Thompson *The Poverty of Theory and Other Essays* London, Merlin Press, 1978 and Allan Sokal and Jean Bricmont *Fashionable Nonsense* New York, Picador, 1998.

12 Ludwig Wittgenstein *Tractatus Logico-Philosophicus* trans. P. Klossowski, Paris, Gallimard, 1961, p.107 (emphasis added).

13 Gilles Deleuze and Félix Guattari *What is Philosophy?* trans. H. Tomlinson and G. Burchell, London, Verso, 1994, p.8.

14 'One ought carefully to distinguish between the neurotic encirclement of the subjectivity engaged in a process of personological *individuation* and the group idiosyncrasies that harbour possibilities of rehandling and transformation', Guattari *La révolution moléculaire* Paris, Recherches, 1977, p.287. See also the argument proposed by Isabelle Stengers, a one time habituée of Guattari's seminars, regarding idioms and idiocy in *La vierge et le neutrino* Paris, Les Empêcheurs de penser en rond, 2006.

15 Guattari *The Anti-Oedipus Papers* op. cit. p.400.

16 See the chapter on the 'Time of Refrains' in Guattari *L'Inconscient machinique* op. cit. pp.117–65.

17 See the comments to this effect in Alain Badiou's *Theory of the Subject* London, Continuum, 2009.

18 Félix Guattari *Psychanalyse et transversalité* Paris, François Maspero/La Découverte, 1972/2003, p.161.

19 *Psychanalyse et transversalité* op. cit. p.55.

20 Gilles Deleuze and Félix Guattari *The Anti-Oedipus* trans. R. Hurley, M. Seem, H. R. Lane, Minneapolis, University of Minnesota Press, 1983, p.38.

21 Specifically in the long essay 'Les échaffaudages semiotiques' that makes up the second half of the book. Regrettably, this long essay – which develops ideas that one can also see being worked out in *The Anti-Oedipus Papers* – has not yet been translated in its entirety. See *La révolution moléculaire* op. cit. pp.241–384.

22 Guattari *The Anti-Oedipus Papers* op. cit. p.149.

23 He comments that the problem of existence is only posed retroactively when 'an extrinsic experimental effect calls into question the whole semiotic system' Guattari *La révolution moléculaire* op. cit. p.244.

24 Guattari's relationship to science is a complex one but generally follows a consistent development. The comments from *La révolution moléculaire* cited above are in many respects prefigured in his essay 'D'un signe à l'autre' in *Psychanalyse et transversalité*: 'The *collective enunciation* of theoretical physics…permanently composes and recomposes a gigantic signifying machine in which machines properly so-called and the signifier are indissolubly linked, able to intercept and interpret all the theoretically aberrant manifestations of elementary particles…' (Guattari *Psychanalyse et transversalité* op. cit. p.142). The obvious difference, of course, is the calling into question of the all-powerful despotism of the signifier, still partly evident here.

25 Guattari *La révolution moléculaire* op. cit. p.244.

26 Guattari *L'Inconscient machinique* op. cit. p.207.

27 See below p.204.

28 On the necessity of Guattari's work to Deleuze's own development of 'a philosophy', see Éric Alliez 'The Guattari-Deleuze Effect' in Alliez and Goffey *The Guattari Effect* op. cit. pp.260–74.

29 Gilles Deleuze *Essays Critical and Clinical* trans. D. Smith and M. Greco, London, Verso, 1998, p.113.

Preliminary

1 Nano-second: 10^{-9} second; pico-second: 10^{-12} second. On all the futurological themes mentioned here, see 'Rapport sur l'état de la technique' in Thierry Gaudin (ed.) CPE, special edition of *Science et technique*.

Chapter 1

1 Guattari is playing with the well-known expression 'il ne faut pas mélanger torchons et serviettes' [TN].

2 It's not without a certain perplexity that I'm using the old term 'analyser' again. I had introduced it in the 1960s and it was 'recuperated' (along with 'institutional analysis', 'transversality', etc.) by the therapeutic current of Lourau, Lobrot and Lapassade, from a point of view that was much too psychosocial for my liking.

3 'Roseau pensant' – the allusion is to Pascal [TN].

4 This formula for the unconscious could be compared to the 'primary process' such as Freud saw it at the time of the *Traumdeutung*: the dreamwork 'does not think, calculate or judge in any way at all' Sigmund Freud *The Interpretation of Dreams* op. cit. p.507.

5 The first Freud, of the *Traumdeutung*, also admirably grasped the nature of this treatment 'against the grain' of the significations of the dream: 'speeches in dreams have a structure similar to that of breccia, in which largish blocks of various kinds of stone are cemented together by a binding medium' Freud *The Interpretation of Dreams* op. cit. p.419.

> [e]verything that appears in dreams as the ostensible activity of the function of judgement is to be regarded not as an intellectual achievement of the dream-work but as belonging to the material of the dream thoughts and as having been lifted from them into the manifest content of the dream as a ready-made structure.
>
> Ibid. p.414.

But this micropolitics of reading 'against the grain' does not just belong to psychic life – it can also be found to be at work in artistic creation; I'm thinking in particular of the way in which, in his 'gestural music', Georges Aperghis only retains what contributes to his a-signifying compositions from semantic contents.

6 Sigmund Freud 'Mourning and Melancholia' in the *Standard Edition* XIV, pp.243–58. Also Karl Abraham *Oeuvres complètes* I, Paris, Payot, 1965, pp.99–113.

7 [Psychose hallucinatoire de désir] Sigmund Freud 'A Metapsychological Supplement to the Theory of Dreams' in the *Standard Edition* XIV, London, Hogarth Press, p.231 and 'Mourning and Melancholia' op. cit. p.234. For Freud, this is identical to the hallucinatory confusion, or 'amentia', of Meynert.

8 'I am tormented by two aims: to examine what shape the theory of mental functioning takes if one introduces quantitative considerations, a sort of economics of nerve forces; and second, to peel off from psychopathology a gain for normal psychology' 'Letter to Fliess May 25th 1895' in Sigmund Freud *The Complete Letters of Sigmund Freud to Wilhelm Fliess 1887–1904* trans. Jeffrey Masson, Cambridge MA, Belknap Press, 1985, p.129.

9 One example among a hundred others: 'physical sexual tension above a certain value arouses psychical libido, which then leads to coitus, etc.' Freud 'Project for a Scientific Psychology' *Standard Edition* I, London, Hogarth Press, 1966, p.192.

10 For example: 'I insist that the whole scale of estimates of certainty shall be abandoned and that the faintest possibility that something of this or that sort may have occurred in the dream shall be treated as complete certainty' Freud *The Interpretation of Dreams* op. cit. p.516.

11 Freud 'Project for a Scientific Psychology' op. cit. pp. 295–387.

12 With a rare frankness for an analyst invoking the Freudian heritage, Lacan explicitly acknowledged it. See Jacques Lacan *Écrits* trans. Bruce Fink, Heloise Fink and Russell Grigg, New York NY, Norton, 2006, p.728.

13 'Reflex processes remains the model for every psychical function' Freud *The Intepretation of Dreams* op. cit. p.538.

14 Ibid. p.542.

15 Far from accepting the singularizing powers of the collective unconscious, which renders them actively processual, Jung makes them uniform, 'archetypifies' them, makes them undergo a reductionistic detotalization: 'although individuals are widely separated by the differences of their consciousness, they are closely alike in their unconscious psychology. It is a significant impression for one working in practical psychoanalysis when he realizes how uniform are the typical unconscious complexes' Carl Gustav Jung *The Psychology of the Unconscious* trans. Beatrice Hinkle, Princeton, Princeton University Press, 1991, p.173. Despite that, one can find some very interesting things in Jung's method: his conception of the opening on to the future on the basis of 'subliminal combinations', his practice of 'historical amplication'; his refusal of the myth of 'analytic neutrality'; his technique of the interpretation of dreams according to the oneiric context instead of simple association…

16 'It is filled with energy reaching it from the instincts, but it has no organisation, produces no collective will, but only a striving to bring about the satisfaction of the instinctual needs subject to the observance of the pleasure principle' Sigmund Freud *New Lectures on Psychoanalysis* in the *Standard Edition* XXII, p.73.

17 'In the unconscious, nothing can be brought to an end, nothing is past or forgotten' Freud *The Interpretation of Dreams* op. cit. p.577. 'In the Id there is nothing that corresponds to the concept of time; there is no recognition of the passage of time' Freud *New Lectures on Psychoanalysis* op. cit. p.74.

18 Freud *The Interpretation of Dreams* op. cit. p.292.

19 Ibid. p.320.

20 Ibid. p.283.

21 Ibid. p.525.

22 Ludwig von Bertalanffy *General System Theory: Foundations, Development, Applications,* New York, George Braziller, 1976.

23 Karl Popper *Unended Quest. An Intellectual Autobiography* revised edn, London, Fontana, 1976.

24 Guattari is referring to a scandal involving the petrol giant Elf in the late 1970s. The 'sniffer planes' [avions renifleurs] were planes on which a device was mounted that was supposedly able to detect the whereabouts of oil simply by flying over ground in which it existed [TN].

25 Maurice Merleau-Ponty *Phenomenology of Perception* trans. Colin Smith, London, Routledge and Kegan Paul, 1962, p.viii.

26 Not only does the map start here to refer indefinitely to its own cartography, as Alfred Korzybski has seen, but the distinction between the map and 'the thing mapped' starts to disappear. Alfred Korzybksi *Science and Sanity* New York, International Non-Aristotelian Library, 1973, pp.58, 247, 498.

27 See the description by J. L Borges of a cartographic activity that engenders the territory to which it refers. See J. L. Borges *Fictions* London, Calder, 1965.

28 Léon Krier 'La reconstitution de la ville' in *Rationale architecture. Rationelle 1978. L'aprés-modernisme* Paris, Éditions de l'Équerre, 1981.

29 Robert Venturi *Learning from Las Vegas* Cambridge MA, MIT Press, 1972, *Complexity and Contradiction in Architecture* London, Architectural Press, 1977. See also Charles Jenks *The Language of Postmodern Architecture* New York NY, Rizzoli, 1977.

30 Jean-François Lyotard *The Postmodern Condition. A Report on Knowledge* trans. B. Massumi and G. Bennington, Minneapolis MA, Minnesota University Press, 1984.

31 A theme that was bought to line in 1935 by Walter Benjamin in 'The Work of Art in the Age of Mechanical Reproduction' in *Illuminations*, trans. Harry Zohn, London, Fontana Press, 1972.

32 J. L. Austin, Emile Benveniste, John Searle, Oswald Ducrot, Antoine Culioli, etc.

33 Although I can't develop this point at length here, it also implies an exit from a whole dualistic ontological tradition, which makes existence depend on a law of all or nothing 'to be or not to be'. By way of an indispensable transitory return to animist thought, the quality of being takes primacy over a 'neutral' essentiality of being, which can be allocated universally and is thus exchangeable, that one might characterize as capitalistic facticity. Existence here gains, loses, intensifies, crosses qualitative thresholds, because of its adherence to such and such an incorporeal Universe of endo-reference.

Chapter 2

1   Epicurus 'Letter to Menoeceus' 134 [Guattari cites from Sextus Empiricus. The translation here is taken from Cyril Bailey's 1926 translation, in *Epicurus. The Extant Remains* Oxford, Clarendon, 1926, p.91].

2   I will leave to one side Freud's characterization of certain drives as non-sexual – the drives of self-preservation or, in his last theoretical approach, the death drive – to the extent that they always arise essentially from a dualistic energetics that establishes them in a bipolar relation to the sexual drives.

3   This capital will sometimes be mentioned in the rest of this text under the term 'Energetico-Spatio-Temporal complexes' or EST for short.

4   Examples of these transfers: Capital, at the heart of the labour process; the semiotic substance of the drive (the Freudian *Vorstellungrepräsentanz*, reduced by Lacan to the state of the Signifier) at the heart of the libido; 'binary digits' at the heart of Flows of information…It will be noted that Marxists never attempted the quantification of Capital in the economic sphere and that Freudians quickly put the libido back in the cupboard of pious relics, or 'miraculated' it in different ways.

5   Everything started with the bringing to light of an identical formula for calculating a quantity of information and for establishing a relationship between entropy and thermodynamic probability. But as Karl Popper remarks 'all that has been shown is that entropy and lack of information can be measured by *probabilities*, or interpreted as probabilities. It has not been shown that they are probabilities of the same attributes as the system'. See Popper *Unended Quest* op. cit. p.163.

6   Edgar Morin notes that taking into account the observer calls for a recharacterization of disorder able to give it back its capacity to cooperate in what he calls the 'generation of organizational order'. Edgar Morin *Science avec conscience*, Paris, Fayard, 1982.

7   'the intra-subjective field tends to be conceived of after the fashion of intersubjective relations, and the systems are pictured as relatively autonomous persons-within-persons…To this extent then, the scientific theory of the psychical apparatus tends to resemble the way the subject comprehends and perhaps even constructs himself in his phantasy life' Jean Laplanche and Jean-Bertrand Pontalis *The Vocabulary of Psychoanalysis* London, Hogarth, 1973, p.452.

8 'As an *energetic concept*...the libido is merely the symbolic notation for the equivalence between the dynamisms invested by images in behaviour' Lacan *Écrits* op. cit. p.73.

9 'Whatever the ingenous hearts of engineers believe, energy is absolutely nothing other than the cladding of the world with the network of signifiers' Lacan, seminar of 14 January 1970, personal notes.

10 'The lIbid.o is to be conceived as an organ, in both senses of the term, as organ-part of the organism and as organ-instrument' Jacques Lacan *The Four Fundamental Concepts of Psychoanalysis* trans. Alan Sheridan, London, Penguin, 1979, p.187 and *Écrits* op. cit. p.692.

11 Lacan *Écrits* op. cit. p.692.

12 Ibid. p.719 and *The Four Fundamental Concepts* op. cit. p.197.

13 Lacan *Écrits* op. cit. p.722.

14 Charles Sanders Peirce *Écrits sur le signe*, Paris, Seuil, 1978.

15 Louis Hjelmslev *Prolegomena to a Theory of Language* Madison WI, University of Wisconsin Press, 1963, pp.114–25.Although he refused any possible translation of systems of expression outside 'everyday language', Louis Hjelmslev and the Copenhagen School had as their project the elaboration of a 'glossematic algebra' of the presuppositions between semiotic magnitudes (or 'ordered relations of dependency') which was, they intended, to be distinguished as much from the linguistics of current languages as from 'symbolic' logic: 'the matter of logic is open, unlimited and the logical approach presupposes an atomistic conception of the universe, or a prior analysis that is situated outside logic itself. Glossematic algebra is addressed to closed structures and presupposes the existence of a coherent material the analysis of which is a coherent part of glossematics itself...' H. J. Uldall *Outline of Glossematics*, Copenhagen, Munksgaard, 1957.

16 Alfred North Whitehead uses the term 'grasp' to define concrescent processes: 'the ground, or origin, of the concrescent process is the multiplicity of data in the universe, actual entities and eternal objects and propositions and nexūs. Each new phase in the concrescence means the retreat of mere propositional unity before the growing *grasp* of real unity of feeling' Alfred North Whitehead *Process and Reality* London, The Free Press, 1978, p.224.

17 Pierre-Maxime Schuhl, Preface to *Les Stoïciens*, Paris, Gallimard/La Pléiade, p.xxi.

18 'The sign function is in itself a solidarity. Expression and content are solidary – they necessarily presuppose one another' Hjelmslev *Prolegomena* op. cit. Louis Hjelmslev had divided up the Saussurean notion of substance into matter and substance, we have additionally divided up the notion of form into incorporeal Universes and abstract machinic Phyla. Thus, by transposing the formula according to which *substance* is the manifestation of *form* in *matter* (with regard to the French translation of this term as 'sense', cf. the observations of Oswald Ducrot and Tvetzan Todorov *Encyclopaedic Dictionary of the Sciences of Language* Baltimore MA, The Johns Hopkins University Press, 1979). We might say here existential *Territories* are the manifestation of incorporeal *Universes* and machinic and machinic *Phyla* in energetico-signaletic *Flows*. Consequently, in our model the level of the secondary unconscious corresponds to the Hjelmslevian function of solidarity, whilst the conjunction of tertiary and primary levels corresponds to that of manifestation. I recall that for Hjelmslev manifestation consists in the articulation of extra-linguistic forms (the 'sense' of Content and Expression) with linguistic formalism (schema and use of language, two notions that he substitutes for the classic Saussurean couple of langue and parole. Cf. Hjelmslev *Essais de linguistique* Paris, Minuit, 1971, pp.77, 89).

19 Cf. C. S.Peirce's category of *suchness* 'mere may-being' 'without any realisation at all'.

20 Ilya Prigogine proposes the very suggestive term *hypnon* to designate the entities arising from an equilibrium state. Ilya Prigogine 'La lecture du complexe', paper given at the colloquium *Culture et développement*, Paris, February 1983.

21 Cf. 'Réseaux-Systèmes-Agencements' in *Cahiers critiques de thérapie familiale et de pratique de réseaux*.

22 That of Australian aboriginals, for example, who on the basis of a collective labour on their dreams and from a very pragmatic point of view which isn't in the slightest mystical, endeavour to localize the potentials for the transformation of their real and/or incorporeal Universe: 'the dream, as law, is not a divine synchronic model frozen in an image, but almost a diachronic, but non-causal, method. What counts is the principle of adaptation as a *transformational potential* represented by the mythical metamorphoses of totemic species' Barbara Glowczewski *Le rêve et la terre*. Thèse de 3e cycle en ethnologie, Paris, Université de Paris VII, p.44.

Chapter 3

1 'Changer de Kelton' was part of a slogan for an advertising campaign for a brand of watches in the 1970s [TN].

2 Guattari uses the term 'constat' throughout this passage. It means 'report' or 'observation' (amongst other things). The English term 'registration' captures the impersonality of the action in question [TN].

3 Martin Heidegger *Les concepts fondamentaux de la métaphysique* Paris, Gallimard, 1992, p.42.

4 See the first module of sensible smoothing, Figures 3.11 and 3.12.

5 Noam Chomsky *Aspects of the Theory of Syntax* Cambridge MA, MIT Press, 1965

Chapter 4

1 And as we will see later, that of Expression.

2 Lubert Stryer *Biochemistry*, San Francisco, W. H. Freeman and Co, 1981, pp.103–14 and 'Les reacteurs biologies' *La Recherche* special issue on the future of biotechnologies 188, May 1987, p.614 et seq.

3 [Guattari makes systematic use here of the terms 'croisement' and 'décroisement' in his discussion, which we have translated broadly as 'crossing (over)' and 'uncrossing'. Elsewhere we have also used the term 'intersection' when a systematic contrast between 'croisement' and 'décroisement' is not at play].

4 Cf. Jacques Schotte *Une pensée du Clinique. L'oeuvre de Viktor von Weizsäcker*, Louvain, The Catholic University of Louvain, Faculty of Psychology and the Sciences of Education, May 1985. Course notes taken by Ph. Lekeuche and reviewed by the author.

Chapter 5

1 Let's mention the processionary caterpillars of the pine or the oak tree (*Thaumatopoea*). These hairy caterpillars with a nasty sting leave their nest together to follow each other in a line with one individual at the front playing the role of leader. They leave a thread of silk behind them which serves as a guide (*Encyclopaedia Universalis* X, p.1127).

2 On the base FT, heterogenesis will later be characterized as necessitation, the correlate of energization, whilst the term heterogenesis will be reserved for the pathic operations of the axis TU.

3 Ivar Ekeland *Le calcul, l'imprévu, les figures du temps. De Kepler à Thom*, Paris, Seuil, 1984, p.128.

Chapter 6

1 'Transformation-peau-de-chagrin du boulanger': 'Peau de Chagrin' or 'Magic Skin' is the title of a novel by Honoré de Balzac. A 'transformation du boulanger' or 'baker transformation' is an operation in dynamic systems theory [TN].

2 On these ideas of partialization and the entry of stochastic elements into deterministic systems, see the commentaries of Ivar Ekeland (*Le calcul* op. cit.) relating to 'truncated multiplications' (p.74) and to the 'baker transformation'. 'The aleatory aspect comes from the fact that one has exact but incomplete information. Part of the information is hidden' (p.78). However, it would be a good idea to give the concepts of information and completeness acceptable limits…

3 '[L]linguistic theory doesn't rest on specific axioms, as language is a fundamental prior element of thought. As a consequence, linguistic theory must be deeply rooted in the hierarchy of the theory of knowledge', Hjelmslev *Nouveaux essais* op. cit. p.75.

4 Cf. Félix Guattari *The Machinic Unconscious* New York NY, Semiotext(e), 2010 and 'Refrains and Existential Affects' in this volume.

5 In other texts I have related the active setting into a-signifiance of a chain of signification to this diagrammatic function.

6 'Which means that the human has not faced up to its face and that it is up to the painter to do so' Antonin Artaud, 1947, in the exhibition catalogue *Antonin Artaud. Dessins* Paris, Centre Georges-Pompidou, 1987.

7 Cf. the chapter of the same title in my book *The Machinic Unconscious* op. cit.

Chapter 7

1 According to a relation that, as Hjelmslev had established, is in one aspect, reversible – in so far as a permutation between E (Expression)

and C (Content) is always virtually possible – and irreversible, in another aspect, in so far as it is 'incarnated' in an existential function (cf. Figure 6.8).

2 'In classical theory, symmetry only concerns ordinary three-dimensional space. It is generalized to spatio-temporal symmetries, discrete symmetries, symmetry through the permutation of identical particles and, finally, internal symmetries which act on the fibres, the space of degrees of freedom internal to quantum fields' Gilles Cohen-Tannoudji and Michel Spiro *La Matière-Espace-Temps* Paris, Fayard, 1987, p.38.

3 'The eternity of art would thus be a differentiated eternity, because the return of this instant is the return of an instant in which a difference is affirmed, an absolutely unique quality which, wishing itself such, escapes from universalization for all time' Daniel Charles, entry 'Esthétique' in *Encyclopaedia Universalis* VIII, p.296.

4 Thomas Kuhn *The Structure of Scientific Revolutions* 3rd edn Chicago IL, University of Chicago Press, 1996.

5 In his tripartite division of cognitive, ethical and aesthetic enunciations, Mikhail Bakhtin has perfectly grasped the aesthetic dimension that haunts scientific enunciation: 'from within the world of cognition, no conflict is possible, for in that world one cannot meet with anything axiologically different in kind. Not science, but a scientist can enter into conflict, and do so, moreover, not *ex cathedra*, but as an ethical *subiectum* for whom cognition is *the performed act of* cognition' Mikhail Bakhtin 'The Problem of Content, Material, and Form in Verbal Art' in *Art and Answerability* Austin, University of Texas Press, 1990, p.278. [The French translation of Bakhtin that Guattari cites has 'aesthetic' rather than 'ethical'.]

6 Arthur Tatossian *Phénoménologie des psychoses* (Congrès de psychiatrie et de neurologie de langue française, Angers, 77th meeting) Paris, Masson, 1979.

7 The original French has 'consistence' rather than 'contingence'. However, the abbreviation P^c implies the latter [TN].

Chapter 8

1 In English in the original [TN].

2 *Les penseurs grecs avant Socrate* trans. Jean Voilquin, Paris, Garnier-Flammarion, 1974, p.95. [Given the enormous variability of translations of Ancient Greek philosophy, the translation here is directly from the Voilquin translation used by Guattari.]

3 The lesson that we retain from Parmenidean being is that it is nowhere susceptible of the more or the less. Everything in it is inviolable; it is innate, undying, suffering neither generation nor destruction. Complete in the instant one and continuous. What is more, it necessarily either absolutely is or is nothing at all. Thus it escapes from the notion of lack and, as a consequence, that of the infinite, because that would imply that that lacks everything. See Parmenides in *Les penseurs grecs avant Socrate* op. cit. pp.94, 96.

4 Emile Brehier 'Kant' in *Commentaires d'Emile Brehier* t.II *Histoire de la philosophie* Paris, PUF, 1981, p.468. For its part, the possible is defined as universal and necessary.

5 'Le formalisme de V. Chklovksi', interview with Jean-Pierre Faye in *La Quinzaine litteraire* 39 (15 November 1967).

6 Ibid. [I have followed the standard English translation of 'Priëm ostranenie' as 'defamiliarization'.]

The refrains of being and sense

1 Presented at the colloquium 'Temps et devenir à partir de l'oeuvre de Prigogine' at Cerisy-la-Salle, June 1983.

2 Felix Guattari *Psychanalyse et transversalité* Paris, Maspero, 1972.

3 Archaic societies, in particular Australian Aboriginals, are customary in that each oneiric performance refers not only to an individual diachronic succession of dreams but additionally to dreams with a collective reference, playing a fundamental role in establishing filiative relations, ritual itineraries and the fixing of performances of all kinds. Cf. Barbara Glowczewski op. cit and *Chimères* 1.

4 In a place that, even longer ago, I regularly met Lucien Sebag, Pierre Clastres and a whole group of other students.

5 Guattari uses the shortened form 'auto', as in 'automobile', here, in relation to the notion of self-analysis ('auto-analyse') [TN].

6 Mikhail Bakhtin *Art and Answerability* op. cit.

Refrains and existential affects

1 Sigmund Freud *The Interpretation of Dreams* op. cit. p.460. The phrase Guattari refers to is itself a quotation from Salomon Stricker's *Studien uber das Bewusstsein* [TN].

2 With regard to schizophrenic alienation, phenomenological psychiatry advocates a diagnosis based on praecox feeling (Rumke), feeling (Binswanger), intuition (*Weitbrecht*). Tellenbach envisages a 'diagnostic atmosphere' as acknowledgement of the dissonance between the atmospheres proper to the two 'partners' [in the diagnosis], without seeking to amass isolated symptoms. Cf. Arthur Tatossian *Phénoménologie des psychoses* op. cit.

3 'All syntactic verbal connections, in order to become compositional connections that realize form in the artistic object, must be permeated by the unity of the feeling of connecting activity which is directed toward the unity (realized through compositional components) of object-related and meaning-related connections of a cognitive or ethical character, that is, by the unity of the feeling of tension and form-giving encompassing from the outside of cognitive content' Mikhail Bakhtin 'The Problem of Content' in *Art and Answerability* op. cit. p.313.

4 Ibid. p.316.

5 Ibid. pp.308–9.

6 Ibid. pp.306, 309.

7 Ibid. p.309.

8 Here virtuality is correlated with a fractal deterritorialization, which has an infinite speed on a temporal plane and generates infinitesimal intervals on a spatial plane (cf. Chapter 3 'The Cycle of Assemblages').

9 Quoted by Tatossian op. cit. p.169.

10 Ibid. p.117.

11 Ibid. p.103.

12 Robert Musil *The Man without Qualities* v.III trans. E. Wilkins and E. Kaiser, London, Pan, 1973, pp.421–2.

13 Tatossian op. cit. p.186.

14 See the chapter 'Refrains of Lost Time' in my book *The Machininc Unconscious* op. cit.

15 Louis Hjelmslev *Nouveaux essais* op. cit. pp.74–5.

16 Walter Benjamin *Illuminations* New York, Harcourt Brace and World, 1968.

17 Roland Barthes *Camera Lucida* New York, Farrar Strauss and Giroux, 1981.

18 Christian Girard *Architecture et concepts nomades* Brussels, Mardaga, 1986. In *La ville de Richelieu* Paris, AREA, 1972, Philippe Boudon distinguished 20 types of scale considered as space of reference for architectural thinking: technical, functional, symbolic, formal, model-dimensional, semantic, socio-cultural, of neighbourhood, of visibility, optic, of division, geographical, of extension, human, global, economic. One can think of other classifications and groupings but what matters here is the respect for the heterogeneity of viewpoints.

19 See the chapter entitled 'The Ethology of Sonorous, Visual and Behavioural Refrains in the Animal World' in *The Machinic Unconscious* op. cit.

20 Marcel Granet shows the complementarity between refrains of social demarcation in ancient China and the affects, or virtues, as he calls them, borne by names, written forms, emblems, etc: 'the specific virtue of a stately race is expressed in the chant (with an animal or vegetable motif) of a dance. Without doubt it is appropriate to see a sort of musical emblem in ancient family names – an emblem that is translated graphically into a sort of heraldic form – all the effectiveness of the dance and of the chants inhabiting as much the graphic as the vocal emblem' Marcel Granet *La pensée chinoise* Paris, Albin Michel, 1950, pp.50–1.

21 This is only true for the icons whose manufacture was spread out between the eleventh and sixteenth centuries, centred on a mysterious, quasi-sacramental faciality. Subsequently, icons were overloaded with details of clothing, personae multiplied and were given metal coverings (oklad). Cf. the article 'Icone' by Jean Blankoff and Olivier Clement in *Encyclopaedia Universalis* IX, 1984, pp.739–42.

22 'La coupure leniniste' in Guattari *Psychanalyse et transversalité* op. cit. pp.183–94.

23 Benoît Mandelbrot *Les objets fractals* 2nd edn Paris, Flammarion, 1984; 'Les fractals' in *Encyclopaedia Universalis* [no edition or volume], pp. 319–23.

24 Mikhail Bakhtin 'The Problem of Content' op. cit. p.308.

25 Ibid. p.281 [Bakhtin refers to 'concretisation', not 'totalisation', as Guattari suggests].

26   Ilya Prigogine and Isabelle Stengers *Order from Chaos. Man's Dialogue with Nature* New York, Bantam, 1984; Ivan Ekelard *Le calcul, l'imprévu* op. cit.

27   Emmanuel Levinas: 'I think rather that access to the face is straightaway ethical...' *Ethics and Infinity: Conversations with Philippe Nemo* Pittsburgh, Duquesne University Press, 1985, p.85. 'The signification of the face is not a species for which indication or symbolism would be the genre' *Heidegger ou la question de Dieu* Paris, Grasset, 1981, p.243. 'Responsibility for the other is not an accident occurring to the subject, but precedes the subject's Essence, its engagement for the other' *Humanisme de l'autre homme* Paris, Livre de Poche, 1987.

28   Cf. Jean Delumeau *Le péché et la peur. La culpabilisation en Occident* Paris, Fayard, 1983.

29   Max Weber associated the idea of the disenchantment (*Entzau berung*) of the world with a devaluing (*Entwertung*) of the sacraments as a message of salvation and with a loss of sacramental magic, consecutive to the growth of capitalist subjectivity. Max Weber *The Protestant Ethic and 'The Spirit of Capitalism'* London, Penguin, 2002.

Genet regained

1   Jean Genet *Prisoner of Love* translated by B. Bray New York, New York Review of Books, 2003 p.429.

2   Ibid.

3   Ibid. pp.166, 381.

4   Ibid. p.364.

5   Ibid. p.5.

6   Ibid. p.358.

7   Ibid. p.381, translation modified.

8   Jean-Paul Sartre *Saint Genet. Comedian and Martyr* trans. Bernard Frechtman, London, W. H. Allen, 1964, especially the chapter 'On the Fine Arts Considered as Murder'.

9   Ibid. p.423.

10   Ibid. p.535.

11   Ibid. p.568

12 Ibid. p.422.

13 Ibid. p.485.

14 Ibid. p. 544.

15 Ibid. p.449.

16 Ibid. p.544.

17 Ibid. p.642.

18 Genet *Prisoner of Love*. p.367.

19 Ibid. pp.369, 425.

20 Jean Genet *The Thief's Journal* p.243.

21 Ibid. p.250.

22 Rudiger Wischenbart 'Conversations avec Jean Genet et Leila Chahid' in *Revue d'études palestiniennes*.

23 Ibid.

24 Genet *Prisoner of Love* p.237.

25 'Anyone who's never experienced the pleasure of betrayal doesn't know what pleasure is' *The Prisoner of Love* p.312.

26 Ibid. p.355.

27 Ibid. p.392.

28 Ibid. pp. 388, 392, 414.

29 Ibid. p.414.

30 'The malicious, slightly timid word, eclipse, allows everything to be a star occluding something else' Genet *Prisoner of Love* p.376 [translation modified].

31 Ibid. p.375.

32 Ibid.

33 Ibid. p.23.

34 Ibid. p.24.

35 Ibid. p.134.

36 Ibid. p.347.

37 Jean Genet *Lettres à Roger Blin* Paris, Gallimard, 1986, p.11.

38 Genet, *Prisoner of Love* op. cit. p.362.

39 Ibid. p.146.

40 Genet *The Thief's Journal* p.86ff.

41   Genet, *Prisoner of Love* op. cit. p.376.

42   Ibid. p.332 [translation modified].

43   On this point, there are numerous references. See in particular ibid. pp.105, 107, 145, 238, 262, 333, 391, 393.

44   Ibid. p.376.

45   Ibid. p.301.

46   Sartre, *Saint-Genet* op. cit. p.5.

47   Genet, *Prisoner of Love* op. cit. p.301.

48   Ibid. p.300.

49   Wischenbart op. cit.

50   Ibid.

51   Genet *The Thief's Journal* op. cit. p.5.

52   Genet, *Prisoner of Love* op. cit. p.376.

53   Ibid. p.81 [Translation modified].

54   Ibid. p.23.

55   Ibid. p. 23.

56   This phrase does not appear in the Bray translation of the text.

57   Ibid. p.378

58   Ibid. p.399.

59   Genet *Prisoner of Love* op. cit. p.245. See also pp.5, 251.

60   Ibid. pp. 75, 390. But sometimes Genet cannot stop himself from launching into frightful 'praise' [coups de chapeau] for the cruellest adversaries of the Palestinian refugees. Witness this very fine passage on the dancing of Bedouin soldiers (pp.79 et seq.) and the incredible 'hommage' to Israeli brutality: 'it would be unfair to deny Israel the thrills of bravery, pillage and torture' (p.382) or even the tender description of the 'six curly blonde wigs' of the fake (or real!) Israeli homosexuals who had gone to Beirut to assassinate the Palestinian leaders (pp.182–6).

61   Ibid. pp.136, 380.

62   Ibid. p.407.

63   Cf. Felix Guattari 'The Refrains of Lost Time' in *The Machinic Unconscious* op. cit.

64   Genet, *Prisoner of Love* op. cit. pp.388, 391.

65   Jean Genet *Oeuvres complètes* t.III Paris, Gallimard, 1985, p.10.

66 Marcel Proust *In Search of Lost Time* v.2 'Cities of the Plains'.

67 Genet *The Thief's Journal* op. cit. p.5.

68 Genet, *Prisoner of Love* op. cit. p.30.

69 Ibid. p.34.

70 Ibid. p.235.

71 Ibid. p.245.

72 Ibid. p.31.

73 Ibid. pp.:163, 165, 174, 177, 223, 229, 235, 244, 245, 337, 339, 342, 346, 360, 381–2.

74 Ibid. p.223.

75 Ibid. p.165.

76 Ibid. p.244.

77 Ibid. p.339.

78 The illustration that comes to mind of its own accord would seem to me to be the series by the painter Gerard Fromanger called 'Un balayeur noir à la porte de sa benne' (1974).

79 Jean Genet *The Blacks* trans. B. Frechtman New York, Grove Press, 1960, p.52.

80 Genet, *Prisoner of Love* op. cit. p. 252.

81 Sartre *Saint Genet* op. cit. p.464.

82 Genet, *Prisoner of Love* op. cit. p.382.

83 Ibid. p.392.

84 Ibid. p.202.

85 P.296 and above all p.203: 'Amidst that world, that language, that people, those faces, those animals, plants and lands all exuding the spirit of Islam, what preoccupied me was a group embodying the image of the *mater dolorosa*. The mother and the son, but not as Christian artists have depicted them, painted or sculptured in marble or wood, with the dead son lying across the knees of a mother younger than the son de-crucified, but one of them always protecting the other'.

86 Genet *The Thief's Journal* op. cit. p.254.

87 Ibid. p.86.

88 Sartre *Saint-Genet* op. cit. pp.183–4.

89 A theme which returns several times, with the inversion of the age

relation between mother and son, pp.192 and 202 or via a slip that makes Mary the wife of Jesus, *Prisoner of Love*, p.260.

90 'More and more I believe I exist in order to be the terrain and proof which show other men that life consists in the uninterrupted emotions flowing through all creation', ibid. p.361.

91 Ibid. p.204.

92 Ibid. p. 244.

93 Ibid. p.269.

Architectural enunciation

1 Léon Krier, for example, considers that faced with the 'holocaust that is all the rage in our cities (…) a responsible architect can no longer build today' Krier in *Babylone* 1, Paris, UGE, 1983 p.132.

2 For example, Daniel Liebeskind's work, or even the landscape compositions of Vittorio Gregotti, such as his Cefalu housing project, which has little chance of ever succeeding.

3 See in this regard the interesting position of Henri Gaudin on regional architecture, in *La cabane et le labyrinth* Brussels, Pierre Mardaga, 1984.

4 I refer here to the passionate analyses of Christian Girard in *Architecture et concepts nomads. Traité d'interdiscipline* op. cit.

5 On the sometimes decisive position of the planner and the architect in the modelling of psychiatric institutions, see the special issue of the journal *Recherches* 'Planning, Architecture and Psychiatry' *Recherches* June 1967.

6 Philippe Boudon *La ville de Richelieu* Paris, AREA, 1972; *Architecture et architecturologie* Paris, AREA, 1975; *Sur l'espace architectural. Essai d'épistémologie de l'architecture* Paris, Dunod, 1971.

7 Henri von Lier *Encyclopaedia Universalis* vII, 1 Paris, 1985, p.554.

8 Fernand Braudel *Le temps du monde, Civilisation matérielle, économie et capitalisme, XVe – XVIIIe siècle* vIII, Paris, Armand Colin, 1979, pp.61–4.

9 Ibid. p.20.

10 Ibid. pp.12–14, 62–8. The world economy is the largest zone of coherence at a given given epoch, in a part of the globe, a sum of individualized economic and non-economic spaces, which ordinarily transgresses the limits of other massive historical groupings. Using the term 'eco-world'

François Fourquet has undertaken a more systematic theorization of the concepts of Fernand Braudel and Immanuel Wallerstein in François Fourquet *La richesse et la puissance*, draft publication, the Commissariat général du Plan, Convention d'Etude 984, Paris, 1987.

11 Cf. my study with Éric Alliez 'Systems, Structures and Capitalist Processes' (published, amongst other places, in Félix Guattari *Soft Subversions* New York, Semiotext(e), 1996, pp.248–61).

12 Paul Virilio *The Lost Dimension* New York, Semiotext(e) 1991, p.21–2.

13 Boudon *La ville de Richelieu* op. cit. p.17.

14 Vittorio Ugo 'Une hutte, une clairière' *Critique* 476/477, special issue 'L'object architecture' Jan–Feb 1987.

15 In the sense given to this term by Heidegger in his essay 'Building, Dwelling, Thinking'. Martin Heidegger *Poetry, Language, Thought* trans. A. Hofstadter, New York, Harper and Row, 1971, pp.145–61.

16 Massimo Cacciari in 'L'objet architecture' in *Critique* op. cit.

17 I refer to the tripartite division of enunciation (cognitive, ethical, aesthetic) proposed by Mikhail Bakhtin in 'The Problem of Content' in *Art and Answerability* op. cit.

18 Melanie Klein *Contributions to Psychoanalysis* London, The Hogarth Press, 1950.

19 D. W. Winnicott *La psychanalyse* Paris, PUF, 1959. The French text refers to 'les objets partiels de Winnicott'. The reference however makes it obvious that Guattari meant 'transitional objects' [TN].

Ethico-aesthetic refrains in the theatre of Witkiewicz

1 Stanislaw Witkiewicz *The Pragmatists. A Play in Three Acts*. All quotations come from the translation by Daniel Gerould in *Witkiewicz: Seven Plays* New York, Martin E. Segal Theater Center, 2004, pp.12–38.

2 Witkiewicz 'The Pragmatists' op. cit. p.13.

3 Ibid. p.28.

4 *Cahiers Witkiewicz* 4, 1982, Lausanne, 'L'Age d'Homme' pp.129–45, *Witkiewicz et la Russie* op. cit. p.70.

5 Witkiewicz *The Pragmatists* op. cit. pp.15, 18.

6 Ibid. pp.23, 25, 29.

7 Ibid. pp.22, 23.

8 Ibid. p.31.

9 S. I. Witkiewicz *The Water Hen* in *The Madman and the Nun and Other Plays* trans. and ed. D. C. Gerould and C. S Durer, Seattle, University of Washington Press, 1968, p.53.

10 Witkiewicz 'Gyubal Wahazar' in *Witkiewicz: Seven Plays* op. cit. p.115.

11 Ibid. p.116.

Keiichi Tahara's faciality machine

1 Presentation for a collection of portraits by the Japanese photographer Keiichi Tahara *Keiichi Tahara* Paris, Audiovisuel, 1991. In the presentation of this text for *Cartographies Schizoanalytiques* Guattari footnotes the many portraits he is referring to by proper name. Here a footnoted name is provided only if it is not clear from the context to whom Guattari is referring [TN].

2 Christian Boltanski, Philippe Sollers.

3 Roy Lichtenstein or Laura Betti.

4 Bernard Lamarche-Vadel, Pierre Klossowski.

5 Tadeus Kantor.

6 Iannis Xenakis or Mario Merz.

7 'Plan americain' is a term from French film criticism that refers to a framing of a character in three-quarter length, medium-long shot [TN].

8 Daniel Buren, Lamarche-Vadel, Sollers, Iris Clert.

9 Louise Nevelson.

10 Joseph Beuys.

11 Alain Robbe-Grillet, Joseph Beuys, Brian Gysin, Christian de Posampac.

12 Jean Degottex, Jannis Kounelis.

13 Xenakis, William Burroughs.

14 Philippe Soupault and Romain Weingarten.

15 Jean Carzou and Roland Torpor.

16 Roland Barthes *Camera Obscura* op. cit. p.77.

17 Romain Weingarten.

18 Laura Betti, Adolphe Spier.

19 Philippe Soupault.

20 Barthes *Camera Lucida* op. cit. p.27.

21 Cited by Susan Sontag *On Photography* New York NY, Farrar, Strauss and Giroux, 1973, p.122.

'Cracks in the street'

1 Lecture given at the meeting of Modern Language Association in New York, 28 December 1986. A version of this paper was translated in the journal *Flash Art* 135 (1987), pp.82–5.

2 Georg Büchner 'Lenz' in *Complete Plays and Prose,* New York, Hill & Wang, 1963, p.141.

3 Augustin Berque *Le Sauvage et l'artifice. Les Japonais devant la nature* Paris, Gallimard, 1986, p.279.

4 John Russell, preface to *Balthus: A Retrospective Exhibition* London, The Tate Gallery, 1968.

5 Pierre Klossowski 'Balthus beyond realism' *Art News* v.55/8 New York, pp.26–31.

6 Martin Heidegger *The Fundamental Concepts of Metaphysics* trans. W. McNeill and N. Walker Bloomington, Indiana University Press, 1995.

7 F. Ferrier et P. Clair *Clefs pour la théologie*, Paris Seghers, 1974, p.25. [The reference is to Tertullians's credo quia absurdum (*De Carne Christi* V, 4).]

8 Benoît Mandelbrot *Les objets fractals* Paris, Flammarion, 1984 and 'Les fractals', *Encyclopaedia Universalis* Symposium, pp. 319–23.

9 As in 'discourse conveyed in language' and not the discourse 'of linguists' [TN].

10 The 'Diabolus in musica' [TN].

11 Cf. the thesis of the musician Abel Muguerza, which is very illuminating on this point, Université de Paris X, Nanterre, UER de Philosophie et Esthétique des Formes, October 1983.

INDEX

Integrated World Capitalism
(IWC) 14, 49
irreversibilization 163, 170, 188, 208
Islam 7
Israel 224
Italy 15, 37

Jakobson, Roman 257
Janet, Pierre 213
Japan 13–14, 225
Jaspers, Karl 213
jealousy 196–7, 201–2
Jospin, Lionel 195, 201
Jung, Gustav 30

Kafka, Franz 192–3, 219, 221, 244
Kant, Immanuel 161
Kao, Micheline 195, 200
Kennedy, John Fitzgerald 94
Klein, Melanie 238
Klossowksi, Pierre 257
knowledge 3–12, 15, 186
    proto-knowledge 136
Krier, Leon 38
Kuhn, Thomas 74, 161

labour 12, 15, 189, 210
Lacan, Jacques 23–4, 40, 43, 50–1,
    176, 251
language 21, 38–41, 209, 222, 224,
    253
latitude 14
Le Corbusier (Charles-Édouard
    Jeanneret) 38, 231
Le Verrier, Urbain 183
Leibniz, Gottfried 4
Levinas, Emmanuel 213
libido 24–5, 29–32, 47, 50, 204,
    242
Lier, Henri von 233
linearization 75, 81, 120, 122, 126,
    130
lines 5, 25, 31, 62, 75, 100, 111, 148,

177, 196–7, 229, 248, 252,
    258–9
    of flight 133, 146, 238
    polyphonic- 199
    processual existential- 202
Loire 193
longitude 14
Louviers (Normandy) 193, 197,
    199–200
love 50, 186, 228
Lyotard, Jean-François 38–9

machines 1–3, 20, 40, 52, 71, 84, 90,
    94–119 passim, 167–8, 209,
    261
    abstract- 74, 89–94, 163, 179,
    185, 241, 256
    chronometric- 10
    concrete- 94–5, 148, 256
    desiring- 74, 202
    of expression 138
    faciality- 247
    of representation 251
    torture- 246
machinic enslavement 22
machinic networks 40
machinic phyla 10, 26, 52, 56, 64,
    73, 77–8, 84, 86, 92–3, 134,
    194
machinic propositions 35, 55, 72,
    83, 89, 92, 127, 143, 150, 158,
    163, 173, 175, 188–9, 199
machinic surges 9
madness 13, 35, 47, 144, 175, 214, 217
magic 32, 203, 214
Mandelbrot, Benoît 211, 259–60
Mann, Thomas 243
maps 24, 35, 251
    of entities and tensors 60
    of flat affects 45
    of flows 149
    speculative- 137
    of subjectivity 31

Ingram Content Group UK Ltd.
Milton Keynes UK
UKHW020009010423
419513UK00010B/392

9 781441 167279